fear*less*

By the same author
Choose to Be Happy: Your step-by-step guide
GoodStress: The life that can be yours

fear*less*

your guide to overcoming anxiety

Wayne Froggatt

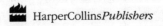

HarperCollins*Publishers*

National Library of New Zealand Cataloguing-in-Publication Data

Froggatt, Wayne.
Fearless : your guide to overcoming anxiety / Wayne Froggatt.
Includes bibliographical references and index.
ISBN 1-86950-465-8
1. Anxiety. 2. Anxiety—Prevention. 3. Anxiety—Treatment. 4. Fear.
I. Title.
152.46—dc21

First published 2003
HarperCollins*Publishers (New Zealand) Limited*
P.O. Box 1, Auckland

ISBN 1 86950 465 8

Designed and typeset by Chris O'Brien/PLP
Set in ITC Garamond and Rotis Semi Sans
Printed by Griffin Press, South Australia, on 79 gsm Bulky Paperback

Publisher's note

This publication is designed to provide accurate and authoritative information on the subject matter covered. It is sold with the understanding that the publisher is not engaged in rendering psychological, financial, legal or other professional services. If expert assistance or counselling is needed, the services of a competent professional should be sought.

Acknowledgements

As with my previous books, *Choose to be Happy* and *GoodStress*, many of those who have added to the present volume will remain anonymous. They are the hundreds of people who have sought assistance from me and who have used the strategies and techniques described herein; and from whom I have learned so much over the years.

Then there are the colleagues who have assisted with encouragement and by reading the manuscript and providing comment: Stefan Thevessen, who assisted with several revisions, along with David Ramsden, Cathi Pharazyn, Sandy Smith, Dr Rod Edwards, Cath Hunter, Louise Lansdown and Lynnette Sudfelt, who each contributed from their various professional perspectives.

Finally, this book, like my others, is based firmly on the theory and practice of Cognitive-Behaviour Therapy, combining in particular the work of Drs Albert Ellis and Aaron Beck, to whom I owe an ongoing and immeasurable debt.

Wayne Froggatt
2003

Contents

Part III Managing specific types of anxiety

Part IV Extra self-help resources

Introduction

Anxiety comes in many forms. It ranges from excessive worrying about day-to-day events and circumstances to panic attacks so severe you think you are about to die. In between, there are social fears, phobias about specific objects, obsessive thoughts that lead to compulsive behaviours, and dreams and flashbacks following a traumatic event.

Your anxiety may have begun recently; or, like most people, you may have been anxious for a long time. Whichever is the case, the fact that you have picked up this book suggests you are thinking it is time to do something about it. You want to be free from excessive anxiety, to live your life without the fear that distresses you and blocks you from achieving your goals.

Over the past 30 years, through my professional work, I have helped many people with all kinds of problems. But the problem that has always fascinated me most is anxiety, for I have a 'proprietary' interest it. I know what it is like to become ill through worrying, to wake in the night with a panic attack, to be overconcerned with cleanliness and order, and to avoid situations for fear of what others might think of me.

While the biological basis of my anxiety remains, I now know what to do about it. This book is my attempt to pass on my knowledge to other sufferers, so they too can learn to overcome and manage the fear that limits their lives. It is about the strategies and methods that I have learned through my professional training, used on myself and then successfully taught to my clients. It is designed to show you, in a step-by-step fashion, how to identify what maintains your anxiety and select strategies to manage it. It presents many choices, because while there are some basics to anxiety management, one size does not fit all — you need to develop an approach that will work for you.

So let's take a brief look at how this book can help you, and how to use it most efficiently and effectively to get the solutions you are seeking.

Part I focuses on the causes of anxiety. You may need to read this section only once. Part II sets the scene for drawing up a self-therapy programme. It shows you how to evaluate your own anxiety problem and develop an action plan. It describes a range of techniques that you can choose from to overcome your fears. Most of what you need for your self-therapy programme is here, and other parts of the book refer back to this section where necessary.

Part III is where you will learn how to apply the skills from Part II to your particular form of anxiety. You may find the whole of this section interesting, but you need study only the one or two chapters relevant to your difficulties. Part IV provides some extra resources: tips on how to sleep well and how to overcome problems with your self-therapy programme, and suggestions for further reading and study. Dip into this part according to your needs.

Above all else, as you work your way through this book, keep in mind a message of hope. Whether your anxiety is recent or lifelong, you are walking a road taken by many others. They are still travelling, but the road is getting easier as they move ahead rather than stand still. From this book you will learn strategies that are based on research, evidence and experience. They work — and they will work for you. All the best with your journey. Now it is time to begin . . .

Part I
Understanding anxiety

1 The many faces of anxiety

For most of human history, there have been two kinds of people — the quick and the dead. Humans lived in the wild, facing many dangers, not the least of which were faster animals with bigger teeth. Those who remained watchful and could quickly raise their heartbeat and breathing rate and increase muscle tension were better able to fight or run. Their anxiety kept them alert, active — and alive.

Things have changed. Today we live in a world where physical dangers are fewer. Unfortunately, our bodies still react as though preparing to fight or flee. The heart speeds up when a bill arrives. Being called to the boss's office leads to hyperventilation. Worry about getting to sleep makes the body tense.

The anxiety that used to be so helpful in aiding survival now often works against us. If it does so only now and again, we get by; but if this becomes a frequent occurrence, we may begin to worry about the anxiety itself. In effect, we become afraid of our own fear. A vicious circle develops and helpful anxiety becomes problem anxiety.

Let's meet some people who know all about this.

Wendy had times when it felt as if she was going to die. Her breathing would speed up, her heart would pound, she had a choking sensation and she would sweat and tremble. These episodes were unpredictable and Wendy worried about losing control and becoming insane.

Linda also experienced panic attacks, but she had found a way to minimise the likelihood of having one — avoidance. She simply stayed away from situations likely to trigger an attack. Unfortunately, this meant that her life had become very limited.

Susan had a long-standing fear of dogs. She became anxious at the thought of being near one. She avoided situations where there was any significant chance of meeting a dog, or tried to arrange in advance for any dogs to be locked up.

Dennis had always been overly anxious in social situations. When he joined the workforce, at age 20, his shyness became worse. His workmates thought he was 'up himself' because he didn't want to eat lunch with them. He forced himself to go to parties, but medicated himself with alcohol beforehand and then stayed in the background, afterwards putting himself down for being 'weak'.

Richard, Janet and Marie had obsessive thoughts that created anxiety. Richard's issue was fear about contamination. He would wash his hands till they were red and sore, insisted on handling money only with plastic gloves and wiped down the passenger seats in his taxi after each use. Janet had repetitive thoughts about her parents dying. She feared that if this happened it would be her fault for thinking about it and telephoned her parents every hour to check on them. Marie hoarded every piece of paper she received, including junk mail, for fear she might throw out something important. Her home had become a fire risk.

Martin had been viciously assaulted for no apparent reason. Several years later, he still became distressed when reminded of the event and had stopped reading the newspaper or watching the television news for fear of reading or hearing about similar incidents. He was depressed and socially isolated. His sleep was disturbed and he had frequent nightmares about being attacked by other people.

Paul had worried since childhood, the tendency becoming worse with age. He worried about money, business security, the health of his wife and children, whether he would have friends in the future, things going wrong with his car, work that might need doing on his house — in fact, just about anything that caught his attention. His worrying created stomach pains, cost him sleep and disrupted his family life.

Finally, Stephen had experienced fears about his health for many years. He had begun seeing doctors and alternative health practitioners about a discoloured patch of skin on his arm. He feared this might signal a major health issue such as cancer. He thought that the patch was growing and refused to accept any reassurance the discoloration was not harmful.

The common threads of fear

Each of these individuals has a different story, yet all had one thing in common: anxiety that was excessive and, to some extent, disabling. But isn't each of their fears valid? Is it not reasonable to be concerned about dying, being attacked by a dog, contamination, the possible death of loved ones, throwing out something important, being assaulted or having a serious health problem?

The answer is yes; it is reasonable to be concerned about such events. There are, though, some common threads to each story that suggest the anxiety was inappropriate. First, each person was *over*-concerned about bad things happening — their anxiety was out of proportion to the actual risks. Second, their anxiety was creating problems with their everyday life and blocking them from their goals. Third, they found it impossible to bring their anxiety under control.

There are several reasons why problem anxiety is hard to contain. If it has been present for a long time, it will have become established as a habit. Perhaps the key reason, though, why many people (and the therapists they visit) have trouble dealing with anxiety is that they fail to identify the real fear.

Susan thought she was afraid of dogs. This is understandable, because she was only anxious when thinking about or in the presence of dogs. But dogs were not the real issue. What she was really afraid of was *how she would feel* if she met a dog. Janet's concern about her parents dying was normal, and of course she wouldn't want to be responsible for that happening — but what she was most afraid of was *how she felt* as she thought about this possibility. Her constant checking-up on her parents was a way of alleviating these feelings. Martin was quite justifiably fearful of being assaulted again — but what he was really trying to avoid were the *feelings* that came when he was reminded of what had happened.

The real fears

What are the feelings these people were so desperately trying to avoid? There are two main types of fear for human beings: the fear of discomfort and the fear of threat to the self-image. We'll deal with both in more depth later, but for now let's look briefly at the first.

Discomfort anxiety may be about such issues as physical pain or loss of lifestyle, but most commonly it is about feeling negative *emotions*. Let's face it, no one wants to feel bad. Our lives are generally geared toward increasing good feelings and minimising bad ones. Unfortunately, this can get out of hand if the *wish* to avoid uncomfortable emotions becomes a *necessity*.

The feeling that sufferers of problem anxiety fear most is anxiety itself. They are anxious about being anxious! This is not usually obvious to the anxious person, but as we shall see later, understanding it is the key to treating problem anxiety. To overcome your fears, you need to know what you are really afraid of.

Why do some of us become afraid of our own anxiety? The next chapter answers this question, but it is worth noting here that a combination of biological make-up — the result of the genes we inherit from our parents and developmental processes in the womb — and learning experiences from early childhood on is involved. Together, these two factors form the basis for a set of beliefs about the world and how to relate to it. The ideas we develop and internalise over the years are known as 'core beliefs'. These guide, usually subconsciously, the way we react to life. Susan, for example, has the core belief 'Large dogs are always dangerous and must be avoided at all costs', which she developed as a child. Carried into adulthood, it causes her to be anxious about dogs in the present.

What is anxiety?

The term 'anxiety' refers to a feeling of uneasiness and apprehension coupled with some uncomfortable physical symptoms. These include tension (tightening of the muscles), increased heartbeat and breathing rate, a dry mouth, an upset stomach, sweating and trembling. If the anxiety worsens, there might be dizziness, faintness, chest pain, blurred vision, a sensation of choking, hot or cold flushes, nausea, the need to urinate frequently or diarrhoea.

As we have seen, a degree of anxiety is appropriate when danger threatens. Moderate anxiety can help you recognise and avoid danger. It can lift your performance by raising alertness and energy levels.

Anxiety becomes dysfunctional only when it is out of proportion to the event that triggers it, is severe, persists, and reduces your performance or even disables you. There are three key symptoms that can alert you to the possibility that anxiety is becoming dysfunctional:

- *Worrying* — you constantly mull over something but do little about it.
- *Avoidance* — you stay away from activities or situations in which you anticipate feeling anxious.
- *Panic* — your anxiety rises dramatically within minutes, the symptoms become extreme and you may even feel as if you are going to die.

Anxiety in its various forms is the most common mental health problem. It appears that in countries such as New Zealand, Australia, Britain and the United States, around one third of the population suffers from generalised anxiety while one tenth has phobias of various types. Anxiety symptoms are also found in other mental health problems, such as depression. Anxiety can have a significant cost. Quite apart from the misery involved, avoidance behaviour can limit a person's lifestyle and even have major consequences — for instance, when fear of being diagnosed with a life-threatening health condition stops a person seeking medical help while there is still time for it to be treated.

Shortly we'll look at how to overcome anxiety. First, though, it will be helpful to identify the particular type of anxiety that creates difficulty for you.

2 What type of anxiety troubles you?

As we have already seen, anxiety has many faces. It is helpful to know how to distinguish between them, because although some approaches can be used for dealing with all of them, there are special strategies for specific kinds of anxiety. Use the following guide to identify your problems and where in this book to find solutions.

Panic attacks and avoidance behaviour

Do you experience feelings of *panic* and worry about having further attacks in the future? Do you also *avoid* situations where you fear that attacks may occur?

Panic can be highly unpleasant. Attacks involve intense fear or discomfort that begins suddenly and peaks within about 10 minutes. Typical symptoms include: the heart pounding, racing or skipping beats; shortness of breath or a smothering sensation; chills, hot flushes, chest pain, sweating, trembling and/or a choking sensation; numbness or tingling; nausea or other abdominal discomfort; dizziness, light-headedness, faintness, or unsteadiness; and fear of dying, losing control or becoming insane.

Panic attacks usually last less than 30 minutes. They may be triggered by a specific situation or take place spontaneously. They may occur only a few times in a person's life or many times a week. They might be interpreted as meaning one is physically ill or perhaps insane.

Panic attacks are common — possibly 30 per cent of adults have experienced at least one. They are not as difficult to deal with as you might think (once you know how!) but untreated, can be disabling to some degree.

Avoidance is often associated with panic attacks. A person may fear situations or places where they anticipate they might have an attack and escape will be difficult or embarrassing, or help unavailable. They therefore avoid such situations, or endure them with intense anxiety, or require someone to be with them. This kind of fear is common in relation to open or public places such as theatres and supermarkets, being alone at home, being away from home, or travelling by car or public transport.

Wendy experienced major panic attacks; Linda did too, but less frequently as she tended to avoid situations that might trigger them. This problem and what to do about it is described on page 162.

Social anxiety

Do you have persistent fears about appearing clumsy, silly or shameful while being observed by others, worry that this may lead to humiliation or embarrassment, and have a strong desire to avoid such an experience? Anxiety of this kind may be associated with eating or writing in front of others, speaking to people or performing in public. People with social anxiety worry that others might see their anxiety, or that they will behave in some way that will cause other people to think they are stupid or weak.

Sufferers either avoid the situations they fear, or face them with a great deal of distress. They know that their fear is excessive and are likely to feel distressed about having the problem. It might interfere significantly with their social, work or personal lives. Dennis' story illustrates social anxiety and its consequences. See page 181 for guidance on this problem.

Specific fears

If you have a persistent fear of specific objects or situations, and a strong desire to avoid them, you may suffer from what is known as a *specific phobia*. Anxiety can be triggered by whatever is feared, or even just by thinking about it. The fear response is immediate, and may involve a panic attack. Sufferers realise their fear is excessive.

They either avoid the triggers, which may interfere with day-to-day life, or endure them with severe anxiety or distress.

Phobias are usually about such things as animals, insects, heights, darkness, earthquakes, dental treatment, blood, air travel and enclosed spaces. Susan's fear of dogs was a phobia, and created typical problems. Phobias are addressed on page 200.

Unwanted thoughts and compulsive behaviours

Do you experience *obsessions*— recurrent thoughts, ideas, images or impulses that create anxiety and that you see as senseless or repugnant? You probably know that the unwanted ideas are a product of your own mind and try to disregard or suppress them but find they eventually come back.

People who experience such thoughts usually feel a pressure to repeat physical behaviours (such as checking or washing) or mental behaviours (such as counting things or silently repeating words). These behaviours, known as *compulsions*, are a response to the unwanted obsessive thoughts, rituals aimed at reducing or eliminating distress, or preventing some dreaded happening. Sufferers know compulsive behaviours are unreasonable or excessive, but still find them hard to control. Compulsions, while providing temporary relief, cause distress in the long run, take up considerable time and interfere with daily living.

Fear of contamination leading to excessive hand-washing is the most common manifestation, followed by doubts that lead to excessive, repetitive checking. Less common are obsessive thoughts without the compulsive behaviour, or obsessive thoughts that the thinker tries to neutralise with other thoughts.

Richard, Janet and Marie demonstrated three variations of this problem, with, respectively, their fears of contamination, of causing harm to others and of throwing out something important. See page 216 if you suffer from obsessive thoughts and compulsive behaviours.

Reliving traumatic experiences

Have you experienced a *traumatic event* that you consider to have been life-threatening, such as an accident, assault or sustained abuse? And do you keep *reliving* the experience via dreams or intrusive thoughts, and go out of your way to avoid reminders of it? This may happen if you witnessed or were involved in an event in which someone died or could have died — or in which you or others suffered, or could have suffered, serious physical injury — and you felt intense fear, horror or helplessness at the time.

In response to such reminders, a person may relive the event in a number of ways: intrusive, distressing thoughts, images or repeated dreams; flashbacks, hallucinations or illusions; or feeling or acting as if the event were recurring. They may try to avoid feelings, thoughts, conversations, activities, people or places that recall the event. They might also become emotionally numb, withdraw from social contact or lose interest in many aspects of life. When the symptoms are severe and last for more than a month, this problem is known as 'post-traumatic stress disorder'.

Martin's nightmares and avoidance behaviour after he was assaulted illustrate how severe anxiety can develop after a traumatic experience. See page 236 to learn what to do about this problem.

Generalised anxiety

Do you worry over just about everything, or experience unfocused, *generalised*, low-key feelings of *anxiety* that are persistent and excessive? You may be able to identify specific triggers to your worrying, or it may just seem to go on and on without any obvious cause.

Most people worry, and at times find this hard to control; but some people have a more general tendency to worry excessively. Typical concerns may involve such things as finances, work performance, social coping or the possibility of illness or accident involving oneself or a relative. Such worrying, and the symptoms of anxiety that result, can leave a person distressed or impair their work, social or personal functioning.

For Paul, as for most sufferers, excessive worrying was a lifetime burden. This problem is addressed on page 138.

Worrying about health

Do you tend to focus on *bodily symptoms*, and regard these as evidence of some serious illness — despite reassurance or medical evidence to the contrary? Such anxiety commonly involves fear of heart disease or cancer. The preoccupation can create distress or affect an individual's personal, social or work functioning. Stephen's anxiety about his skin discoloration illustrates this problem. See page 258 for information on what to do about it.

From identification to understanding

So far we have looked at what is wrong: soon we will see how you can put it right. At this stage you are still building your understanding, so the next step is to learn more about what is causing your anxiety, especially the part played by self-defeating attitudes and beliefs.

3 Why human beings get anxious

If you are alive, then you almost certainly experience some anxiety. It acts as a warning bell, alerting you to danger and providing the physiological boost needed for action. From an evolutionary viewpoint, you and I are the offspring of humans who possess the ability to detect danger and react quickly to it. How does this work?

When you perceive danger, your mind becomes more alert and sends messages to various parts of your body with instructions to commence a number of changes. Your heart speeds up and your blood pressure increases in order to supply more blood to your muscles. This blood is diverted from other parts of your body, which explains why your skin becomes pale when you are anxious. Increased sweating cools your body. Your muscles tense in preparation for physical action. Your breathing speeds up to provide them with more oxygen. Your digestion slows so that energy is refocused where it is most needed.

Not all anxiety is problematical. Each of these changes is necessary to deal with an immediate threat. They are harmful, though, if they become too severe or continue beyond the time they are needed. Too much anxiety overloads the system and makes it hard to think clearly. Persistent high blood pressure will put your health at risk. Tension that continues after you go to bed will stop you sleeping. Too much anxiety can lead you to focus on the feelings instead of the external problem.

Unfortunately, excessive anxiety is common. In modern industrialised societies the need to respond with physical action is much less than when humans lived in the wild, surrounded by physical dangers. Today, we usually need to use our minds rather than our bodies. For many of us, though, the body still reacts in the old ways.

Why do some people develop an excessive dose of what is supposed to be productive and life-preserving? The answer requires us to take a 'bio-psycho-social' approach; that is, to see anxiety as resulting from a combination of biological, psychological and social factors.

Your biology

As we saw earlier, your biochemical make-up is involved. Human beings are born with a variety of temperaments. We all have different levels of mental activity and physical sensitivity. It has been suggested that an overreactive autonomic nervous system (the part of the nervous system that controls automatic functions such as heartbeat and breathing) is the principal factor in problem anxiety, [2] conferring what is known as *high arousability.*

Some people are born with a higher level of arousability than others. That is, their bodies secrete higher than normal levels of adrenaline when they perceive danger.

This explains why some people come to fear their own anxiety. A person with high arousability is more aware of their anxious feelings. Because the alarm bell is always going off (and ringing loudly), they interpret a greater number of life situations as being dangerous. As a result, they experience more episodes of anxiety. As time goes by, because their anxiety occurs more often and at higher levels, they begin to fear their own feelings.

High arousability is the key to understanding the difference between helpful and problem anxiety. Helpful anxiety acts as a warning bell, alerting you to the need for protective action. When the danger is past, the feelings go away. With problem anxiety, the alarm becomes worse than the fire.[3] The anxiety grows out of proportion to the danger, overwhelms your ability to take action, and persists long after it has served its purpose. Gradually, it takes on a life of its own and becomes a source of fear in itself. The inevitable happens: fearing anxiety makes it happen, which leads to more fear, then more anxiety, then more fear — and so begins the vicious circle.

Your learning and life experiences

The circular nature of anxiety shows that there is more to a person than their biochemistry: learning is involved. What you experience in your life, from birth on, combines with your biological inheritance to influence how you react to life in general.

Your physical temperament affects how you learn from experience. Let's take Susan as an example. At age three she is playing with another child when a large dog comes near. Her friend experiences a slight increase in adrenaline secretion, which leads her to think there might be some danger, but her concern is not enough to overwhelm her natural childhood curiosity. She greets the dog, discovers it is friendly, and therefore concludes that large dogs can be fun. Susan, by contrast, experiences a much higher surge of adrenaline, which she interprets as meaning there is great danger present. She runs away. The dog, thinking Susan is playing a game, starts to follow — which increases her terror. Susan concludes from all this that large dogs are dangerous and must be avoided at all costs. This belief is built on and reinforced progressively through childhood, because whenever she sees a large dog she becomes anxious, each time a little more than the time before. She treats her gradually increasing anxiety as 'proof' of her belief about the dangerousness of dogs.

Susan's story shows that as well as learning beliefs from external sources (such as caregivers, peers, books, television, teachers, etc.), we create our own. This happens when we draw conclusions about *external* events (for example, the presence of a large dog) by observing our *internal* reactions (such as the heart beating faster). A person with high arousability is more likely to develop unhelpful beliefs about danger. Susan learned to fear dogs because her inbuilt tendency to high levels of anxiety caused her to mistakenly conclude that every dog she met was dangerous — which led, over time, to the ultimate conclusion that dogs were always dangerous and must be avoided at all costs.

In addition to this kind of *self-teaching*, learning also occurs via teaching from others and through modelling, as Susan's experience also illustrates. Her father, whom she adored, was an anxious man who showed fear in many situations — fear that Susan observed from her earliest years. He also instilled in her the idea that one must be constantly on watch for danger and avoid it at all costs.

To sum up, biological inheritance combines with learning experiences to create a set of beliefs about the world and how one is to relate to it. Learning begins at birth and continues throughout life via teaching by parents and others, observing and modelling off other people, and self-teaching.

Early childhood learning is crucial, as it occurs before children have developed the capacity to reason logically and question what they are learning. Early beliefs therefore seem like givens — 'Laws of the Universe' — that are unquestionable. As a result, they are hard to change.

We continue to learn throughout life. The beliefs we develop and internalise over the years guide, mainly without our awareness, the way we react to life. The bad news is that a predisposition to high arousability is made worse by negative lessons drawn from experience. The good news is that it is possible to moderate the effects of your biological inheritance and unhelpful childhood learning with new, constructive learning experiences. A key area for new learning is that of beliefs and attitudes.

Thinking

As we have seen, your physically inherited temperament combines with early learning experiences to create a set of beliefs about yourself, the world and life in general. Your belief system is the key factor in determining how you feel and behave in response to events and circumstances. Beliefs are discussed in the next chapter, so what follows is only a brief summary.

Over time, like every other human being, you will have developed a set of *core beliefs*. 'Large dogs must be avoided at all costs' is an example. Although learned in the past, you continue to hold these in the present, mostly at a subconscious level.

Your core beliefs affect how you interpret, or draw *inferences* about what is going on around you. If, for example, you have a core belief that oversensitises you to dogs, you may be inclined to infer that a large black object in the distance 'is probably a dog' (as opposed to a rubbish bag).

Your inferences are followed by one or more *evaluations*; that is, you place some kind of value (that goes beyond the 'facts') on an inference. Again, your core beliefs affect how you do this. For example, an oversensitivity to dogs leads to the evaluation 'It would be "awful" if that were a dog and it got near me, so I "must" avoid it.'

The ABCs of anxiety

How the three levels of thinking — core beliefs, inferences and evaluations — operate in specific situations can be shown using the well-known *ABC* model developed by American psychologist Albert Ellis. Variations of this are widely used within cognitive-behaviour therapy (on which this book is based). *A* refers to the activating event or trigger that starts things off. *B* refers to the beliefs or thoughts that follow from *A*. *C* is the consequence — how the person feels and what they do as a result of *B*. Here is an example:

A **Activating event (what started things off)**
Felt uneasy while in supermarket.

B **Beliefs (what I told myself about A)**
Core belief is activated
1. I can't stand bad feelings and must avoid them at all costs.
An inference is drawn
2. I'm going to have a panic attack.
The inference is evaluated
3. It would be *awful* to have a panic attack.
4. I *must* stop this happening — so I *have* to get out of here.

C **Consequence (how I felt and/or behaved)**
Felt panic.
Left groceries in trolley and ran out of supermarket.

Remember, underlying this episode is the person's inherited temperament and lifetime learning. The core belief that was activated did not suddenly come about — it was always there, albeit subconsciously.

Once triggered, it influenced how the person interpreted and evaluated the triggering situation. This thinking then caused their emotional response and the behaviour.

Putting it all together

Let's summarise all of this information about the causes of anxiety. We'll return to Susan as an example of how it all works.

Biological inheritance affects *early learning*. Both contribute to the development of *core beliefs*. Susan is biologically predisposed to high levels of anxiety. She has a childhood confrontation with a large dog and begins to develop the core belief 'Large dogs are always dangerous'.

An *activating event* (A) occurs: Susan, in adulthood, is out walking and comes across a large dog. This triggers the *core belief* (B1), which generates *current thinking* (B2): 'This is a large dog, it is probably dangerous, I must avoid it'. The current thinking in turn creates a *consequence* (C) — emotions and behaviours — in this case, anxiety and a deviation across the road.

Feedback loops operate. How we feel and behave affects our current thinking and in turn our underlying core beliefs. Susan observes her anxiety and avoidance behaviour and concludes that the situation really must be dangerous. This reinforces her pre-existing core belief 'Large dogs are always dangerous'.

All of this explains why you and I are as we are. There is, though, a message of hope. *Having a predisposition which arises from your biological inheritance and childhood learning does not mean you are stuck with problem anxiety.* While there will be some work involved, it is within your power to learn how to compensate for such a predisposition. Many people have successfully done this.

Helping you learn the required skills is what this book is all about. Before we move on to this, though, there is one further thing to do: take a more detailed look at the important subject of self-defeating thinking.

4 What is self-defeating thinking?

As we have seen, a significant cause of your problem anxiety is what you think. By now it will be pretty clear that managing anxiety involves changing anxiety-producing thinking. To do this, you first need to know what to look for.

Let's meet Paul again, the man with the worry problem. He became very upset when his wife said she wanted to take a break from the household and go away for a weekend alone.

Paul *inferred* that his wife was unhappy and thinking of leaving him. He then *evaluated* this as 'awful' and something that 'must not happen'. Both his inference and his evaluation resulted from two *core beliefs*, namely 'It would be awful to be rejected by anyone significant in my life, so this must never happen to me', and 'I must worry about bad things happening, otherwise they might occur.'

Drawing inferences about your world

Inferences are interpretations of reality — that is, *supposedly* factual statements about what has happened, is happening or might happen. Faulty inferences represent conclusions about a situation that are drawn prematurely, without a complete understanding of the situation. There are seven ways in which people tend to misinterpret events and circumstances:

Type of inference	Example
Black-and-white thinking (also known as *all-or-nothing thinking*) — viewing things in extremes, with no middle ground.	'If I don't do this perfectly, it will be a total waste of time.'
Filtering — seeing all that is wrong while ignoring (filtering out) the positives.	'If she were to leave me, there would be nothing worth living for.'

Overgeneralising — assuming that one event or circumstance represents the situation in total, or that something is happening 'all the time' or will happen 'forever'.

'All large dogs are always dangerous.'

Mind-reading — jumping to conclusions, without evidence, about what other people are thinking.

'They're all looking at me. They think I'm stupid.'

Fortune-telling — treating beliefs about the future as realities rather than predictions.

'If I go into the supermarket and faint, people will think I'm mental.'

Emotional reasoning — believing that because you *feel* a certain way, this is how it really *is*.

'The fact that I feel anxious proves that something bad is going to happen.'

Personalising — jumping to the conclusion, without evidence, that an event or circumstance is directly connected with you.

'He was really referring to me when he said the office was getting slack.'

Evaluating what you think is happening

Evaluations are assessments, or judgments, of events or circumstances — or, to be more specific, assessments of inferences. Faulty evaluations, like faulty inferences, represent premature conclusions about a situation. Both evaluations and inferences are influenced by core beliefs.

There are four types of evaluation that typically contribute to problem anxiety: *demanding, awfulising, can't-stand-it-itis* and *self-rating*.

Demanding

This is thinking in terms of unconditional 'shoulds' and 'musts'. By thinking in this absolutist way you place demands on yourself, others and the world in general. There are two main kinds of demanding.

Moralising involves words like 'should' or 'ought', e.g. 'I *should* not have this anxiety problem' or 'I *ought* to be able to pass this examination.' *Musturbating* involves words like 'must', 'need' or 'have to', e.g. 'This elevator *must* be totally safe', 'I *need* a route which avoids the park where they walk dogs' or 'I *have to* ensure that nothing bad could ever happen to my family.' Demands create internal pressure and escalate feelings of anxiety. Can you feel the difference between 'I would *like to* succeed' and 'I *have to* succeed'?

Awfulising

This is thinking that exaggerates the badness of events and circumstances, e.g. 'It would be *terrifying* if this elevator made noises while I was in it', 'It would be *awful* to fail this exam' or 'It would be *horrible* to be near that large dog.' Awfulising escalates anxiety by causing you to see things as worse than they really are.

Can't-stand-it-itis

This is thinking about particular experiences as 'unbearable' because you see them as involving high levels of discomfort, such as frustration, boredom, physical pain, embarrassment or sadness. Here are some examples: 'I *couldn't stand* to be in an elevator that made noises'; 'It would be *unbearable* to fail this exam'; 'I *couldn't stand* to have that large dog near me'. You may mix can't-stand-it-itis with awfulising and demanding, e.g. 'It's *awful* and *unbearable* to feel anxious, so I *must* avoid any situation where this might happen.'

Self-rating

Rating or evaluating your individual actions — e.g. 'I failed this exam' — is functional because it enables you to learn from experience. Unfortunately, a common human tendency is to rate the *entire self*, e.g. 'I failed this exam, therefore *I* am a failure.'

Self-rating leads to *self-image anxiety* — emotional upset resulting from anticipation of self-downing, e.g. 'If I freak out in an elevator, I will look stupid in front of others and they will think I am a weak person.' It also creates secondary problems, such as downing oneself for having an anxiety problem, e.g. 'I'm afraid of elevators, which shows I'm weak.' Finally, it leads to avoidance, e.g. 'If I stay away from elevators, I can avoid going to pieces and feeling bad about myself.'

Here are some anxiety-inducing evaluations of the inferences in the previous table:

Inference	Possible evaluation
If I don't do this perfectly, it will be a total waste of time.	It will prove I'm useless. (*self-rating*)
If she were to leave me, there would be nothing worth living for.	She must not leave me. (*demanding*)
All large dogs are always dangerous.	I couldn't bear to be near a dog. (*can't-stand-it-itis*)
They're all looking at me. They think I'm stupid.	If they think I'm stupid, it proves I am. (*self-rating*)
If I go into the supermarket and faint, people will think I'm mental.	That's the worst thing that could ever happen to me. (*awfulising*)
The fact that I feel anxious proves that something bad is going to happen.	I must worry about this, otherwise it may happen. (*demanding*)
He was really referring to me when he said the office was getting slack.	It's horrible that he thinks I'm slack. (*awfulising*)

Two ways to be anxious

The way in which you evaluate your experiences can lead to two types of psychological disturbance: *discomfort anxiety*, where the fear is about such things as physical or emotional pain; and *self-image anxiety*, where you fear any threat to your view of yourself. Most people have elements of both, but usually one is predominant.

Discomfort anxiety

As we saw earlier, we can fear a particular situation not so much because of the situation itself, but because of what we anticipate we will *feel* should we be exposed to it. Here are some examples:

- Fear of anxiety: 'I couldn't stand another episode of panic.'
- Fear of having a heart attack: 'I will experience excruciating pain.'
- Fear of flying: 'I will panic in such a confined place.'
- Fear of loss of lifestyle: 'I would feel miserable if I lost my job and we had to sell our house.'

Because it creates anxiety about anxiety, the fear of discomfort is a key factor in turning normal anxiety into problem anxiety.

Self-image anxiety

Self-image anxiety is the emotional tension that results if you think that your 'self', or your personal worth, is threatened. You might perceive such a threat if you fear that you may fail at something, that you may act badly or stupidly, or that other people might disapprove of you. This will lead to *unpleasant emotions* such as guilt or shame, and you may engage in *avoidance behaviour*, keeping away from situations where you anticipate failure or disapproval.

Having a problem about having a problem

These two types of anxiety lead to *secondary emotional problems*, or 'having a problem about having a problem'. This is another key reason why anxiety becomes self-perpetuating. Secondary emotional problems come in two varieties, determined by the type of disturbance involved. Here are some examples:

- *Anxiety about anxiety* is a secondary emotional problem based on discomfort. Its usual effect is to make a person anxious and set up a vicious circle of anxiety breeding anxiety — which explains why short-term anxiety becomes long-term and chronic.
- *Anger, bitterness or resentment at having an anxiety problem* is also based on discomfort. It can perpetuate anxiety by locking you into self-pity rather than motivating change.

- *Self-labelling as 'weak' or 'useless' for having an anxiety problem* is based on self-image anxiety. This, too, can perpetuate problem anxiety, because, in effect, you tell yourself you are incapable of learning how to manage it.
- *Shame because other people know* you have an anxiety problem is another secondary emotional problem related to self-image.

The underlying cause: core beliefs

Underlying your inferences and the evaluations you place on them are your core beliefs. These are ideas and attitudes that are general, global and relatively enduring. They are with you all the time, albeit in your subconscious. Here are some anxiety-inducing core beliefs that may underlie the evaluations we have been looking at:

1. My performance defines what kind of person I am.
2. It would be awful to be rejected by anyone significant in my life.
3. Discomfort and pain are unbearable.
4. What people think of me proves what kind of person I am.
5. I must never give myself or other people cause to believe I'm crazy.
6. If I worry about things, I can stop them happening.
7. It's awful to be criticised.

Note how core beliefs are stated in general terms. Each can be applied in many situations. Your *general* beliefs largely determine how you interpret and evaluate *specific* situations.

It is helpful to see core beliefs as of two types: *assumptions* and *rules*. Assumptions are a person's beliefs about how the world is — how it works, what to watch out for, etc. They reflect the inferential type of thinking. Rules are more prescriptive. Irrational rules usually contain a demand (a 'should' or a 'must'). Here are some examples:

Assumptions	Rules
I can get respect from other people by always agreeing with them.	I *need* to get love, respect and approval from those significant to me, and I *must* avoid disapproval from any source.

My performance defines what kind of person I am.	I *must* be worthwhile as a person, and to be worthwhile I *must* achieve, succeed at whatever I do and make no mistakes.
Large dogs are always dangerous and will usually bite if you get near them.	To be bitten by a dog would be the *worst thing* I could ever experience, so I *must* prevent this from happening at all costs.
If I worry about bad things, I can stop them happening.	I *have to* worry about things that could be dangerous, unpleasant or frightening in order to stop them happening.

Twelve self-defeating beliefs

Albert Ellis has suggested that most irrational core beliefs are variations of just a few universal beliefs. Here is a slightly expanded and modified version of his list:

1. I need to get love, respect and approval from those significant to me, and I must avoid disapproval from any source.
2. To be worthwhile as a person I must achieve, succeed at whatever I do and make no mistakes.
3. People should always do the right thing. When they behave obnoxiously, unfairly or selfishly, they must be blamed and punished.
4. Things must be the way I want them to be, otherwise life will be intolerable.
5. My unhappiness is caused by things outside my control, so there's little I can do to feel any better.
6. I must worry about things that could be dangerous, unpleasant or frightening, otherwise they might happen.
7. I can be happier by avoiding life's difficulties, unpleasantnesses and responsibilities.
8. Everyone needs to depend on someone stronger than themselves.
9. Events in my past are the cause of my problems, and they continue to influence my feelings and behaviours now.
10. I should become upset when other people have problems and feel unhappy when they're sad.
11. I shouldn't have to feel discomfort and pain. I can't stand them and must avoid them at all costs.

12. Every problem should have an ideal solution, and it's intolerable when one can't be found.

Each of us holds our own individual set of beliefs. Which of the above do you think you hold? It is your personal array of core beliefs that determines how you interpret and evaluate what happens to you. To improve the quality of your life it is necessary to identify and change any underlying assumptions and rules that are dysfunctional. How to change them, and what to change them to in order to free yourself from excessive anxiety, is the subject of Part II.

Part II
Managing your anxiety:
Strategies and techniques

5 An introduction to anxiety self-help

To get control over your problem anxiety you need a powerful method of personal change. This book is based on such a method: Cognitive-Behaviour Therapy (CBT). Since CBT was first developed in the 1950s, it has been steadily underpinned by a solid research base and become the most-used method of psychotherapy throughout the world.

The primary assumption of CBT is that people are most likely to overcome their emotional and behavioural difficulties by changing the beliefs that create and maintain them. Although human beings appear to have a biologically based propensity to develop irrational beliefs, they also possess an innate capacity to use reason and logic to challenge dysfunctional thinking.

Why the label 'cognitive-behaviour'? 'Cognitive' refers to the processes by which we acquire knowledge and develop beliefs. The main aim of CBT is to help people make lasting changes to their generalised core beliefs that will in turn lead to changes in the way they typically think about specific day-to-day events and circumstances. Many of the techniques used are 'cognitive' in that their purpose is to achieve changes in thinking; for example, collecting evidence about a belief to see whether it is true or false.

Other CBT techniques are 'behavioural', their purpose being to encourage new ways of acting in order to reinforce changes in thinking and gradually bring about lasting changes in behaviour. A common behavioural technique is deliberately to go into a feared situation to establish that it is not as dangerous as originally perceived.

There is a third type of CBT technique — 'emotive' techniques. These involve the use of strategies, such as humour or imagery, that affect the emotions — again, with the aim of achieving long-term changes in thinking.

Our approach, then, might be referred to more accurately as 'cognitive-emotive-behavioural'. Because change in one area causes changes in the others, we will address all three — thoughts, feelings and behaviours.

Principles of cognitive-behavioural self-treatment

It is not a good idea simply to pick techniques from here and there without a guiding framework of some kind. Here are some basic principles that you can use to direct your own self-help work.

First, your primary aim is to achieve the freedom to choose your emotions, behaviours and lifestyle — as much as is realistically possible within physical, social and economic restraints — and to establish a method of self-observation and personal change that will help you maintain your gains.

Second, not all negative emotions are unhelpful. Nor are all pleasant emotions helpful. This book is not about so-called 'positive thinking'; rather, it is concerned with realistic thoughts, emotions and behaviours that are in proportion to the events and circumstances you experience in your day-to-day life.

Third, developing emotional control does not mean you will become limited in what your feel. Quite the opposite: learning to use cognitive-behavioural strategies will help you become open to a range of emotions and experiences that in the past have been blocked by your fears.

Fourth, the approach to anxiety management you are about to adopt is based on the methods of science. Behaviour is viewed as 'functional' or 'dysfunctional', rather than 'good' or 'bad'. You will be developing ways of thinking based on reason and evidence rather than 'magic'.

Finally, you are aiming for *management* rather than *cure*; in other words, you are trying to bring your problem under control, not get rid of it altogether. While the underlying causes will remain they will no longer have a significant effect on your life and happiness. This may not be acceptable to you. You may, understandably, wish to be entirely free of your problem anxiety for ever. Why not aim for a complete and permanent cure? Well, the experience of many sufferers

FearLess

and therapists shows that it is rare for problem anxiety to be dealt with quite so thoroughly. It is almost certain to return on occasion, usually at times of stress. If you thought you were permanently cured, you could become disillusioned at the reappearance of symptoms. You might think that because you had relapsed the therapy wasn't working for you so you might as well give the whole thing up. If, on the other hand, you expect to slip back from time to time, you will be prepared when it happens — and ready to brush up your self-help skills and get working on yourself again.

The process of self-help therapy

Cognitive-behavioural therapy is effective because it is structured and directed. Therapy is always going somewhere — it is not random or ad-hoc. Here's a brief summary of the process:

- The beginning phase consists of checking out your problem, then developing a plan for self-treatment.
- The middle part is where you carry out the treatment plan. This may take anything from a few months to several years.
- In the end stage you evaluate how successful the treatment has been and prepare yourself to maintain your gains in the long term.

The three-step programme

Broadly speaking, the treatment of all types of problem anxiety involves the use of three key strategies:

1. *Learning specific skills* to help you cope with your particular anxiety symptoms. This will give you some initial relief and let you feel more in control, and will also prepare you for the next step.
2. *Exposure* — facing feared situations in a planned and structured manner, using your new coping skills.
3. *Developing new core beliefs* — this involves identifying and changing any underlying dysfunctional assumptions and rules.

42

You are about to begin using the most powerful method of personal change known to behavioural science. How do we know this? There is a huge research literature that attests to the effectiveness of CBT. See page 299 for a sample.

How far can you go with self-help? You can take yourself a long way, but there are limitations.[1] Sometimes a problem is so ingrained, severe or complex that it seems impossible to make headway with it. It is then wise to consider supplementing self-help with professional assistance from an appropriately qualified and experienced cognitive-behaviour therapist. Remember, to seek help is not an indication of weakness, nor does it signal failure. For guidance on choosing a therapist see page 290.

Whether used alone or with assistance, CBT has gained so much credibility that it has become the treatment of choice for a range of problems, including anxiety.[2] As you move from understanding anxiety to learning how to manage it, you can be assured you are taking a well-travelled and well-proven road.

6 Check out your problem and make a plan

Before getting to work on your anxiety, take a little time to assess the problem and draw up a clear plan of action. This will make success more likely and save time in the long run.

Gather information

Begin by putting together what you know about the problem and the factors that may be contributing to it.

What is the problem?

- What exactly are your symptoms? List all of them. It may help to keep a diary for a few weeks, noting carefully what form they take. People are often surprised by what they discover when they stop relying on their memory and keep a structured record of their symptoms.
- Decide what kind of problem anxiety you may be dealing with. Refer to the categories in chapter 2 (page 19) for help with this. Make sure you avoid jumping to conclusions and making too hasty a diagnosis, and consider consulting an appropriate health professional for confirmation if there is any reason for uncertainty as to what you are dealing with.

Identify your protection strategies

Everyone has their own ways of trying to reduce anxiety. There are three main protective strategies to be aware of:

1. *Avoidance.* Do you stay away from situations where you anticipate feeling anxious, or leave them as soon as you can?

2. *Checking*. Do you keep trying to reassure yourself that danger is not present? For example, do you repeatedly check locks, visit the doctor, read medical information or ask others whether you have said or done anything wrong?
3. *Freezing*. Do you become immobilised when you sense danger? Do your muscles tense uncontrollably?

You will probably identify your protection strategies in the course of checking your symptoms.

Check for any risk factors

- *Depression*. It is not uncommon for depression to coexist with anxiety. Watch for signs such as a persistent low mood, tiredness and lack of energy, loss of interest in things you used to enjoy, poor concentration, change in appetite and sleeping patterns, and a sense of hopelessness. Unless you are fully confident you know what to do, consult a health professional if it appears you may be depressed. It is usually necessary to treat depression before trying to deal with anxiety.
- *Suicidal thinking*. The risk of suicide among sufferers of anxiety is substantially greater than in the general population.[1] If you have thoughts of harming yourself, don't delay: seek help now — either from an appropriate professional or, at the very least, from a supportive friend or relative. Your anxiety problem *can* be overcome, but you need to stay alive long enough to discover this!
- *Relationship break-up*. If an important relationship is in imminent danger of breaking up because of your anxiety, consider obtaining appropriate professional help.
- *Other risks*. Is your avoidance behaviour creating risks in other areas of your life? For example, are you in danger of losing your job, getting into financial difficulty or leaving medical problems untreated? Take whatever action is needed to avert the risk while you deal with your anxiety. Talk to your employer, seek financial guidance, see your doctor or do whatever else is appropriate to minimise the risk.

Note any historical factors

- What has been your experience of anxiety and/or other emotional difficulties during your life? Are there any patterns that may shed additional light on your current anxiety problems?
- Are there any family members, especially parents or siblings, who have suffered from anxiety or other mental health problems that may point to either inherited factors or early learning of dysfunctional behaviours?

Establish baselines

Before you begin tackling your problem anxiety you need to establish 'baselines'. These are records of the current frequency and severity of your symptoms, and are best kept in a *diary* or *log* (p. 47), possibly in combination with the symptom check described above. Use the scale on page 95 to measure your levels of anxiety. Baselines give you something to measure your progress against. Don't overlook this step — it can make a big difference to the effectiveness of treatment.

Do you have a secondary disturbance?

Do you feel ashamed, down yourself, get angry or feel depressed about having an anxiety problem? Any such secondary disturbance may need attention before you are able to get far with the primary problem of the anxiety itself. See page 34 for a discussion of secondary problems. There are suggestions for dealing with common issues at the end of this chapter.

Check for any nonpsychological factors

Is there anything else that may be contributing to your problem anxiety? For example:

- *Physical health conditions*, including poor general fitness.
- *Side effects of medications.*
- *Substance use*, including caffeine (more than five cups per day), alcohol (more than two standard drinks per day) and any mind-altering drugs.
- *Lifestyle/environmental factors*, e.g. relationship problems, lack

of social contact, lack of interesting and absorbing hobbies, lack of goals or direction.

If you identify any of these factors, add into your self-treatment plan steps to deal with them, including professional help if necessary.

Techniques for gathering information

Keeping a log or diary of anxious episodes for a short period, perhaps a week or two, should be sufficient to clarify your symptoms and their current baseline. However, you may want to keep a diary throughout your self-therapy programme for ongoing monitoring of symptoms.

One type of diary is the *episode record*, in which you record the occasions when your symptoms occur. Include such information as:

- What happened.
- When and where it happened and whom you were with.
- What aspect of the situation you were responding to.
- The severity of the symptoms (using a scale of 1–10) and how long they lasted.
- What you tried to do to alleviate the symptoms.

Here is an example of an episode record:

Date	What happened, when, where, whom with, which part I reacted to	Symptoms	What I did to alleviate
Tues.	Went to supermarket; lots of people, car park full.	Panic 7/10	Did not get out of car – drove straight home.
Wed.	Walked round block; started to feel faint	Panic 5/10	Turned round, went home.

A variation of this is the *ABC diary*, in which you keep a record of the *A*s, *B*s and *C*s of your anxiety. This can be used to monitor self-defeating thoughts or to check out perceptions of reality (e.g. 'How much of the time am I really failing?'), or as the first stage of *rational self-analysis* (p. 52). The first three columns of the *daily thought record* (p. 57) can be used for this purpose.

You might also try using *imagery*. Picture a situation about which you feel anxious and write down what you see happening. This can provide useful information about the more specific content of your fears. Build the scene in your mind carefully: consider where you are, who else is there, what is happening and what you can hear, smell and feel.

Develop your plan

Your next step is to develop a plan of action for your self-therapy. This usually involves setting goals, deciding on strategies or subgoals that will move you towards these, and choosing specific techniques with which to implement each strategy. The self-treatment plan developed by Linda, the woman prone to panic attacks whom we met in chapter 1, is a good example.

Decide on your self-therapy goals
In what ways do you want to feel and behave differently? State your goals in concrete, specific terms that can be measured. 'To feel better' is too broad. 'To be able to go into supermarkets and stay till I have completed my shopping' is much better. The supermarket goal was one of several Linda set herself.

Decide on strategies for treatment
Strategies are basic guidelines that determine the choice of tactics and techniques. They arise from your understanding of your problem and your therapy goals. Some will be aimed at countering old protective devices. For example:

- If you typically avoid anxiety-associated situations, one strategy could be 'To confront what I fear.'
- If repeated checking is one of your protective devices, a useful strategy could be 'To check once only.'

- If you tend to freeze (i.e. become very tense) when anxiety strikes, your strategy might be 'To let go.'

To achieve her supermarket goal, Linda developed two strategies:

1. To increase my tolerance for feelings of anxiety by confronting what I fear.
2. To manage my feelings of anxiety so they stay below 60% on the catastrophe scale.

(For details of the anxiety scale, see page 95.)

Decide on the key techniques you will use
Choose techniques with which you are most likely to achieve the aims of your strategies:

- *Exposure* (p. 90) and other behavioural techniques would help you implement the strategy 'To confront what I fear.'
- *Response-prevention* (p. 99) might help with 'To check once only.'
- *Relaxation training* (p. 114) or *breathing control* (p. 126) could help with 'To let go.'

To achieve her first strategy, Linda chose two techniques: *imagery exposure* (p. 92) and *graduated real-life exposure* (p. 94). To achieve the second strategy, she chose three: *relaxation training* (p. 114), *rational self-analysis* (p. 52) and *rational cards* (p. 87).

Identify any obstacles to carrying out your plan
Try to identify any difficulties you might encounter in carrying out your self-therapy plan. See page 285 for a checklist of potential blocks and solutions. Keep these in mind as you proceed.

Prepare for your self-therapy programme

Increase your knowledge about anxiety
Learning about anxiety in general, and your specific problem anxiety in particular, will help you in a number of ways. It will increase your

motivation to overcome the inevitable discomfort of change, by show-
ing, first, how exposure to the feeling of anxiety is a necessary part of
treatment, and, second, how getting better depends mostly on your
own efforts. It can also correct the common misunderstanding that
having an anxiety problem proves you are 'weak' or 'crazy', by show-
ing that extreme anxiety is a result of a combination of hereditary,
learning and environmental factors; and how it differs from psychotic
illness.

To make the most of your self-therapy keep the following key
points in mind:

- Anxiety is a *normal* and usually *helpful* human emotion.
- It is designed to alert us to possible danger.
- It is unpleasant by necessity — so that we take notice and act
  on it.
- Hyperarousability or dysfunctional thinking (or both) commonly
  means 'the alarm becomes worse than the fire'.

Enhance your motivation to change

The effort to overcome anxiety is uncomfortable and usually leads to
a temporary increase in anxiety. To help yourself stick with your self-
therapy programme, clarify why you would want to put yourself
through the work and discomfort involved in learning to cope with
your anxiety. This will get you thinking about the possible advantages of facing an increase in discomfort. Use the *benefits calculation*
(p. 65) to draw up a complete list of advantages and disadvantages of
doing the work and making lasting change.

Deal with any secondary emotional problems

If you have identified any 'problems about having your problem', it is
usually a good idea to deal with them early in your programme,
because they may affect your commitment to making change. For
example, self-downing will tend to lower your confidence, thereby
undermining your determination to succeed.

Here are some of the more common secondary emotional problems, with suggested solutions:

- *Self-downing and labelling yourself for being anxious.* Adopt the principle of *self-acceptance* (p. 78). 'Normalise' anxiety by considering its bio-psycho-social nature. Use *rational self-analysis* (p. 52) to identify and challenge self-downing thoughts.
- *Fear of disapproval and shame* is usually based on self-downing: you fear what others will think of you because subconsciously you believe it will prove something bad about you. Sometimes, though, it relates more to fear of the practical consequences of rejection; for example, that you will be without friends, or that people will in some way make life difficult for you. Techniques to use here include *shame attacking* (p. 99), which might entail telling someone else about your anxiety problem, the *blow-up technique* (p. 72), the *catastrophe scale* (p. 70) and *time projection* (p. 72).
- *Anxiety about becoming anxious.* Study the principles of *high tolerance for discomfort* (p. 80) and *long-term enjoyment* (p. 80). Techniques that can help include the *catastrophe scale*, *graduated exposure* (p. 90), the *benefits calculation* (p. 65), *imagery* (p. 73) and *reframing* (p. 71).
- *Anger about, and nonacceptance of, having an anxiety problem.* 'Normalise' your anxiety (see above under *self-downing*) and study the principle of *acceptance of reality* (p. 82). Techniques to use include *reading* (p. 86), the *catastrophe scale* and *reframing*.

You have assessed the problem, set your goals and prepared an action plan. Now it's time to start developing specific techniques to take control of your anxiety. We'll start with the most important: how to deal with self-defeating thinking.

7 How to analyse your thoughts

It is possible to change your feelings. You can get power over your emotions so that they no longer distress and disable you. The question is how do you deal with beliefs that you have held for many years and that are resistant to change? What you need is a structure or process that helps you make sense of what goes on in your mind when you are anxious.

Rational self-analysis is such a structure. You can use it to identify and change the thoughts involved when you experience distress or behave in self-defeating ways. Analysing your thinking can serve two useful purposes. First, it can help you alleviate distress when it occurs. Second, and even better, it can help you reduce the likelihood of reacting the same way in future. Rational self-analysis is an extension of the *ABC* model introduced on page 28.[1]

How to complete a self-analysis

When you are feeling overanxious or engaging in avoidance behaviour, *stop.* Interrupt the episode. Get your brain working on the problem. Take a good-sized sheet of paper and write down the following sequence:

1. Identify the *Activating event* (*A*) — the trigger that set things off.
2. Identify the *Consequence* (*C*) — your reaction, how you felt and/or behaved.
3. Identify your *Beliefs* (*B*) — what you told yourself about *A* that prompted *C*.
4. Decide on a new *Effect* (*E*) — how you would rather feel and/or behave.
5. *Dispute* (*D*) and replace any self-defeating beliefs.

6. Develop some *Further action* (*F*) to reinforce your new thinking.

Let's expand each of these steps:

A **Identify and write down the** *Activating event* **— the trigger to your current anxiety response.**
   - What were you reacting to? Note that *A* could be an *external* event, i.e. something that occurred in your environment (such as entering a crowded room or seeing a large dog), or it could be *internal*, i.e. something that happened inside you, such as a change in your heart rate or a sudden pain.
   - Be brief — summarise *A* only.

C **Identify the** *Consequence* **— how you felt and/or behaved in reaction to** *A*.
   - What did you feel (your emotional response)?
   - What did you do (your behavioural response)?

B **Identify your** *Beliefs*. **What did you tell yourself about** *A* **that prompted your reaction at** *C*?
   - Watch for any of the *inferential* distortions of reality described on page 30 — black-and-white thinking, filtering, over-generalising, mind-reading, fortune-telling, emotional reasoning, personalising.
   - Even more important, identify your *evaluative* beliefs. Look for the four types described on page 31. Ask questions like:
     * What am I telling myself 'must'/'should' be (or not be)? (*demanding*).
     * What is 'terrible'? (*awfulising*).
     * What is 'unbearable'? (*can't-stand-it-itis*).
     * What am I labelling myself? (*self-rating*).

   Most importantly, identify the *core beliefs* according to which you are operating. Most will be variations of the self-defeating attitudes listed on page 36 — you could use these as a checklist.

E **Identify a new and better** *Effect*. **How would you prefer to feel or behave differently from** *C*?
   - Your goal is to replace the self-defeating reaction with a more

53

appropriate emotion or behaviour.

- Make sure any new emotion you wish to feel is realistic. Rather than attempt to replace an intense negative emotion with a strongly positive one — for example, 'terrified' with 'relaxed' — aim to substitute a more moderate negative feeling, such as 'uncomfortable'. If you are anxious, don't make your goal 'To feel great' — that would be unrealistic. It would be better to aim for 'To be concerned.' Concern is still a negative emotion, but more in proportion with *A* and less disabling than anxiety.

D *Dispute* each of your beliefs.

Before developing a new belief it is essential to fully dispute the old one you wish to replace so you are convinced it is irrational. Ask these three questions about each belief:

1. *Does it help?* 'Does believing this help me to be effective, achieve my goals and be happy? Or does it create unneeded distress, difficulties with other people or blocks to achieving my goals?'
2. *What does the evidence say?* 'Where is the proof? What evidence is there? Is there a law of nature that says this is so? Or do the facts really point to some other conclusion?'
3. *Does it logically follow?* 'Because (it's unpleasant/I made a mistake/etc.) does it follow that (it's awful/I'm a total failure/etc.)?'

After disputing each belief, develop a *new rational alternative*. Ensure this adequately contradicts the old belief, and that it is realistic (not meaningless 'positive thinking' or 'affirmation').

F Finally, develop a plan for *Further action*.

Consider: What can I do to reduce the chance of thinking and reacting in the same unhelpful way in future? There are three main types of further action. Try to develop at least one item from each:

- *Re-educative* action — e.g. rereading a chapter of this book that is relevant to the problem you have analysed, researching the problem on the internet, listening to a self-help audiotape.
- *Rethinking* action — using techniques to reinforce new beliefs, e.g. writing them on a card and rereading the card eight to 10 times a day for a few weeks.
- *Behavioural* action — deliberately acting in new ways to

develop more functional behaviours, e.g. entering a situation you usually avoid.

An example

Let's see how this might work in practice by meeting Linda again. With her two children at high school, she returned to working full time as a clerical worker, but found her long-standing fears about entering public situations in case she experienced a panic attack becoming worse. Here's a self-analysis she completed early in her treatment programme:

A   **Activating event**
Felt uneasy while in supermarket.

C   **Consequence**
Emotion Panicky.
Behaviour Left groceries in trolley and ran out of supermarket.

B   **Beliefs**
Inferences
1. I'm going to have a panic attack. (*fortune-telling*)
Evaluations
2. I can't bear this feeling. (*can't-stand-it-itis*)
3. I must stop this happening, so I have to get out of here. (*demanding*)
Core belief
4. I can't stand bad feelings and must avoid them at all costs.

E   **New** *Effect* **I want**
I would prefer to feel concerned rather than panicky so I can stay in the situation and ride out my anxiety.

D   **Disputation**

New beliefs

Does it help me to see an attack as inevitable?
I may have a panic attack, but this is not inevitable.

How do I know it is definitely going to happen?

Does it follow that because I feel uncomfortable a panic attack is inevitable?

D Disputation

Does it help my anxiety to think that I *can't stand* some feelings?

Does my experience show that attacks kill me?

Does it follow that because I dislike something I *can't stand* it?

Is it good for me in the long run to tell myself I *must* stop this happening?

Where is it written that I *must* stop it?

Does it follow that because I *want* to get out of the situation I absolutely *must*?

Does it help me cope to believe that I *can't stand* bad feelings and that I *must* avoid them?

Where is it written that I *must* avoid them?

Does it follow that because I would *prefer* not to feel something I *must* not?

New beliefs

I dislike this feeling but I can stand it. After all, I've felt panic many times before and I'm still alive to tell the tale.

I'd prefer to stop this happening, but demanding it stop will only wind me up and keep it going. And while I certainly feel like leaving, in the long run I'd be better off to stay and see my anxiety through.

I dislike bad feelings but I can — and do — stand them, and facing short-term pain will give me long-term gain.

Notes on disputation

- In this example Linda has disputed *all* the beliefs she listed; however, often all you need to do is dispute the *core belief(s)*, because that is how you will gain the most benefit. Whether you dispute other beliefs is a matter of judgment as to their relative importance and the time available.

- Linda's disputing questions are recorded here to show the process she went through, but usually there is no need to write these down — just record the new belief(s).

F Further action

1. Reread material on catastrophising and how I can combat it.
2. Write my new core beliefs on a rational card and read it eight to 10 times a day for three weeks.
3. Once daily for the next month go somewhere where I am likely to

have a panic attack and stay till the attack happens and then passes, using my rational thinking skills — and the card — to help see me through.

Learning to use rational self-analysis

The best way to learn how to use rational self-analysis is to practise it in writing. Later you will be able to do it in your head, although at times you will still find it helpful to get out pen and paper and analyse an episode more formally.

If you are like most people, you will start by doing an analysis after an episode of anxiety has come and gone. Later you will be able to do it during an episode. Eventually, you will begin to anticipate dysfunctional reactions and interrupt them at the start.

Try the daily thought record

The *daily thought record* is a slimmed-down version of the rational self-analysis format, useful for identifying and changing irrational thinking on a regular basis.

A Activating event/ situation	B Beliefs/thoughts	C Consequence	D Disputation/ rational response
Sensation of dizziness.	I'm going to faint and look foolish. That would be unbearable.	Panic 7/10	This is just anxiety — it will lead to nothing.
Asked for opinion at parents' meeting.	They'll all think I'm stupid if I say the wrong thing.	Anxious 5/10	How do I know they'll think I'm stupid? Even if they did, it would prove nothing about me.

Don't forget the further action

Try to finish every analysis with some relevant further action — especially *behavioural* action — so you consolidate your new beliefs by 'walking the talk'.

8 How to identify fearful thinking

Let's turn to the *B* of the *ABC* model. Although it is not always easy to identify accurately what we are thinking, especially our underlying core beliefs, there are some techniques that can help us do this.

Follow a process

You will find it easier to identify your thoughts if you follow a structured process. A recommended set of steps is as follows:

1. Collect thoughts.
2. Select the critical thought.
3. Inference-chain from the critical thought.
4. Ascertain the evaluations.
5. Get out the core beliefs.

The example that follows shows how Paul, the chronic worrier we met in chapter 1, used this process to identify his thoughts. As you read, consider how you would apply this process to yourself.

Collect thoughts

Start by listing whatever thoughts you can easily bring to consciousness, using questions like the following:

- 'What was I telling myself about *A* to make myself disturbed at *C*?'
- 'What was going through my mind?' or 'What was on my mind then?'
- 'What was I thinking at that moment?'

Usually (but not always) these early thoughts will be in the form of *inferences* (p. 30). Here is an example:

Question: What was going through my mind when she said she wanted time out and I felt that strong feeling of anxiety?
Answer: She's telling me the relationship is over.
Question: What else was I thinking?
Answer: She's going to leave me.
Question: What other thoughts did I have?
Answer: Perhaps she's got another man.
Question: What else went through my mind?
Answer: She'll take the kids.
Question: And what else?
Answer: She hates me.
Question: What else was I thinking?
Answer: I guess that's about it.

Select the critical thought

The next step is to select the *critical thought* — the one you sense is most involved in your reaction. Follow your intuition or gut feelings here. For example:

Question: Which of these do I think is most related to my feeling of anxiety?
Answer: Probably the thought that she hates me.

Chain from the critical thought

Uncover and run down the 'chain' of inferences that follows on from the critical thought until you arrive at the evaluation. This involves *assuming* that the inference is true, then asking what you think about it, e.g. 'If I assume that is true, then what . . .?' You can do this in several ways:

- *Use open-ended questions* such as 'What do I think about that?' or 'What did I think then?'
- *Look for the meaning* — 'What did/does this mean to me?'
- *Refer to the consequence* — 'What is anxiety-provoking/anger-creating/depressing/etc. about this for me?'

Here is an example of inference-chaining:

Thought: She was deliberately nasty to me.
Question: Assuming that is true, what does that mean to me?

Answer:	That she hates me.
Question:	And if she does really hate me, what is anxiety-creating about that?

And so on. You will often find that the chain comes to an end when it seems to 'run out of steam'.

To complicate things, sometimes there will be more than one chain, in which case pick the one you think is most relevant to your reaction at *C*. Also, sometimes there will be inferences that are not connected in a chain: use your judgment as to whether they are important to the analysis. Keep in mind that you are aiming to identify the thoughts that led you from *A*, the activating event, to *C*, the emotional and behavioural consequence.

Ascertain the evaluations

Eventually the chain will end in one or two evaluations. If *open* questions don't get you to that point, try some *direct* questions, based on your knowledge of what you are looking for, i.e. the four types of evaluative thinking — demanding, awfulising, can't-stand-it-itis and self-rating:

- 'What *demand* was I making to . . .?' or 'What *should* or *must* is involved here?'
- 'How *awful* was it to . . .?'
- 'How *unbearable* was it to . . .?'
- 'What *kind of person* do I think I am?' or 'What am I telling myself that says *about me* as a person?'

Here is an example of direct questioning:

Question:	What am I thinking it says about me if she hates me?
Answer:	That I'm worthless.
Question:	What 'should' or 'must' am I holding here?
Answer:	That I need her love.

Get out the core beliefs

Deduce the core belief(s) from the evaluations you have identified. A typical question to ask yourself might be: 'Given that I was thinking (the inferences and evaluations), what core belief(s) does this suggest I might be holding?' For example:

Question: If I am telling myself that I must have her love, and that without it I am worthless, what kind of core belief might I be holding about love and about myself as a person?

Answer: What I've always believed, I guess — that to feel OK about myself I have to be loved by people that matter to me.

In case you have difficulty formulating the core belief(s), here are some suggestions:

- Consider alternatives, e.g. 'Could it be I have a core belief something like . . .?'
- Read through the list of 12 self-defeating core beliefs on page 36, using it as a prompt. Ask yourself: 'Given what I have been telling myself about this situation, which of these might be involved?'

Tips for identifying beliefs

Replace 'Why?' with 'How?' and 'What?'
Do you sometimes get stuck with 'Why?' questions: 'Why am I so anxious?', 'Why am I like this?', etc. The perpetual search for 'Why?' will divert you from understanding how you create and maintain your reactions and from taking steps to change the unwanted ones. The solution is to move from 'Why am I like this?' to 'What am I telling myself that makes me anxious/depressed/etc.?' You are then more likely to move, ultimately, to the really important question: 'What do I need to do to help myself?'

Consider which type of disturbance predominates
At an early stage in the process of eliciting beliefs, consider whether the 'flavour' of those ascertained thus far suggests *self-image anxiety* or *discomfort anxiety* (p. 33). This will provide some guidance as to what to look for.

If, for instance, you uncover thoughts that are mainly about disapproval from others, you might ask yourself a leading question to elicit thoughts to do with self-image anxiety, e.g. 'What would it say about me if they were to disapprove?' Alternatively, if you elicit thoughts about having a heart attack, you might suspect discomfort anxiety and ask yourself about such things as pain or restriction of lifestyle.

Use imagery to identify thoughts

There are two ways you can use imagery as an aid to identifying your thoughts.

With *past imagery*, you consciously think about a feared event by imagining it had already occurred. With *future imagery* you consciously think about a feared situation you are avoiding by imagining you are actually in it. In either case, when you experience the emotions associated with the event or situation, note what is going through your mind.

Replace questions with direct statements

It is common, when recording thoughts, to write down questions, e.g. 'Will I be able to cope with this?' or 'Am I going to go crazy?' Usually these are not questions at all, but statements masquerading as such. For inference-chaining and disputation to work, it is important to unmask these questions and reveal the statements behind, e.g. 'I may not be able to cope with this' or 'I may go crazy.' One way to do this is to answer each question. Alternatively, simply ask yourself what the statement is that lies behind each question.

Keep an ABC diary

A diary of *activating events*, *beliefs* and *consequences* (p. 57) is another way of winkling out your beliefs. Use it for a week or so till you are confident you are able to identify accurately the thinking that prompts your unwanted reactions.

9 How to change your thinking

After identifying your beliefs, the next step is to dispute and change the ones that are self-defeating. Why dispute an old belief? Why not just move on from it and come up with a new one? There are two reasons. First, if the old belief is not thoroughly dealt with, it is most likely to remain active. Second, you are more likely to take on a new way of thinking when you have become convinced that the old one is bad for you. So, take the time to patiently dispute the old belief before moving to the new.

Disputation is the process of questioning a belief, developing arguments against it if it turns out to be faulty, then replacing it with a more functional alternative.

The three questions

Let's begin with the most effective way to check out a belief, which is to ask three key questions about it:[1]

1. Is it useful? (the *pragmatic* question)
2. Is it supported by the evidence? (the *empirical* question)
3. Does it logically follow? (the *logical* question)

For an illustration of this questioning process, see Linda's self-analysis on page 55. What follows now is a detailed description of the three questions, using the example belief 'I must always succeed at whatever I try.'

Pragmatic: 'Is this belief useful?'
Pragmatic disputing focuses on the *usefulness* of a belief. The aim is to check whether it is helpful or unhelpful. Does it lead to negative or positive consequences? Ask yourself questions like the following:

- 'What does telling myself "I must always succeed" do to me?'
- 'Does it help me face my fears to believe "I must always succeed at whatever I try"?'

These will most often lead to the conclusion that the belief is bad for you. However, it is also a good idea to check whether there is any subconscious reason why you still wish to hold on to the belief. Ask yourself:

- 'Do I see some reason for continuing to hold the belief "I must always succeed" that may make it hard for me to give it up?'
- 'Am I telling myself that I "need" this demand to motivate me to try and that without it I would become slack?'

Pragmatic disputation is possibly the most important of the three strategies. You are more likely to change a belief when you see it is harmful for you and serves little or no useful purpose. It is often most effective to use pragmatic disputing first, spending some time on it, before finishing off with the other two strategies.

Empirical: 'Is this belief supported by the evidence?'

The aim here is to see whether the belief is consistent with reality, and what empirical *evidence* there is to support or contradict it; that is, evidence gained from observation and experience rather than speculation or guesswork. Ask yourself:

- 'What evidence do I have for believing "I must always succeed"?'
- 'Where is it written that "I must always succeed"?'
- 'What evidence is there that might contradict this belief?'

You can enhance your empirical analysis with these techniques:

1. *Develop alternative explanations.* Anxiety may lead you to misinterpret what is happening around you. Brainstorm alternative interpretations of your beliefs.
2. *Test your hypotheses.* Record your fears in a diary or notebook, then review them every week to see which have actually been

realised. Alternatively, use *direct action*. For example, you could disprove the belief 'I can't talk to a stranger' by greeting one stranger each day for a week.

Logical: 'Does this belief logically follow?'

Here you examine the logic of the belief to see whether it *follows* from the facts. Whereas empiricism is about facts themselves, logic is about putting facts together and drawing conclusions from them. Ask questions like:

- 'How does it follow that because I *want* to succeed I *must*?'
- 'Am I jumping to a conclusion by thinking that I *must* succeed?'

What to dispute

Which beliefs should you focus on? In the early stages of your self-help therapy, it may be easiest to dispute your inferential thinking. As you gain more experience, you can begin to challenge your evaluative thinking, gradually working towards dealing directly with your core beliefs. Ultimately, working with your underlying, generalised core beliefs will give you the most extensive and long-lasting gains.

Rethinking techniques

In addition to the three questions, there are many other techniques for beefing up the disputation process. Don't overwhelm yourself by trying to use them all — it's best to pick and choose. Skim through the following pages to see what's on offer, then return to the techniques that look especially useful to you and study them more closely.

Techniques to increase your motivation

Benefits calculation

This is a procedure for reinforcing in your mind the benefits of changing a dysfunctional belief. It entails examining the pros and cons of continuing to hold a belief and of changing to a new one. Follow these steps:

1. List all the advantages and disadvantages of continuing to hold the old belief.
2. List all the advantages and disadvantages of holding the new belief.
3. Score each advantage (out of +10) and disadvantage (out of –10).
4. Add up the scores.

You can do this by drawing four boxes on a sheet of paper, as below (alternatively, use four separate sheets of paper). The example uses Linda's belief about avoiding discomfort:

	Option 1	Option 2
	Keep the old belief: 'I can't stand bad feelings and must avoid them at all costs.'	Change the belief to: 'I dislike bad feelings, but I can — and do — stand them, and facing short-term pain will give me long-term gain.'
Advantages	It helps me avoid panic attacks. +6 I don't have to meet other people. +4 Total = +10	I'd have a chance of beating my fears. +8 I'd be able to do more with my family. +9 I would stop putting myself down. +6 I could make new friends. +5 Total = +28
Disadvantages	My life is very restricted. –8 I won't overcome my fear of panic. –7 I might lose my job. –6 I don't do much with my family. –9 Total = –30	I could have more panic attacks. –7 I would not have an excuse for playing it safe and avoiding the risk of others rejecting me. –3 Total = –10
	Grand total: +10 – 30 = –20	**Grand total: +28 – 10 = +18**

Note that the advantages of option 1 and the disadvantages of option 2 will often be the obverse of one another. While this may seem like doubling up, it actually aids clarification. Also, you may not always need to score each item: simply listing them may be enough to convince you of the benefits of changing.

Double imagery procedure

The double imagery procedure[2] is a way of increasing your motivation to change by using the power of your imagination.

Imagine avoiding the short-term discomfort of change and staying the same. Think of all the disadvantages and create a vivid picture of these in your mind. Then imagine a future based on facing and dealing with your problems, and the long-term benefits of changing. Think of all the possible advantages. Now compare and contrast the two pictures.

Ways to check facts

Correcting probability estimates

When you suspect you are exaggerating the likelihood of a feared event occurring, rate the probability with a percentage figure. This alone may help you become more realistic. Sometimes it will be necessary to go further and outline the evidence on which you are basing the figure, which will probably make you lower it.

When you have decided that, for example, there is a 10 per cent chance you will be rejected, remind yourself there is a 90 per cent chance you won't.

Susan, the woman we met in chapter 1 with a dog phobia, used this technique to tackle her fear of being bitten. She talked with a number of friends and discovered that while most had occasionally been confronted by an aggressive dog, none had actually ever been bitten. She concluded that the chance of her being bitten was probably about 5 per cent, which meant she had a 95 per cent chance of *not* being bitten. This didn't totally solve her problem — she also needed to use the *catastrophe scale* (p. 70) — but it did help her get the risk in perspective.

Hypothesis testing

One of the best ways to check out and modify a belief is to act. Examining the evidence for your fears and acting in ways that disprove them is commonly known as *hypothesis testing*. The procedure is as follows:

1. Write down what you fear will happen, including a list of the negative consequences you anticipate.
2. Plan an assignment in which you act in a way that you fear will lead to these consequences.
3. Carry out the assignment to see whether the consequences do in fact occur. Check against the list at 1.

After a number of assignments you will see that few or none of the consequences you fear tend to occur, making it easier for you to interrupt unjustified fears.

Sometimes a hypothesis can be checked out quite simply. For example, if you believe you are totally unable to manage the symptoms of anxiety, you could use the *breathing focus* technique (p. 126). By doing so, you will discover that you are in fact able to control your symptoms, at least temporarily.

The worry calculator

This technique is a good way to get worrying into perspective. Draw four boxes as below. List everything about which you typically worry, or are worrying about at the present time. To ensure you don't miss any significant items, you could keep a 'worry diary' for a week or so. Areas to look at may include: *personal* health, well-being, comfort, success and safety; *family* health, finances and welfare; *job-related* concerns, such as your personal performance and the people you work with; *global* issues such as war and natural disasters; and the *little things* to which you react.

	Things I can do something about	Things I can't do anything about
Important to me	1	2
Not important to me	3	4

Be realistic about which box you place an item in. Don't put impossible items (e.g. 'To always avoid disapproval') in boxes 1 or 3, or things about which you could in fact do something (e.g. 'Getting behind with tasks') in boxes 2 or 4. Also, make realistic decisions as to what is important and what is not.

Finally, develop some *problem-solving* strategies (p. 29) for the items in box 1 and work at *accepting* (p. 76) the items in box 2.

Challenging demanding

Double-standard dispute

If you hold an irrational 'should' or 'must', think of someone about whom you care very much, such as your partner, child or best friend, and consider whether you would encourage that person to adopt the same demanding rule. You will almost certainly respond with an emphatic 'No!' You will then see that you are holding a double standard. Ask yourself how you justify this — and the answer will be that you can't!

You could take this a little further by imagining the person you have in mind has adopted the demanding rule. What would you say to convince them of its inappropriateness? You will quickly see the same reasoning applies to you. In effect, you will be arguing against your own irrational belief.

Linda considered whether she would want her adolescent daughter to hold her core belief 'I can't stand bad feelings and must avoid them at all costs.' The answer was an emphatic 'No!' She did not want her own daughter to hold a belief that would make her fearful and limit her life. She rehearsed what she would say to her daughter should she ever admit to thinking in such a way — and ended up arguing quite effectively against her own self-defeating belief.

The double-standard technique is also an excellent way to challenge *self-rating* (p. 77).

How to deal with catastrophising

The techniques in this section will help you deal with awfulising and can't-stand-it-itis.

Catastrophe scale

Here is a technique for getting things back into perspective when you are awfulising. Draw a line down one side of a sheet of paper. Write '100%' at the top, '0%' at the bottom, and 10% intervals in between. Decide where on the scale you would place whatever it is you fear, and write the item down in that position.

At each level on the scale, write something you think could legitimately be rated accordingly. At 0%, for example, you might write 'Having a quiet cup of coffee at home', at 20% 'Having to mow the lawns when the rugby is on television', at 70% 'Being burgled', at 90% 'Being diagnosed with cancer' and at 100% 'Being burned alive.'

As you add each item, compare its rating with that of your feared item. You will find yourself altering the position of your feared item on the scale as you progressively get it into perspective.

Dennis, the young man in chapter 1 with social fears, found this approach helpful. At first he rated approaching a girl at a party and being rejected as 100% bad — the worst thing that could possibly happen to him. As he added other items to his scale, he realised there were many things that were far worse. Gradually, his 'greatest' fear slipped further and further down the scale. His catastrophe scale looked like this:

DENNIS'S CATASTROPHE SCALE
Fear: Being rejected by a woman at a party

100	Becoming a paraplegic	⇐ original placing
90	Being smashed up in a car accident	
80	Being diagnosed with cancer	⇐ 2nd placing
70	Having my Ford stolen	⇐ 3rd placing
60	Losing my job	
50	Being kicked out of home	
40	Having my house burgled	
30	Losing my wallet	
20	*Being rejected by a woman at a party*	⇐ final placing
10	Mowing lawns while rugby on television	
0	Having a coffee at home	

Keep your chart and add to it from time to time. Whenever you are overanxious about something, ascertain the rating you are sub-consciously giving it, pencil it on your chart, then see how it compares to the items already there. Most often you will realise you have been exaggerating how bad it is, and move it down the list until you sense it is in perspective.

Reframing

Another strategy for getting bad events into perspective is to re-evaluate, or reframe, them as 'disappointing', 'concerning' or 'uncomfortable' as opposed to 'awful' or 'unbearable'. This worked for Dennis, who reframed rejection as 'unpleasant' as opposed to 'catastrophic'.

A variation of reframing is to recognise that even negative events almost always have a positive side to them, think of such an event and list all the positives you can come up with. However, take care that you don't pretend a bad experience is really a good one. That won't work, because it's unrealistic.

Preparing to handle feared situations

The following techniques can also be used to deal with catastrophising, but are especially useful for addressing fears about the future.

The worst-case technique

People often try to avoid thinking about the worst that could happen in case it makes them even more anxious than they already are. However, facing the worst, while it may *initially increase* anxiety, usually leads to a *longer-term reduction*. This is because you discover:

1. The 'worst' would be bearable if it happened.
2. As it probably won't happen, whatever does will obviously be even more bearable.
3. If it did happen, you would usually still have some control over how things turned out.

One way to face the worst is the 'So what if' approach. Ask yourself, 'So what if (so and so happens)?'

Dennis found this helpful with his social fears. He made a list of every negative consequence that could possibly result from asking a woman for a date. The worst he could think of initially was that she would think he was stupid. He then asked himself, 'So what if she does think I'm stupid?' His answers followed a chain: 'She'll tell her friends' > 'So what if she does?' > 'They'll laugh and think I'm stupid' > 'So what if they do?' > 'Everyone in town will know about it and laugh at me.' When he finally asked a woman out, she did turn him down but she handled it diplomatically, and Dennis, because he had prepared for a much worse scenario, coped reasonably well.

The blow-up technique

This is a variation of the worst-case technique, coupled with humour to provide a vivid and memorable experience. Imagine whatever it is you fear happening, then blow it up out of all proportion till you can't help but be amused by it. Laughing at fears will help you get control of them.

Dennis used this with his fear of asking a woman for a date. He imagined ringing her up and her being shocked at his cheek, accusing him of being out of his tree for daring to approach her, and calling the police; then the police arriving and taking him away while journalists, photographers and television cameras turned up outside his house; then his picture and an account of his despicable act being broadcast on the television news, the country being in uproar, the government passing an Act to have him restrained from ever asking anyone out again, and the army, complete with tanks and artillery, patrolling his house and workplace to make sure he never tried to talk to another woman.

Time projection

This technique[3] is designed to show that life and the world in general carry on after a feared or unpleasant event has come and gone:

1. Visualise the feared event occurring, then imagine going forward in time one day, then a week, then a month, then six months, then a year, then two years, and so on.

2. Consider how you are likely to be feeling at each of these points in time. You will see that life will go on, even though you may need to make some adjustments.

Time projection can be used to deal with a range of events and circumstances — actual or feared — such as redundancy, loss of a contract, business failure, reduction in income, death of a loved one, disability, failure to pass an examination, and so on.

Marie, the woman in chapter 1 who hoarded every bit of paper that came her way, found this useful for dealing with her obsession. She imagined how she would feel as she dropped a carton of paper into the incinerator — probably 9 out of 10 anxious. Then she considered how she would feel an hour later, half a day later, the next day, in two days' time, in four days' time, a week later, two weeks later, after a month, two months, four months and six months, and then a year later. She realised that on the day following the incineration she would feel slightly less anxious, and that her anxiety would be a little less again at each successive point in time and eventually disappear completely. After she had incinerated her first carton of paper, she discovered that in fact her anxiety reduced within hours and was totally gone within a few days.

Rational-emotive imagery

This imagery technique entails imagining a feared event, feeling the anxiety it prompts, 'forcing' the anxiety to change into a more functional emotion, then noting the thoughts that enabled you to do this. It works because the only way to alter the emotion is to change the thinking behind it. Regular practice will gradually reinforce the new ways of thinking. Here is the procedure, along with an example from Dennis's experience of social fears:

Procedure	Example
Imagine, vividly and clearly, the event or situation with which you have trouble.	Inviting a woman to the movies.
Allow yourself to feel (strongly) the self-defeating emotion that follows.	Anxiety.

Procedure	Example
Note the thoughts creating the emotion.	'She will probably turn me down. I will feel stupid. I couldn't stand that.'
Force the emotion to change to a more functional, but realistic, feeling. It is possible to do this, even if only briefly.	Concern.
Note the thoughts you used to change the emotion.	'It will be uncomfortable, but it won't kill me. While I'd like to avoid emotional discomfort, I will be better off in the long run if I face my fears.'

Practise the technique daily until you find your anxiety has dropped to a manageable level.

Coping rehearsal

Coping rehearsal is a variation of rational-emotive imagery. Imagine experiencing the dysfunctional reaction you fear, then changing the self-defeating thinking involved and feeling and behaving in more functional ways. Begin by completing a *rational self-analysis* (p. 52). Then do the following:

1. Imagine yourself, as vividly as you can, in the situation you fear.
2. Feel the emotions that follow and see yourself behaving in the self-defeating ways you anticipate, repeating the old self-defeating beliefs you listed in the analysis.
3. Stay 'in the situation' and visualise yourself disputing the self-defeating beliefs and replacing them with the rational alternatives you developed in your analysis.
4. Feel your negative emotion falling to a level you can handle.
5. Picture yourself acting more appropriately and functionally.

You can use this technique to prepare yourself for many situations — behaving assertively, giving a talk, coping with a job interview, negotiating a contract, and so on. Regular practice will improve its effectiveness.

Substitution imagery

You can prepare yourself to cope with feared situations by developing new fantasies to replace old, anxiety-producing ones. Here are two variations:

1. *Coping imagery.* If you have a repetitive fantasy of some feared experience:

   - Develop a new fantasy in which you engage in behaviours that help you cope with the situation or achieve a better outcome. Ensure the new fantasy is realistic for you.
   - Practice the new, coping fantasy regularly, i.e. daily for several weeks or until the old fantasy is eliminated.

   Here are some examples:

   * Fear of being hurt: imagine being criticised but not taking the criticism to heart.
   * Fear of poverty: imagine carrying out a plan that brings financial security.
   * Fear of losing control: imagine yourself behaving competently.

2. *Contrasting.* Another way to deal with feared images is to develop a fantasy in which you visualise a different, less feared outcome. For example:

   * Fear of flying: imagine arriving safely at your destination.
   * Fear of children being killed in a road accident: imagine them growing up to live happy, productive lives.

There are pros and cons of substitution imagery. It can be useful when you are facing an imminent issue — for example, flying, meeting an employer or giving a presentation — and you need some quick help to cope. The disadvantage is that a quick fix of this sort is unlikely to address your dysfunctional core beliefs. Use substitution imagery sparingly, preferably in conjunction with techniques that address your core beliefs more directly.

Dealing with past events

Emotional review

This technique can help with catastrophising about actual, i.e. past, or feared, i.e. future, negative experiences. It entails imagining the experience in question and then describing the thoughts and feelings involved, and repeating this procedure until your anxiety is reduced.

The principle behind it is that repeated reviewing of an event or situation will help you accept it, become more objective about it, separate fantasy from reality, clarify just what it is that you fear, see the situation in a wider context, and identify factors that may help you cope better. While you have been thinking obsessively and *un-willingly* about the event, the emotional review is something you *choose* to do, and will thereby help you develop a sense of control. Here is the procedure:

1. Close your eyes and imagine the event or situation.
2. Think about what happened, or what you fear is going to hap-pen, and be aware of how you feel.
3. Stay with the imagery for only a minute or two at first. After a few sessions, gradually increase the time as you feel more in control of your anxiety.
4. After each review, consider possible new ways to view your fears.

You can do the review alone or with another person, by talking into a tape recorder or writing down your thoughts and feelings. If you have more than one issue to deal with, it is best to work on them individually, getting comfortable with one before moving on to an-other. When your anxiety is somewhat reduced, consider whether there is any action you can take on the problem.

Martin, the man in chapter 1 who had been assaulted, found this technique helpful in dealing with post-trauma anxiety. Once a day he allowed his mind to go back to the assault, initially for a few minutes at a time. After each session he wrote down his thoughts about the incident and analysed them. Gradually he found his thinking was becoming less fearful and he was able to extend the length of each review until he could manage 10 minutes or so. After about three weeks he found his nightmares becoming less frequent.

How to challenge self-rating

Double-standard dispute

Described earlier in relation to demanding (p. 69), this technique is also very useful for combating self-rating. If you persistently put yourself down, either over something you have done or in general, think of someone who is important to you, such as your partner, a child or a close friend. Then consider whether you would down *them* for the same thing. You will almost certainly admit that you wouldn't. When you realise you are holding an unjustifiable double standard, you will find it easier to give up the self-rating.

You can go further by reflecting on how you would talk the other person out of such self-downing — in effect, arguing against your own self-downing beliefs.

Reframing

As well as helping combat catastrophising, reframing can also be used to address self-rating. It involves viewing yourself in a different way. For example, instead of being 'a stupid person', you become 'a person who sometimes does stupid things'. You can do the same with all the other labels you attach to yourself — 'bad', 'selfish', 'no good', 'weak', and so on.

Watch that you don't go to the other extreme, though, and start giving yourself purely positive labels. That won't hold up in the long run. Positive self-rating is just as illogical as negative self-rating: if you can be 'totally good', then you can equally well be 'totally bad'. Neither makes sense, because human beings are never one thing or the other — they are mixtures of many characteristics and tendencies.

10 Developing new beliefs

You are only likely to let go of a self-defeating belief when an alternative, rational one is available. Accordingly, after identifying and disputing an old, dysfunctional belief, it is important to develop a new, functional one that is logical, consistent with reality, and likely to have productive consequences.

New inferences

Here are rational alternatives to the seven types of inferential thinking:

Black-and-white thinking	See things as falling along a continuum rather than at extremes.
Filtering	See life as consisting of both negatives and positives.
Overgeneralising	Keep negative experiences in perspective.
Mind-reading	Look at alternative explanations for the behaviour of other people.
Fortune-telling	Treat all beliefs about the future as predictions and nothing more.
Emotional reasoning	Know that emotions are caused by your own thinking about situations, not situations themselves.
Personalising	Remember that the universe doesn't revolve around one person, and that events may have many explanations.

New evaluations

Here are rational alternatives to the four types of evaluative thinking:

Demanding	View what you want as *preferable* or *desirable* rather than as absolutely *necessary*.

Awfulising	See negative experiences and situations as *bad* or *unpleasant* rather than *terrifying* or *horrific*.
Can't-stand-it-itis	View discomfort and frustration as *unpleasant* but *bearable*.
Self-rating	Accept your*self* even though you rate your *actions*.

Key rational values for managing anxiety

To expand our catalogue of alternative, rational ways of thinking, a list of values follows that, judging by the research literature on the attitudes of people who cope well with stress, appear to be useful aims for human beings.[1] You might find it helpful when you are developing new, rational beliefs.

Self-acceptance

If you have suffered from problem anxiety for a long time, you may be downing yourself for having the problem and labelling yourself 'weak', 'hopeless' or 'crazy'. Such labels create a self-fulfilling prophecy that reduces the motivation for change. Learning to accept yourself *with* your anxiety problem may be a crucial first step if self-treatment is to succeed. Moving from self-rating to self-acceptance involves taking on a new philosophical position along the following lines:

- 'I don't like some things about the way I feel and act, and I would prefer to change these, and will work hard to do so, but there is no "Law of the Universe" that says I *should* be different from how I am.'
- 'I'm not a weak person/hopeless person/crazy person — I'm just a person who *sometimes* behaves weakly/acts in a hopeless way/does crazy things.'

See page 77, and consult the index, for more about techniques for combating self-rating.[2]

Ability confidence

If you lack confidence in your ability to change, this will slow down your progress. Many people think that the solution is to develop *self-confidence*, but this implies you can do everything well, which is unrealistic and will only set you up to be disillusioned. A better approach is to develop confidence in your *abilities*. This will help you evaluate your behaviours in terms of how they help you reach your goals, not what they 'prove' about you as a person. It will enable you to take calculated risks to reach those goals, instead of giving in to the anxiety and avoiding even trying. And it will help you learn from your experiences in order to improve your abilities and, in turn, build your confidence even further.

High tolerance for discomfort

Because people with problem anxiety usually come to fear their own feelings of discomfort, it is important to:

1. Accept the reality of frustration and discomfort rather than demand these not exist, and see them as *unpleasant* rather than *awful* or *unbearable*.
2. Expect to experience, and regard as a part of normal life, some degree of concern, remorse, regret, sadness, annoyance, disappointment and pain.

Long-term enjoyment

High discomfort-tolerance may also involve being able to postpone pleasure at times and accept short-term discomfort in order to increase the likelihood of enjoyment in the longer term.

Risk-taking

Anxious people often have an aversion to taking risks even when avoidance limits their life and happiness. Be willing to take sensible risks to get more out of life and avoid the distress of boredom, listlessness and dissatisfaction, and accept that uncertainty is a part of normal life and can be tolerated.

Moderation

Moving from a restricted lifestyle of avoidance means, to some degree, stepping into the unknown. Remind yourself that this does not mean going to the other extreme, of being 'out of control'. The principle of moderation — that is, avoidance of extremes in thinking, feeling and behaving — provides a middle path. Moderation can be usefully and widely applied — to the use of caffeine, alcohol and drugs, to exercise and diet, to sexual activity, or to anything else that might affect your anxiety levels and your ability to manage them.

Emotional and behavioural responsibility

Change in the way you feel and act can occur only when you acknowledge that, for the most part, you create your own emotions and behaviours and are responsible for them, even though you may not always have control over the external events and circumstances that trigger your reactions. Taking such responsibility may require overcoming some common blocks.

Emotional reasoning may lead you to believe that, because your feelings of anxiety are usually triggered by external events and circumstances, these externals are the *primary cause*. Remind yourself that the real cause is your own thoughts about events and circumstances.

Continuing to be anxious may deliver *secondary gains* or payoffs. Be aware of any that are operating for you so that you can prepare to give them up. Typical payoffs include:[3]

- *Avoidance of responsibility.* Do you find that being anxious means less is expected of you and fewer demands are placed on you?
- *Dependency.* Are others stepping in to do things for you because you are anxiety-prone and therefore 'helpless'?
- *Avoidance of risk.* Does anxiety provide a means of rationalising not doing things when the outcome is unpredictable?
- *Justifying behaviour.* Does anxiety provide a means of justifying the overuse of alcohol, drugs, food or tobacco?
- *Special privileges.* Are you using anxiety to get special treatment from others, e.g. to avoid irksome social or family responsibilities?

- *Being a victim.* Do you blame circumstances or others, including the friends or therapists who have tried to help you in the past, to avoid taking responsibility for your own life? Do you fear that overcoming your anxiety would mean ceasing to be a 'victim'?

To deal with any secondary-gain problems, try to be aware when you are operating in the role of victim. Compare the advantages and disadvantages of your secondary gains — the benefits calculation, described on page 65, can assist you with this. Finally, impress on the significant people in your life the importance of maintaining firm boundaries and of avoiding the temptation to rush in and 'rescue' you.

Objective/flexible/preferential thinking

Anxious people often engage in 'magical' thinking; they assume, for example, that no matter what the available evidence says, their worrying, obsessive thinking and ritualistic or avoidance behaviour somehow ward off danger. It is important to reorient your thinking so it is based on evidence gained from observation and experience, rather than on subjective feelings or uncritical belief. Stick with conclusions that follow logically from the evidence available. Critique your beliefs: do they help or harm you?

Acceptance of reality

Acceptance of *reality* is just as important to the success of therapy as the acceptance of *self.* Quite naturally, you may want to be totally free of your symptoms. Unfortunately, demanding total freedom from anxiety *creates* anxiety, and leads to overreaction when the symptoms appear, thereby escalating them.

Anxiety about anxiety is the prime reason why temporary anxiety becomes persistent anxiety. After their first panic attack, a person is likely to be anxious about having another one — which leads to exactly that.

Self-downing for having an anxiety problem simply ensures it persists, while catastrophising about the symptoms simply keeps them coming. Accepting your anxiety condition and its symptoms will help you break this vicious circle.

People sometimes misunderstand the concept of acceptance. It is important to realise that acceptance is not the same as resignation. It doesn't mean giving in. Furthermore, to accept something doesn't mean you have to like it — you can dislike something, and strongly *prefer* it not exist, while realistically accepting there is no 'Law of the Universe' that says it *should* not exist.

Finally, accepting something needn't mean you stop trying to improve on it. You can continue to seek better solutions to your anxiety, but without the guilt-inducing demand 'I should not have this problem.'

What, then, is acceptance? To accept something is to acknowledge three things:

1. That it is a reality.
2. That although it may be unpleasant, it is bearable.
3. That even though it may be undesirable, there is nothing to say it *should* not be as it is. Paradoxically, accepting your anxiety — getting rid of the demand that you *should* or *must* not have it — is the first step to overcoming it.

From self-defeat to rational thinking

Here are rational alternatives to the 12 self-defeating beliefs:

Self-defeating beliefs	Rational alternatives
I need to get love, respect and approval from those significant to me, and I must avoid disapproval from any source.	Love and approval are good things to have, and I'll seek them when I can. But they're not necessities — I can survive, albeit uncomfortably, without them.
To be worthwhile as a person I must achieve, succeed at what ever I do and make no mistakes.	I'll always seek to achieve as much as I can, but to expect unfailing success and competence is unrealistic. Better I just accept myself as a person, separate from my performance.

Self-defeating beliefs	Rational alternatives
People should always do the right thing. When they behave obnoxiously, unfairly or selfishly, they must be blamed and punished.	It's unfortunate that people sometimes do bad things. But humans aren't perfect, and upsetting myself won't change that reality.
Things must be the way I want them to be, otherwise life will be intolerable.	There's no law that says things have to be the way I want. It's disappointing, but I can stand it — especially if I avoid catastrophising.
My unhappiness is caused by things outside my control, so there's little I can do to feel any better.	Many external factors are outside my control. But it's my thoughts, not the externals, that cause my feelings. And I can learn to control my thoughts.
I must worry about things that could be dangerous, unpleasant or frightening, otherwise they might happen.	Worrying about things that might go wrong won't stop them happening. It will, though, ensure I get upset and anxious right now.
I can be happier by avoiding life's difficulties, unpleasantnesses and responsibilities.	Avoiding problems is easier only in the short term — putting them off can make them even worse later on. It also gives me more time to worry about them.
Everyone needs to depend on someone stronger than themselves.	Relying on someone else can lead to dependent behaviour. It's OK to seek help, just as long as I learn to trust myself and my own judgment.
Events in my past are the cause of my problems, and they continue to influence my feelings and behaviours now.	The past can't influence me now. My current beliefs cause my reactions. I may have learned these beliefs in the past, but I can choose to analyse and change them in the present.
I should become upset when other people have problems and feel unhappy when they're sad.	I can't change other people's problems and bad feelings by getting myself upset.
I shouldn't have to feel discomfort and pain. I can't stand them and must avoid them at all costs.	Why should I be exempt from discomfort and pain? I am better to tolerate them, otherwise my life would be very restricted.

Self-defeating beliefs	Rational alternatives
Every problem should have an ideal solution, and it's intolerable when one can't be found.	Problems usually have many possible solutions. It's better to stop waiting for the perfect one and get on with the best available. I can live with less than the ideal.

11 Making new thinking stick: Follow-up work

If you succeeded in changing a belief and then did nothing more, how long would your new way of thinking last? Probably about as long as it took for one of those familiar activating events to come along and trigger the old self-defeating belief. What you need to do is consolidate and extend your new belief. There are three main types of follow-up work that can help:

1. *Self-education* on topics relevant to your problem.
2. *Rethinking techniques* to consolidate new thinking.
3. *Behavioural strategies* to rectify avoidance or develop new ways of reacting to events.

Self-education

Understanding something usually makes one less fearful of it. Having done some work on a particular fear, you will find it helpful to educate yourself about the issue. Here are some approaches to self-education:

- *Reading.* As well as increasing understanding, reading can speed up the learning of new rational principles and self-help techniques. Sources of written information include books, magazine articles, pamphlets and the internet. See the extensive bibliography, which includes websites, at the back of this book.
- *Audiotapes.* You can listen to tapes while doing housework, driving, gardening, walking or undertaking other physical activities.[1] You can also record your own with passages from books or pamphlets you find helpful.
- *Essays.* Research and write about a particular problem area,

86

covering questions such as: What is known about the problem? What are the possible causes? What can be done about it? What blocks might get in the way of dealing with it? How can I overcome these?

Rethinking techniques

Rational cards

The rational card is an elegantly simple yet surprisingly useful aid. Follow these steps:

1. Dispute the self-defeating belief and develop a rational alternative.
2. Take a small card and write the old belief above the new.
3. Carry the card for a week or so, and read it eight to 10 times a day.

Here's the card Linda wrote following her self-analysis:

> **Old belief**
> I can't stand bad feelings and must avoid them at all costs.
>
> **New belief**
> I dislike bad feelings, but I can — and do — stand them, and facing short-term pain will give me long-term gain.

Reading the card will take only 10 seconds or so, but the repetition can be a great help in establishing a new, rational belief. Here are some tips to make it more effective:

- Ensure the old belief is on the card as well as the new one. If you simply repeat the new belief, the old one will be left untouched. Every time you read both together, the new one challenges the old.
- Note that a new thought requires daily practice for several weeks to become a habit. Also, using the card 10 times a day for, say,

two weeks seems to be more effective than using it once a day for 20 weeks.

Don't be misled by the simplicity of this technique: the best solutions are often the simplest. How does it work? It seems that the repetition keeps the brain both consciously and subconsciously processing the information.

The 'Why change?' card

This is a variation of the rational card. It can help if you are having trouble overcoming unhealthy habits or dysfunctional behaviours. Follow these steps:

1. List in detail the disadvantages of these behaviours.
2. List the advantages of new behaviours.
3. Summarise both lists on a card.
4. Read the card eight to 10 times a day for two weeks.

You might find it helpful to use a 'Why change?' card in conjunction with a *benefits calculation* (p. 65).

Disputation essays

If a self-defeating belief is of particular significance or especially resistant to change, you could dispute it in detail by writing an essay that considers both sides of the issue.

Tape-recordings

As an aid to exposure work, make a tape recording of old and new beliefs, then listen to the tape on a portable player while carrying out anxiety-provoking behavioural assignments. Here are some possible variations:

- *Record new beliefs.* Put forceful rational statements on your tape.
- *Record a disputation sequence.* Talk from both the self-defeating and the rational points of view so you record both sides of the argument. Make the rational argument more forceful.

- *Repeating tape*. Use a repeating loop tape so you can play rational statements over and over again. (Loop tapes, about 30 seconds long, are usually sold by commercial stationers for use in answering machines.)

Behavioural techniques

Probably the most important follow-up techniques involve behavioural tasks, in which you act in ways that oppose old thinking and reinforce new. Because behavioural follow-up is so important to the success of therapy, it forms the subject of several chapters.

12 New behaviour: Walking the talk

Why is Cognitive-Behaviour Therapy so effective? The main reason is that as well as working on what a person *thinks* — the cognitive part — it entails putting new thinking into *practice* — the behavioural part. With CBT you learn the walk as well as the talk. Behavioural strategies involve *deliberately acting in new ways*: confronting fears to discover that you can cope with them; raising your tolerance for discomfort through controlled exposure; opposing old beliefs to prove they are invalid; reinforcing new beliefs by acting on them; and experimenting with new ways to handle problematical situations.

Sounds like hard work? Well, yes, there is work involved, but rewarding work; work you will find increasingly exciting and fulfilling as you realise you are steadily overcoming negative tendencies that have held you back for years.

Facing your fears

Exposure is the most common type of behavioural strategy. It involves entering anxious situations you would normally avoid (after learning skills to cope with your anxiety). The main purposes of this are:

- To test out your beliefs.
- To increase your tolerance for discomfort.
- To develop confidence in your ability to cope.

Exposure is usually graduated, beginning with situations of which you are only a little afraid, continuing with those about which you are moderately anxious, and finishing with those of which you are most fearful. The usual process is to list feared situations, rate each according to the level of anxiety associated with it, and arrange them in a hierarchy. The lowest in the hierarchy is the least frightening, the highest the one you fear most. You enter the lowest and remain in it until your anxiety has reduced to about half. You do this repeatedly, preferably daily, until you feel little anxiety either before or during exposure. Then you move up to the next situation in the hierarchy and repeat the process.

You may well ask why you need to go out of your way to be anxious. After all, you are already fearful enough of these situations. It is important, though, to set up the situations deliberately rather than wait for them to occur. Then you can prepare to manage your reaction. Practice like this, under controlled conditions, will equip you to cope when the situations occur naturally and unexpectedly.

Furthermore, your previously unplanned exposure will most likely have occurred while you were thinking your old fear-inducing thoughts. Consequently, you will have gained little from the experience — you may, in fact, have had your fears reinforced. It is important that you carry out exposure using *new* beliefs.

There are three main types of exposure:

1. *Inducing the symptoms* — using physical techniques to precipitate the symptoms of panic in order to practise coping outside the real-life situations that trigger attacks.
2. *Imagery exposure* — facing a feared situation in your imagination to practise coping before doing it for real.
3. *Real-life exposure* — deliberately facing, in a graduated fashion, the actual situations you fear and avoid.

Inducing the symptoms

As we have seen, a key aspect of problem anxiety is the fear of anxiety itself. Symptom induction involves using physiological procedures to generate feelings of panic deliberately. The purpose of this is to practice coping with panic under controlled conditions. You will also discover that the symptoms, while unpleasant, are harmless. You can use symptom induction to practise self-help techniques such as

91

breathing control, relaxation and rethinking. Here are some ways to induce symptoms:[1]

- Hyperventilate, i.e. breathe deeply and rapidly, for two minutes, then stand up suddenly.
- Breathe through a straw for one minute while holding your nose.
- Walk up and down stairs rapidly, or use an exercise machine, for a minute or two.
- Shake your head from side-to-side for 30 seconds.
- Place your head between your legs for 30 seconds.
- Hold your breath for 30 seconds.
- Spin on a swivel chair for one minute. (Have a comfortable chair to sit down in afterwards.)
- Tense every part of your body and hold yourself like that for about one minute.

Experiment with these options until you find the one that works best for you. Make sure you keep going long enough to induce increased (though not overwhelming) anxiety. Practise once a day until you can use the technique without feeling significantly anxious.

Don't use these procedures if you have any condition that may be compromised, such as a chronic respiratory problem, a heart condition, epilepsy, pregnancy, etc. Consult your doctor if in any doubt.

Remember to use symptom induction *after* you have already developed and practised appropriate strategies for coping with the panic you will induce. Your main purpose is to practise using coping skills to manage your panic.

Imagery exposure

If you are like most people, you will be able to face a fear in your imagination and practise coping with it before doing it for real. The idea is to visualise a feared object or situation and then use relaxation and rethinking skills to reduce the anxiety it induces. The steps are as follows:

1. Prepare

Carry out the same preparatory steps as for *real-life exposure* (pp. 94–95) before proceeding:

1. Make sure you are practised and ready to cope, using relaxation, breathing control and rethinking skills.
2. Measure your anxiety.
3. List the problems and establish goals.
4. Develop a hierarchy (the steps can usually be larger than for real-life exposure).
5. Select and practise a safe, peaceful scene in which you can imagine feeling relaxed and calm, such as lying on a beach or sitting in front of a cosy fire.

2. Relax

1. Spend a few minutes fully relaxing your body.

3. Visualise the first anxious scene

1. Visualise being in the first scene in your hierarchy. Picture as much detail as possible, as vividly as you can.
2. See yourself feeling calm and confident, and behaving in the situation in the way you would like to.
3. As you feel yourself tensing up or getting anxious, consciously relax your body, breathe deeply and slowly, and use your rethinking techniques.
4. Stay in the scene for about one minute, unless your anxiety goes above 4/10, in which case stop and replace the scene with the peaceful one.
5. Try again, either with the same scene or another one that is easier to manage.

4. Switch to the peaceful scene

1. After about a minute, stop visualising the anxious scene and visualise the peaceful one instead, using the relaxation and rethinking techniques you have developed. Do this for about one minute or until you become fully relaxed.

5. Repeat the anxious scene

1. Repeat the visualisation of the anxious scene.

6. Move to the next scene

1. When you can visualise a scene with minimal anxiety, move to the next scene up the hierarchy and repeat the procedure.

Two or three scenes from a hierarchy are usually enough for one practice session (unless they elicit little or no anxiety, in which case it is appropriate to move further ahead). *Continue practising on a daily basis*, progressively moving up the hierarchy with each session. Remember to fully relax your body and mind before commencing each session.

While imagery is not a replacement for real-life exposure, it can be useful preparation. If daily access to the feared object or situation is impractical, it might be the only option, e.g. with fear of flying.

Real-life exposure

Also known as 'in-vivo' exposure, this involves deliberately facing the actual situations you fear and avoid. It will help you correct misperceptions of danger, develop tolerance for discomfort and gain confidence that you can handle your anxiety. The usual way to carry out real-life exposure is in graduated steps, starting with a fairly low-anxiety situation and working your way up, step-by-step, to the higher-anxiety ones. Here's a summary of the process:

1. *Prepare yourself.* Ensure you understand the purpose of exposure, have some relevant coping strategies and know how to measure your anxiety.
2. *Develop an exposure hierarchy.* List the problems, set your goals, choose a goal, develop a series of steps for reaching it, and order these into a hierarchy according to the degree of anxiety you associate with each.
3. *Carry out each step on the hierarchy* using your various coping strategies.

Let's look at these steps in more detail.

Make sure you are ready to cope

Remind yourself that you will feel an increase in anxiety, and that this is not just a side effect but an essential part of the exercise. The aim is to develop tolerance for anxiety through deliberate and controlled exposure to situations that trigger it.

First, though, make sure you are proficient with some techniques for coping with anxiety — relaxation, breathing control, rethinking and imagery.

Measure your anxiety

You will need some way of measuring the level of anxiety you associate with various situations. A 1–10 scale like the following is a useful way to do this:

Low	Moderate	Getting high	High	Severe

| 1 | 2 | 3 | 4 | 5 | 6 | 7 | 8 | 9 | 10 |

Clarify upper and lower anxiety target levels

Establish the *lower level* that is your desired aim (usually 3) and the *upper level* at which you will retreat from any particular exposure exercise (usually 7).

List the problems

1. List the situations you typically avoid because of anxiety, e.g. supermarkets, meetings, dogs, acting assertively.
2. Identify the level of anxiety you associate with each using the 1–10 scale.
3. Select a lower-anxiety situation to deal with first.

If there is only one thing you are avoiding, you can skip this step and proceed straight to the next.

Set a goal

Turn each problem into a goal. For example:

- 'To do my supermarket shopping alone.'
- 'To fly home for the holidays.'
- 'To check the locks before bedtime no more than twice.'

Ensure your goals are *specific*. For example:

- 'To fly home for the holidays' is better than 'To not be afraid of flying.'
- 'To do my supermarket shopping alone' is better than 'To get rid of my agoraphobia.'

Set a realistic timeframe for achieving each goal, i.e. by when do you want to achieve it?

Develop a hierarchy

Plan a series of steps for gradually reaching each goal. For example, for 'To do my supermarket shopping alone' you could have:

Step	Item	Anticipated anxiety level
1.	Sit in car outside supermarket with helper	3
2.	Sit in car outside supermarket alone	3.5
3.	Stand outside supermarket with helper	4
4.	Stand outside supermarket alone	5
5.	Walk through supermarket with helper without buying	6
6.	Walk through supermarket with helper and buy one item	7
7.	Walk through supermarket alone	8
8.	Walk through supermarket alone and buy one item	9
9.	Do full supermarket shopping with helper	9.5
10.	Do full supermarket shopping alone	10

Prepare separate hierarchies for each goal. Note that the gains from working on one will usually carry over to others, so your progress will tend to speed up as you do more exposure work. You probably won't need hierarchies for all the situations on your problem list.

Here are some tips on preparing hierarchies:

- Imagine being near to but not fully immersed in the feared situation, e.g. sitting in your car outside the supermarket rather than being in the supermarket shopping, or reading an invitation to a party rather than being at the party. This can be the first step. Then imagine the most anxiety-provoking thing, e.g. waiting in a long queue at the supermarket checkout or approaching an attractive stranger at the party. This can be the highest step. Clarify what specific aspects of the situation are anxiety-provoking, e.g. the number of people in the supermarket, the difficulty exiting quickly, and use these to formulate the in-between steps.
- Ensure each step is challenging, i.e. produces some anxiety, but not overwhelming, i.e. doesn't produce so much anxiety you will simply avoid it. Anything less than a 2 on your anxiety won't be severe enough to serve much purpose; conversely, a 5 or 6 would probably be too high to begin with.
- It may be useful to have a helper — a person who accompanies you on some of the steps (see page 102).
- A real-life hierarchy will usually have eight to 20 steps that are closer together than those in an imagery hierarchy.

Keep an exposure log

Keep a record of all your exposure sessions:

Date	Step	Anxiety level		Coping techniques used	Comments
		Before	After		

This will help you analyse any difficulties and allow you to refer back to progress already made when the going seems hard and never-ending.

Carry out each step in the hierarchy

- Start at the lowest level in the hierarchy. Enter the situation using your coping skills to manage the resulting anxiety.
- Stay in the situation long enough for your anxiety to reduce, if only slightly. If you leave prematurely, it is important to return soon and try again. If this doesn't work, develop an in-between, lower-anxiety step.
- When you can manage the situation with minimal anxiety (2 or less on the scale), move to the next one up.

Here are some tips for working through a hierarchy:

- In a single practice session you may advance anywhere from one to five steps, depending on the anxiety experienced, tiredness, time available, etc.
- Regular practice is important — daily if possible.
- Don't try to move ahead too fast. Early successes may lead you to think you can miss out intermediate steps, but you will run the risk of becoming overwhelmed, which may then discourage you. On the other hand, if it turns out that some steps are too small, rearrange them so they are sufficiently challenging.
- Remember that success will vary day by day, and that slipping back is common. Some days you will progress rapidly through many steps, other days you will manage only one, and sometimes you won't even cope with steps you managed the day before. If you anticipate slipping back on occasion, you will be better equipped to combat the disappointment you will feel.

When to finish exposure

Exposure work finishes when you are able to enter all the situations you previously feared and avoided and you regard your anxiety as manageable and tolerable.

Response-prevention

Exposure is often associated with response-prevention. This involves inhibiting any dysfunctional strategies you usually use to handle a feared situation. Here are some examples:

- If you rely on alcohol to give you courage in social situations, refrain from drinking.
- If you fear being in public places, instead of giving in to the impulse to run away, stay till the panic subsides.
- If you have an obsessive-compulsive disorder, carry out exposure exercises that trigger the anxiety-producing obsessions while resisting the impulse to engage in anxiety-reducing rituals.

Kinds of exposure work

There are many kinds of exposure work.

Shame attacking

Shame attacking involves doing things you usually avoid through fear of what other people might think. The purpose is to reduce concern about disapproval and raise tolerance for the feeling of shame. The action needs to be something you fear other people are likely to notice and disapprove of.

For example, if you are obsessive about your appearance, you could go out in unmatched items of clothing or without grooming to your usual standard. If you are overly worried about behaving correctly in front of others, you could break some minor social convention. If you fear being regarded as stupid, you might express an opinion to a group of people.

Risk-taking

The purpose of risk-taking is to challenge the belief that a certain behaviour is too dangerous when reason says that while a safe outcome isn't guaranteed the behaviour is worth the risk. For example, if perfectionism or fear of failure is the problem, undertake a task at which you have a reasonable chance of failing or not fulfilling your aspirations; or, if you fear being rebuffed, talk to an attractive person at a party, ask someone on a date, disagree with someone's opinion or state your own.

Sample hierarchies

There are further examples of hierarchies and instructions for exposure work in the chapters relating to specific types of problem anxiety:[2]

- Panic and avoidance: see page 177.
- Specific fears: see pages 209–210.
- Social fears: see pages 194–195.
- Obsessions and compulsions: see pages 227–228.
- Post-trauma anxiety: see pages 247–250.
- Health anxiety: see page 267.

Flooding

Although graduated exposure is the standard procedure for dealing with anxiety, some people benefit from experiencing their symptoms in full. This involves exposure to a high-anxiety situation without any preliminary steps, staying with the feelings, no matter how intense, until they have run their course, and resisting the impulse to fight the panic, instead just 'going with it'. The purpose is to discover that far from being fatal, panic-type anxiety actually comes to nothing. The only way to really appreciate this is to allow an attack to run its course.

This approach, known as flooding, can be useful when there is panic but little or no avoidance of situations. Panic can be induced using the techniques described earlier (p. 91). As with any form of exposure, prepare yourself first by clarifying why you are doing it and by developing cognitive, relaxation and breathing-control strategies that will help you manage, but not distract you from, your anxiety.

13 Making exposure work

While a temporary increase in discomfort is necessary for exposure work to serve its purpose, you don't want this to become overwhelming. There are a number of techniques for calming yourself in advance, and for keeping discomfort at a manageable level while you are in the exposure situation.

Relaxation

Once you have learned a relaxation technique and practised it sufficiently, you will be able consciously to let go of your rising tension while in the feared situation. This can break the vicious circle in which the mind observes the body tensing and concludes that there is danger, thereby increasing the tension. See page 114 for further details.

Rational cards

Read a rational card immediately prior to exposure, take it into the feared situation and reread it there, and reread it again afterwards. See page 87 for further details.

Self-instruction

Repeat to yourself phrases that summarise appropriate self-help concepts, such as 'Stick with it', 'Concentrate on your actions, not your feelings', 'Anxiety is uncomfortable, not terminal', 'If I stay here my anxiety will lessen', 'I don't like it but I can stand it.'[1] Alternatively, use meaningful images; see, for example, *substitution imagery* (p. 75) and the *blow-up technique* (p. 72).

Reframing

Relabel your anxious feelings as 'uncomfortable' rather than 'unbearable'. This will be more effective if you have already thought through the difference between these two ways of characterising an emotion. You will also benefit from thinking about the discomfort involved as therapeutic — which it is — rather than as an unnecessary side effect. See page 71 for further details.

Benefits calculation

Complete a benefits calculation for facing a situation versus avoiding it, then take a written record of this into the situation to read as a reminder that while it is uncomfortable to face the fear, the short-term pain will lead to long-term gain. You can also use this technique to overcome resistance to getting started. See page 65 for further details.

Other techniques

You may find it helpful to prepare with *coping rehearsal* (p. 74). You could also use rewards: give yourself a small prize for each step you manage, and a larger one for completing a hierarchy.

Using a helper

Consider taking someone into a feared situation with you, such as a family member or close friend. They can help you stay there until your anxiety lessens, and remind you of the coping strategies you can use. The helper can gradually reduce their involvement as you develop confidence in your ability to cope.

Tips for helpers

Show the following list to anyone you plan to use as a helper:[2]

- Be caring and supportive in your approach to the person you are assisting; be nonjudgmental concerning their problem; be patient and persistent in encouraging them to confront feared situations.

- Make yourself familiar with the purpose and procedures of exposure, and with the strategies the anxious person will use to cope.
- Ask what the person wants of you in each practice session, e.g. is it to stay with them, to wait nearby, or something else?
- Allow the person to decide the aims of a practice session.
- Know what to watch for that may indicate the person is becoming overly disturbed. Ask them to list typical signs and symptoms.
- Know what to do to help the person with mounting anxiety, reminding them of what coping skills they can use.
- Carry out your role as agreed at the start of a session; for example, if you are to be waiting at the main door of a supermarket when the person comes out, ensure you are actually there.
- Encourage the person to confront their fears, but don't push them.
- Act supportively, but don't take over or encourage the person to avoid *all* anxious feelings.

Strategic withdrawal

A basic principle of exposure is to remain in the feared situation until you get your anxiety down to the target level (usually about 3 on the anxiety scale). However, if it rises above about 6, it is quite appropriate to leave the situation temporarily. Note, though, that temporary withdrawal entails returning as soon as your anxiety has subsided, and not escaping never to return.

Difficulty moving to the next step

If you find it hard to move to the next step in a hierarchy, there are several things you can do:

- The most common option is to spend more time on the previous step.

- If there is too big a gap between steps, develop some intermediate ones. For example, if you are now able to drive to a neighbouring suburb but feel unable to get out of your car, you could, as an intermediate step, stop the car and sit with the radio playing for two minutes. Or, if you are able to enter an airport building but not sit in the viewing area, you could try walking around the terminal for three minutes.
- Using a helper is another way to provide intermediate steps.
- If you have trouble with even the lowest step in a hierarchy, consider formulating a lower first step.

14 Other behavioural strategies

Although exposure is the most-used behavioural strategy, there are others that can form a useful part of your self-treatment armoury. Let's look at some of the more common.

Stimulus control

Sometimes behaviours become conditioned to particular triggers, or stimuli. For example, if you have trouble sleeping, your mind can develop a connection between being in bed and lying awake; or chronic worrying can become associated with the belief that the act of worrying somehow helps to keep bad things from happening, thereby appearing to ward off acute anxiety.

The purpose of stimulus control is to lengthen the time between a stimulus and the response to it and thus weaken the connection. Here are some examples:

Old conditioned behaviour	Stimulus control tactic
Lying in bed awake	If you are unable to sleep for 20 minutes or more, get up and remain up for 30–60 minutes until you feel tired. This will gradually break the connection in your mind that bed is a place in which to be awake.
Worrying	Whenever you catch yourself worrying, postpone the worry until a set time in the evening. This will gradually break the connection between a worry and its trigger.

Develop ways to make this tactic work. For example, to help you get up and stay up in the night, try reading, doing housework, having a snack, etc.; or, to postpone worrying, record the worry in a notebook and then get active with an absorbing task or enjoyable activity until the allotted time.

Contradictory behaviour

When you wish to change a self-defeating tendency, deliberately behave in a way that is contradictory to it — don't wait till you 'feel like' doing it. Even though practice isn't spontaneous, it will gradually make a habit of the new behaviour. Two common types of contradictory behaviour are *stepping out of character* and *postponing gratification*.

Stepping out of character
If you have perfectionist tendencies, deliberately do some things to less than your usual standard. If you are prone to guilt and believe that to care for yourself is selfish, indulge in a personal treat each day for a week. If you tend to rush around but get little done, deliberately slow down and take long breaks, doing nothing but relax. When you feel depressed, keep a log for a day or two of anything that happens to you that you consider pleasant, noting the everyday things that you might usually take for granted, such as the sun, a comfortable chair, a cup of tea, a food item, or a piece of music on the radio.

Postponing gratification
If you suffer undue frustration when you have to wait for what you want, or you have a tendency to seek quick relief from discomfort, deliberately delay gratification with one act or activity each day, continuing this for a month or so until you can manage the frustration or discomfort.

Activity-scheduling

Anxiety may become so overwhelming that you find it hard to keep functioning. This can have a compounding effect: as functioning decreases, so does confidence, leading to even lower performance. Activity-scheduling, originally developed by psychiatrist Aaron Beck to help depressed people become more active, can also help the anxious person regain confidence.

A *weekly activity plan and record* is a useful way of scheduling your activities. Draw up a table like the one below, with a cell for each hour of the day you are usually awake. Plan and record activities for each segment of time. After completing each activity, rate it for *pleasure*, i.e. how much you enjoyed doing it (e.g. P5/10), and *achievement*, i.e. how well you did it (e.g. A7/10).

Weekly Activity Plan & Record for week beginning ....

	Mon	Tues	Wed	Thurs	Fri	Sat	Sun
8–9							
9–10							
10–11							
11–12							

Challenge any fear of failure: remember, the objective is to be active, not to do things perfectly. Here are some suggestions for activity-scheduling more effectively:

- Plan for one day at a time. Make your final activity for each day planning for the next.
- Develop a mixture of tasks and pleasurable activities.
- Try, as far as possible, to select activities you find absorbing.
- When you are carrying out your schedule, focus on one task at a time, putting future tasks out of your mind.
- Change the plan as necessary to accommodate unexpected developments.

At first it may take a while to plan for the next day, but you will gradually get quicker at it. For further ideas on using activity to control anxiety, see the section on *coping plans* on page 134.

Distraction and thought-stopping

While not behavioural strategies in the strict sense of the term, distraction and thought-stopping can aid exposure and help deal with residual unwanted thoughts that remain after you have done more extensive rethinking work.

Distraction

Distraction has only a temporary effect, but can nevertheless be useful in some circumstances. For example, you can use it to help yourself cope with fearful thoughts. What will successfully distract varies from person to person — find out what works for you. Here are some of the more common diversions:

- Pleasant activities that involve concentration or help focus your thoughts elsewhere: watching TV, walking, gardening, telephoning a friend, doing a puzzle, etc.
- Pleasant thoughts (whatever works for you).
- Relaxation and meditation techniques, e.g. *breathing focus* (p. 126), which combines both deep-muscle relaxation and a type of 'secular' meditation.

Linda used distraction to help her cope with going into public places she had been avoiding. Before entering a supermarket, for instance, she reread a rational card she'd written after one of her self-analyses. Then, while inside, she distracted herself from her fear-inducing thoughts by concentrating on using a hand-held calculator to work out the savings she might make by buying alternatives for each item on her shopping list.

There is a variation of distraction called *counting thoughts*, developed by Aaron Beck and his associates, that you may find helpful.[1] Counting your automatic dysfunctional thoughts can help distance yourself from them, gain a sense of mastery over them and recognise their automatic quality. One way to count thoughts is to carry a small card on which you make a mark every time you recognise a particular automatic thought. Alternatively, you can use a counter, like a wrist golf counter (obtainable from a sports store) or a stitch counter (obtainable from a knitting shop). There are numerous ways this technique can be used. For example:

- Count specific types of dysfunctional thought, e.g. those concerning self-downing or discomfort.
- Count thoughts during an anxiety episode.
- Count thoughts during specified times.
- Set an alarm, for every hour or so, as a reminder to count thoughts.

Whatever type of distraction you use, don't fall into the trap of using it as an easy replacement for in-depth work on your self-defeating thinking; rather, use it as a supplement.

Thought-stopping

Thought-stopping, like distraction, will only provide temporary benefit, but can help break repetitive patterns of thinking. The basic strategy is to stop an unwanted thought or image by interrupting it. Here is the procedure:

- Hold the thought in your mind, then shout 'Stop!'
- Repeat this 10–20 times, so you become used to it.
- Practise for a few days at home or in other situations where you can shout without others noticing.
- When you are ready, shout 'Stop!' in your mind only. From this point on you will be able to use thought-stopping wherever you happen to be when anxious thoughts intrude.

There are alternative ways to do this:

- *Focus on the environment.* Instead of saying 'Stop!', concentrate on your surroundings and describe them — aloud when possible — in painstaking detail.
- *Traffic-light approach.* When you have the unwanted thought, visualise a big set of traffic lights with the red light coming on.
- *Rubber band technique.* Place a rubber band round one of your wrists. Whenever you have the unwanted thought, flick the band just hard enough to sting. The pain will interrupt the thought.

- *Alternative imagery.* After inhibiting the anxious thought or image, substitute a coping thought or pleasant fantasy.

Bear in mind that thought-stopping will appear superficially attractive because it can be quickly learned and involves little discomfort. It may, however, be a way of simply avoiding uncomfortable thoughts. It is therefore best used when self-defeating beliefs have been fully analysed and you just need to combat some remaining habitual thoughts.

15 Overcoming blocks to using behavioural techniques

Although 'walking the talk' is important, you may be tempted to neglect taking action on your problems in favour of simply reading or thinking about them. Here are the most common blocks to carrying out behavioural work, with suggestions for overcoming them.

You make little progress

It may be that the exposures you have chosen are too easy.

As we have seen, you can either start at the deep end and tackle the things that bother you most, or you can take a gradual approach. If you choose the latter, remember that you need to experience *some* degree of discomfort. If you make it too easy, you will do nothing to increase your tolerance. Ensure, therefore, that while your assignments are not overwhelming, they are still challenging. For the same reason, ensure that you don't cheat by resorting to strategies that help you avoid discomfort, e.g. using alcohol, drugs or distraction techniques.

You avoid carrying out tasks or do not see them through

- Check that while tasks are challenging, they are not overwhelming.
- If the steps between exposure assignments are too large, incorporate some intermediate steps.
- Ensure that you are not moving on from one step to the next too soon, before reducing your anxiety with the first to a manageable level. Aim for regular, gradual progress.

- Ensure that you are using self-help techniques such as rethinking and relaxation, both by way of preparation and during exposure.

You overreact to discomfort by giving up

- Remind yourself repeatedly that you have to experience the discomfort of anxiety in order to develop tolerance.
- Remember that it is no use waiting till the next fearful situation presents itself. Newly learned coping skills need to be practised under *controlled* conditions — and practised while you are experiencing at least some anxiety.
- Make sure that you fully understand how a technique works and why it is relevant to your getting better.

Important points on using behavioural techniques

Finally, a few last points to keep in mind as you develop and practise your behavioural strategies.

Avoid foolhardy risks or inappropriate actions
Don't do anything that carries an unreasonable risk of injury, or alarms or disrupts the lives of others.

The object of action assignments is not to 'succeed'
The real purpose of behavioural work is to expose yourself to problematical situations in order to test them out or increase your tolerance for discomfort. Often what you fear will not actually occur — although sometimes it is better if it does! For example, a person is unlikely to develop confidence in their ability to handle rejection until they have actually been rejected a few times.

Repetition
For new behaviours to consolidate, you will usually need to carry them out repetitively over a period of time. Don't just do them once — keep on reinforcing them until they begin to happen naturally.

Finally, keep in mind that 'walking the talk' is an essential component of your self-help work. Cognitive-Behaviour Therapy works so quickly and has such lasting benefits because it involves changing both thinking and behaviour. The two go hand in hand and constitute the most effective route to overcoming problem anxiety.

16 How to relax your body and mind

You can't always rely on what your body is telling you. When it gears up for action, your heart beats faster, your breathing speeds up and your muscles tense. These reactions are designed to meet the *physical* demands of a situation — that is, either to fight off danger or to run from it.

Unfortunately, the body often gets it wrong. Most modern-day problems do not require a physical response. If a child is whining, you need to use your head, not your fists. Running away when the boss criticises you may say a lot for your physical fitness, but not much for your future as an employee.

Relaxation training

Learning an appropriate relaxation technique will enable you to reduce muscular tension when you choose to. When you relax, you slow things down and loosen up your muscles. This can help you do many things: control anxiety, feel less pain, cope with medical procedures, lower your blood pressure, get better sleep, function better under pressure, control anger and feel more confident.

Who will benefit?

You are likely to benefit if you experience any of the following:

- *Symptoms*. Muscle tension anywhere in the body; restlessness or a feeling of being keyed up or easily startled; a pounding heart or raised blood pressure; shortness of breath or speeded-up breathing; headaches or migraines; trembling, nervous tics or grinding of the teeth; a need to pass water frequently, diarrhoea or constipation; indigestion or queasiness in the stomach; poor sleep.
- *Behaviours*. Impatience, hyperactivity or a short temper; being

constantly busy to avoid feeling agitated; using tranquillisers or other drugs to calm yourself down.
- *Health problems.* Hypertension, strokes, angina or heart attacks; chronic pain; stomach or duodenal ulcers; ulcerative colitis; irritable bowel syndrome; digestion problems; rheumatoid arthritis.

Some cautions

If you have a medical condition or mental health problem, you would be wise to discuss relaxation with your health professional before proceeding.

- *Medical conditions.* It would be advisable to have a medical inspection if you experience any of the following: chest pains, hypertension, low blood pressure, cardiac disorder, asthma, diabetes, epilepsy, glaucoma, thyroid disorder, hypoglycaemia, narcolepsy or diseases of the gastrointestinal tract; also if you have recently undergone surgery or injury or have problems with your muscles.
- *Mental health conditions.* It is not usually appropriate to do relaxation training when depressed, because of the slowing-down associated with depression. In cases of psychosis, consultation with an appropriate professional is essential.

Finally, be aware that relaxation training is unlikely to be effective if anxious *attitudes* are not addressed first. If you are actively worrying, it will undercut your ability to relax your muscles. See chapter 18 for help with worrying.

The key principles of relaxation

Relaxation training will be more effective if you understand the following basic principles:

- *Relaxation training involves learning.* It isn't something a therapist does to you: it is something you do.
- *Learning involves practice.* Don't wait for a stressful situation to come along before putting your training to use. Practise —

so you are proficient *before* you need to apply it.

- *Relaxation is something you do.* You are not 'cured' when you have completed the training. You need to consciously *apply* it when you feel stressed. However, the more you use it, the more automatic it will become.

- *Relaxation training focuses on muscles, breathing and mind.* Once you know how to make your muscles relax, regulate your breathing and focus your mind, you will be able to calm both body and mind.

- *Relaxation is a way of taking control.* 'Letting go' of tension is the opposite of what your body tries to do when stressed. As you learn to make your body 'let go' at your command, you will be gaining greater control over it.

Three-stage relaxation training

Why bother with relaxation training? Why not just buy a relaxation tape and play it every time you feel uptight? For one thing, you will frequently experience stress in situations where you are not able to play a tape. Your boss is unlikely to adjourn a business meeting, or your kids stop demanding attention, while you go away for an hour to listen to soothing sounds.

What you need is a way to let go of tension quickly in the midst of a stressful situation, when other people may be around. The method outlined below involves three stages. The many hundreds of people to whom I have taught it have reported major improvement in their stress symptoms.

Stage I is designed to help you make a clear distinction between tension and relaxation. Taking each of the main muscle groups in turn, you first tighten your muscles and concentrate on the exaggerated feeling of tension, then you let go and focus on the contrasting feeling of relaxation. This takes about 30 minutes, and you practise once a day for seven to 10 days. While you will find this stage relaxing in itself, its real purpose is to prepare you for the next.

Stage II is designed to relax the same muscle groups, but without tensing them first. This takes about 15 minutes. Again, you practise each day for seven to 10 days. This will prepare you for the third and final stage.

Stage III is designed to show you (1) how to relax your whole body all at once, without using any exercises at all, and (2) how to keep it relaxed even when carrying out day-to-day tasks. This takes about 10 minutes. You practise for a few minutes each day for a month or so to consolidate the learning.

After following the method all the way through, you won't need to do the exercises again: you will know how to relax more or less instantly in any situation. It is then just a matter of frequently reminding yourself to use what you have learned.

Some important things to keep in mind
You are about to learn a new skill, like driving a car or playing a musical instrument. Don't expect to achieve deep levels of relaxation right away. As you practice, your results will steadily improve.

- Adopt the attitude of 'going with' the process. You don't have to strive to relax: what you need to do is 'let it happen'.
- If you have problems with your knees, back or any other joints, don't strain them when doing the exercises. If you wear contact lenses, take them out. When you tense a muscle, you don't need to tense it as hard as you can — that can hurt. Just tense it to about three-quarters of the maximum possible tension.
- When you let the tension go, release it instantly, and enjoy the sudden feeling of looseness.
- Finally, do not attempt to use the training procedure while you are driving, operating machinery or in any other situation that requires alertness or concentration. Do your practice alone, in a quiet place, when you won't be interrupted.

Getting started
The only requirements are a high-backed chair with arms that fully supports your body, a quiet place in which to practise, and pencil and paper to record your progress. Each time you practise, record the date, how tense you feel before you start, and how tense you are after you have finished. Use this rating scale:

| Asleep | Relaxed | Moderate tension | High tension | Extreme tension |

| 10 | 20 | 30 | 40 | 50 | 60 | 70 | 80 | 90 | 100 |

Relaxation Stage I

Draw up a form with headings as in the example below, then record the date and your current tension rating.

Date	Rating		Comments
	Before	After	e.g. interruptions, worrying, illness, headache, tiredness
22 Jan	55	30	Had a fairly stressful day at work.

You will be working on the main muscle groups of your body. Follow these steps for each group:

1. Tense the muscles.
2. Hold the tension for five seconds and concentrate on it.
3. Release the tension.
4. Concentrate on the feeling of relaxation for five seconds.
5. Repeat steps 1–4.
6. Check you are breathing properly, and wait 10 seconds.
7. Move on to the next muscle group and repeat.

Working through all the main muscle groups of your body in this way will take a little over 30 minutes.

Check your breathing

Right now, check you are breathing correctly. Breathe deeply, taking the air right down into your abdomen. Breathe slowly, naturally and comfortably. Place one hand on your abdomen, the other on your chest. The hand on your stomach should rise each time you breathe in, while the hand on your chest should stay still.

Follow the tense-relax sequence

1. Clench your left fist. Hold it tight and feel the tension in your hand and in your forearm. Concentrate on the tension . . . (*5 second pause*) . . .
2. Now let go. Relax your left hand and let it rest on the arm of the chair. Let your fingers spread out, relaxed, and note the difference between the tension you created before and the relaxation you can feel now . . . (*5 second pause*) . . .
3. Repeat steps 1 and 2.
4. Keep breathing deeply, taking the breath right down into your abdomen. Breathing slowly, naturally and very comfortably . . . (*5 second pause*) . . .

Repeat this *tense–relax–tense–relax–check breathing* sequence with the following muscle groups:

1. Your *right hand.*
2. The *backs of your hands.* Hold both hands in front of you and bend them back at the wrists so your fingers point toward the ceiling.
3. Your *biceps,* the muscles in the upper arm. Close your hands into fists, bend your elbows and bring your fists up toward your shoulders.
4. Your *forehead.* Wrinkle your forehead by raising your eyebrows as high as you can.
5. Your *eyes.* Close your eyes tightly, creating tension around them and in your cheeks.
6. Your *jaws.* Bite your teeth together hard.
7. Your *mouth.* Press your lips together hard, and at the same time press your tongue against the roof of your mouth.
8. The *back of your neck.* Press the back of your head against the chair, creating tension in the back of your neck and your upper back.
9. The *front of your neck.* Bend your head forward and press your chin into your chest, almost as hard as it will go.
10. Your *shoulders.* Shrug them as though you were trying to touch your ears.

11. The muscles around your *shoulder blades*. Push your shoulders back as though you were trying to touch them together.
12. Your *back*. Hold the top of your back against the chair and arch the middle right out, making your lower back quite hollow and creating tension all along your back.
13. Your *chest*. Take a deep breath, filling your lungs, and hold it.
14. Your *stomach*. Pull your stomach in, making it hard and tight.
15. Your *bottom*. Pull your buttocks together.
16. Your *thighs* and *upper legs*. Lift your feet off the floor, straighten your legs and point your toes away from you.
17. Your *calves*. Lift your feet off the floor, straighten your knees and point your toes back towards you.

And now to finish . . .

1. Check back, one at a time, over the muscle groups you have just worked on. With each group, note whether any tension remains. If it does, focus on the muscles and direct them to relax, to loosen. . .(*5 second pause*) . . .
2. Relax the muscles in your feet, ankles and calves . . . (*5 second pause*) . . . shins, knees and thighs . . . (*5 second pause*) . . . buttocks and hips . . . (*5 second pause*) . . . stomach, waist and lower back . . . (*5 second pause*) . . . upper back, chest and shoulders . . . (*5 second pause*) . . . upper arms, forearms and hands, through to your fingertips . . . (*5 second pause*) . . . throat and neck . . . (*5 second pause*) . . . jaw and eyes . . . (*5 second pause*) . . . Let all the muscles of your body relax, more and more, deeper and deeper . . . (*5 second pause*)
3. Now sit quietly with your eyes closed, breathing deeply, slowly, naturally and comfortably. For a few minutes, do nothing more than that . . . (*2 minute pause*) . . .
4. Now consider your overall state of tension/relaxation. Decide approximately where you fall on the tension rating scale of 0–100.
5. Have a good stretch, and be fully alert.
6. Record your score on your record sheet.

From here on . . .

- Perform the same sequence each day for the next seven to 10 days, or at least until you are scoring a relaxation level of 30 or below on two or three consecutive days.

- Remember this is only the first step in a three-stage training process. You will not be ready to apply your new relaxation skills in the outside world for a few weeks yet. Note, too, that at this stage the feeling of relaxation you create is unlikely to last for long after a practice session.

Relaxation Stage II

Once you are used to identifying the difference between tension and relaxation, you are ready to move on. Stage II involves simply *letting go* each muscle group in turn, without first tensing. This will move you closer to the point where you can let your whole body relax instantly, without doing any exercises at all.

Start by recording your present tension level on a form like the one you prepared for Stage I. Then sit comfortably with all parts of your body supported so there is no need for any of your muscles to be tensed.

Follow the breathing–relax sequence

1. Breathe deeply, taking the air right down into your stomach. Breathing slowly, naturally and comfortably ... (*3 second pause*) ...
2. Direct your attention to your *right hand* and let go of any tensions there ... (*3 second pause*) ... Relax the muscles in your right hand as far as you are able ... (*3 second pause*) ... Let go further and further ... (*3 second pause*) ...

Repeat this *breathing–relax–relax* sequence with the following muscle groups:

1. Your *right forearm.*
2. Your *upper right arm.*
3. Your *left hand.*
4. Your *left forearm.*
5. Your *upper left arm.*
6. Your *shoulders.*
7. Your *forehead.*
8. Your *eyes.*

9. Your *cheeks*.
10. Your *jaws*.
11. Your *neck*.
12. Your *chest*.
13. Your *stomach*.
14. Your *hips and buttocks*.
15. Your *thighs*.
16. Your *calves*.
17. Your *feet*.

To finish . . .

1. Even when you are feeling very relaxed, it is often possible to let go just a little bit more. To do this, count from 1 to 10, repeating the following words (or something like them) with each number. At each step, let go a little bit more than before.
2. One, 'Relax, just relax . . . ' (*3 second pause*) . . . Two, 'Deeper and deeper, further and further relaxed . . . ' (*3 second pause*) . . . Three, 'Letting go, more and more, deeper and deeper . . . ' (*3 second pause*) . . . Four, 'Getting heavier and looser, more and more relaxed . . . ' (*3 second pause*) . . . Five, 'Further and further relaxed . . . ' (*3 second pause*) . . . Six, 'More and more, further and further . . . ' (*3 second pause*) . . . Seven, 'Deeper and deeper, more and more relaxed . . . ' (*3 second pause*) . . . Eight, 'Letting go more and more . . . ' (*3 second pause*) . . . Nine, 'My whole body more and more relaxed, deeper and deeper . . . ' (*3 second pause*) . . . Ten, 'Just continuing to relax, more and more, further and further relaxed . . . ' (*3 second pause*) . . .
3. If you are now at 30 or below on your tension rating scale – that is, feeling quite relaxed – you can try an exercise that will help you relax even more. Focus your attention on the point at which your breath leaves your body, and allow your body to relax a little more with each outward breath. This will help you clear and relax your mind, as well as increase the relaxation in your body. Do this now, for a few minutes . . . (*3 minute pause*) . . .
4. Now consider your overall state of tension/relaxation. Decide approximately where you fall on the tension rating scale of 0–100.
5. Have a good stretch, and be fully alert.
6. Record your score on your record sheet.

From here on . . .

- Practise this stage every day until you are regularly achieving a relaxation level of 30 or below (for five to seven days in a row).

Relaxation Stage III

After adequate practice on Stage II, you are ready to learn how to relax your entire body inconspicuously and quickly in just about any situation, even while carrying out tasks and activities or in the presence of other people.

Your aim with Stage III is to learn how to be aware of any unnecessary tension that creeps in, and quickly let it go, in a selective fashion, depending on what the situation requires of your muscles.

Follow the selective relaxation procedure

1. Relax in your chair for five to 10 minutes, or until you have achieved a relaxation level of 30 or below.
2. You need *some* tension in *some* parts of your body to carry out particular day-to-day activities. However, other parts of the body may not need to be tensed, and it is this unneeded tension that is now to be your focus.
3. Fix your gaze on some object on the wall, such as a picture or light switch. Notice that to do this you need to slightly tense your neck (to keep your head upright) and your eyes (to keep them open and focused). However, identify any *other* tension that has crept in (e.g. in your arms, legs or stomach) and let it go while still focusing on the object.
4. Repeat step 3 with a number of more demanding tasks. For example, hold a book in your hands and turn it over and over, or stand and look out of a window. With each task, identify which muscles need to be tensed to carry it out, then be aware of and get rid of any unneeded tension that creeps into other parts of your body. Continue the task for several minutes, until you can remain tension free while carrying it out.

From here on . . .

- Practise the Stage III exercise for a few minutes every day for several months. This will help consolidate the relaxation habit.

Tips for relaxation training

Using a tape recorder

An alternative way to learn the three-stage relaxation procedure is to tape-record the instructions for Stages I and II. Then all you have to do is follow the tape when you practise. You can either record the instructions yourself or ask someone else to do it for you. Speak in a slow, measured, calm manner.

An additional technique

The *breathing focus* technique is a useful add-on to deep-muscle relaxation. See page 126 for full instructions.

Making relaxation work in everyday life

Remember that the skills you have learned are just that — skills. They are not a cure. You will benefit from what you have learned in direct proportion to how much you apply it. Get into the habit of stopping at regular intervals during the day to consider: 'Am I tense or relaxed right now? Could I be more relaxed than I am?'

Develop a reminder system. Get some stick-on coloured dots or stars and place them where you will see them through the day — on the bathroom mirror, above the kitchen sink, on the car speedometer, on your watch-strap, briefcase, purse or wallet. Other people probably won't notice them, but each time you do, it will remind you to check how tense/relaxed you are.

Finally, keep in mind that relaxation training is not a total solution to stress. Don't neglect the self-defeating attitudes and beliefs that create stress in the first place, and which can stop you applying your new-found relaxation skills.

Overcoming blocks to a relaxed body and mind

Lack of time

Probably the most common block to learning and using relaxation techniques is the 'I don't have time' argument. Use the principle of *long-term enjoyment* (p. 80) to help yourself here. Note that being able to relax your body and mind will be cost effective. It will reduce your fatigue, increase your alertness and concentration, and increase your efficiency and productivity. Taking the time to learn and use relaxation techniques, instead of resorting to quick fixes like tranquillisers, alcohol or marijuana, will help you control stress much better in the long run.

When relaxation doesn't seem to work

If relaxation doesn't seem to work for you, you may not be a suitable candidate for relaxation training. (See the suitability criteria on page 114.) Experiment. If none of the suggestions in this chapter sit well with you, check out alternative strategies such as meditation, visualisation or biofeedback. Your doctor, local mental health service or other health professional may be able to advise you where to get information. Use relaxation strategies that work for you.

It may be that your mind is very active, perhaps through worry, while you are trying to relax. Do some work on your tendency to worry before attempting further relaxation training (see chapter 18).

Have you really practised the three-stage relaxation training method — faithfully? Make sure you have taken the time to follow all three stages correctly, and, especially, that you have practised daily. The time spent will almost certainly be cost-effective in the long run.

Do you become panicky?

A small proportion of people who begin relaxation training become more anxious, and possibly even panicky, when they start to relax. This is usually due to a sense of losing control as they begin to let go. If this happens to you, remind yourself that the anxiety is unpleasant but not terrifying, uncomfortable but not unbearable. Persevere: the discomfort will pass. If you feel afraid when you close your eyes during relaxation training, keep them open to begin with. Probably the most helpful thing you can do is use *rational self-analysis* to uncover and deal with the thoughts creating your anxiety.

Breathing control

Many people hyperventilate when they are anxious; that is, they take abnormally rapid, shallow breaths. This is a common symptom of panic attacks. Hyperventilation increases the sense of anxiety; conversely, breathing more slowly and deeply almost always has a calming effect (and is usually the quickest way to stop a panic attack).

The 3–1 technique

This is a simple, easy-to-learn, yet effective way to develop control of your breathing. The procedure is as follows:

1. Place both hands on your abdomen, and ensure they rise and fall with each breath (which indicates you are taking air right down into your diaphragm).
2. Breathe in, silently counting to 3 as you do so.
3. Hold your breath for the count of 1.
4. Breathe out, counting to 3.
5. Wait for the count of 1 before breathing in again.
6. Repeat for 5 minutes if practising, or until all signs of overbreathing have gone if you were hyperventilating.

Some people report symptoms of anxiety when they first use this technique, possibly because they overfocus on their breathing, but these pass with further practice. Practise the technique regularly for several weeks before trying it out during a panic attack or in a feared situation.

The breathing-focus technique

This is very useful for clearing the mind when it is overactive or worry is stopping you from relaxing. It can help you get to sleep, and you can use it for five minutes or so to refresh body and mind during the day. It is a simple yet surprisingly effective procedure.

Follow this sequence:

1. Sit (or lie) in a comfortable position.
2. Breathe in slowly and deeply. Take a good, deep breath right down into your abdomen, filling yourself with health-giving oxygen.
3. Hold your breath for about one second.
4. Slowly breathe out. As you do, focus on your breath as it leaves your

body. Focus on the centre of your face, visualising the breath leaving through your nose and/or mouth.

5. Each time you breathe out, imagine that a little more of the tension leaves your body along with your breath. Let your body, from the top of your head to the tips of your fingers and down to your feet, slump a little more each time you exhale. Breathe right out, expelling all the old air and waste products.

6. Pause for about a second before breathing in again.

To make the procedure more effective:

- Maintain your focus on the centre of your face, where the breath enters and leaves your body. If your attention wanders, bring it back. Holding the one point of focus will help keep your mind from drifting back to stressful thoughts.

- When thoughts intrude, instead of trying to reject them, allow them to pass and return to focusing on your breathing.

- Whenever you become aware of noises around you, instead of trying to shut them out, focus on them briefly, then gradually return your attention to your breathing. Treat noise as a natural part of your environment rather than something to be avoided. Some people find it helpful to think of themselves as 'merging' with the noise, or 'absorbing' it. This strategy can be surprisingly effective when you are trying to work, relax or sleep in a noisy situation.

- Don't become obsessive about getting your breathing 'perfect'. Don't force yourself to breathe deeply. Adopt the attitude of 'allowing' it to happen.

- Set a timer for five or ten minutes so you don't drift off to sleep. If you do drift off and sleep for longer than 15–20 minutes, you may feel groggy when you wake up.

Use the breathing-focus technique:

- When you feel stressed, especially when stressful thoughts keep intruding.

- To get to sleep when your mind is overactive or your body is tense.

- Routinely for five or 10 minutes once or twice a day. This will increase your alertness and concentration, and also act as an anxiety preventative.

Relaxation and breathing tape

If you would like a professionally prepared tape of the three-stage relaxation method, plus a user's manual, visit www.rational.org.nz/public/relaxtape.htm.

17 Coping with the stress in your life

As well as the rethinking, behavioural and relaxation techniques already covered, there are some additional strategies you may find helpful. *Problem-solving, assertiveness training* and *stress management* can reduce the negative activating events in your life. *Coping plans* and *self-instruction* can help you manage day-to-day problems.

Problem-solving

Anxiety may be easier to deal with if you have a structured approach to solving the problems in your life. We engage in problem-solving many times a day. Much of the time we do it unawares, at other times we consciously grapple with a problem. Choosing an ice-cream flavour, balancing a budget and finding care for an elderly parent are all examples of problem-solving.

Sometimes a problem is especially difficult to solve, and calls for a structured approach. This involves going through a series of steps: defining the problem, obtaining information, developing courses of action, putting these into practice and evaluating the results. You can follow the process laid out below when you have problems that require major decisions, or when there is no obvious course of action.

You don't have to go through all the stages with every problem. Some problems can be dealt with quickly. Others, especially those that involve major changes in your life, can warrant spreading the process over days or even weeks.

When faced with a difficult problem — stop! Don't panic and do the first thing that comes to mind. If your emotions are running high, free up your thinking by doing a *rational self-analysis* (p. 52).

Step 1: Spell out the problem

State the problem in concrete terms. Be specific: 'Our average weekly expenditure is $180.00 more than our income' is better than 'We can't make ends meet.' Also, break the problem down into its various parts. This will help you see it more clearly and allow you to work on it in manageable chunks. Be very clear as to exactly what you see as problematical.

Step 2: Collect information

Gather information on the problem. There are some tips on doing this later (see page 133).

Step 3: Set goals

Express the various parts of the problem as goals. State these as specifically as possible so you can know when they have been achieved. 'To be able to keep our spending within our income and save $2000.00 per year' is a goal that can be objectively measured.

Don't settle on your goals until you have considered everything you might wish for, however fanciful. 'I wish our creditors would all disappear' may be asking for the unlikely, but it might trigger some creative thinking that could lead to 'We could reduce the number of creditors by taking no more credit.'

After thinking widely and imaginatively, finalise the goals towards which you are going to work.

Step 4: Develop solutions

First, list a range of possible strategies for reaching the goals you have set. Use the *brainstorming* procedure: write down every potential solution you can think of, no matter how way-out any of them may seem. The idea is to generate the largest number of options you can. Don't criticise any or attempt to analyse how workable they are — go for quantity rather than quality. 'Go busking for money' deserves a place alongside 'Draw up a budget.' Even highly impractical ideas may trigger other, more realistic ones.

Next, decide which strategies to pursue. Carefully examine all the options you have written down, asking three questions about each:

1. What are the likely *consequences* of pursuing this—both negative and positive, for myself and significant others, in both the long and short term?
2. How does this fit with my *personal value system?*
3. How *useful* would this be in helping me achieve the goal I have set? (This is where, if you can't sing very well, you decide that busking is out.)

A single strategy may be enough to achieve a goal, or you may need to follow several courses of action before you get there. Sometimes there will not be any solution that is desirable; the best you can do then is decide which would be the least unsatisfactory option.

Step 5: Identify any blocks to your strategies

Is there anything that might prevent you from applying the strategies you have chosen? Identify them now. For example, if your children are used to an allowance you can no longer afford, think about ways to get them to cooperate with the new financial regime.

Step 6: Develop tactics

By now you will have decided on one or more strategies aimed at achieving your various goals. You could describe these strategies as *subgoals*. Now it is time to generate some *tactics* — that is, specific actions for carrying out your strategies (and so achieving your subgoals). Tactics are what you actually *do*.

Let's say, for example, that your strategy is 'To get budgeting help.' Some tactics might be:

1. Ring Citizens Advice Bureau to see what budgeting organisations exist in our area.
2. Talk to some friends who have had budgeting help.

Once again, use the brainstorming method described in Step 3. Go for the maximum number of ideas. You might consider such actions as consulting the local budgeting service, obtaining a library book or consumer magazine about saving on household costs, or talking to your creditors.

Next, select the tactics to put into action. Be guided in your selection by asking the same questions as at Step 4. What are the likely consequences of each tactic? How does it fit with my personal value system? Will it be useful in implementing the strategy concerned? Also ask yourself: Will this tactic get around the potential blocks I have identified?

Step 7: Put your tactics into action
Carry out the tactics you have chosen.

Step 8: Evaluate the results
If you don't get the results you want, don't give up. Return to an earlier stage of the process and start again from there.

Some problem-solving suggestions

When there is more than one problem
It is usually best to deal with problems in order of needs first, then desires. Satisfaction of a higher-level *desire* is unlikely when lower-level *needs* remain unmet. Social desires or aspirations, for instance, are not likely to be an issue when you lack food. Developing a talent will usually take second place to finding somewhere to live. The following chart, adapted from the hierarchy of needs described by psychologist Abraham Maslow, illustrates the progression from needs to desires:

Desires	*Self-actualisation*	Self-fulfilment through developing talents, abilities and potential.
	Positive view of self	Self-respect, a sense of competence.
	Social connection	Feeling of belonging, receiving affection, intimacy.
	Safety and security	Shelter, avoidance of pain.
Necessities	*Physical survival*	Food, water, rest.

Trying to solve more than one problem at a time may leave you feeling overwhelmed. If you pick off your problems one by one, you will have a much better chance of dealing with them effectively. Separate and prioritise them so the most important get dealt with first. If you are concerned you might forget any, make a record of those you are putting on hold.

Getting information to aid problem-solving

To develop solutions you require information. Here is a process to help you gather information relevant to a problem you are working on:

- *Identify what information you need.* After you have defined the problem, ask: 'What do I need to know to reach a solution?'
- *Identify possible sources of information* — your own experience, other people, community education classes, organisations, books, magazines, audio- or videotapes, the internet, etc.
- *Access the sources you have identified.*
- *Extract the information.* Be selective; try to record only relevant information, and summarise it so you are not overwhelmed by facts.
- *Synthesise the information.* Put together the separate pieces of information to form a new combination that addresses the problem.

Practice on less critical problems

Don't wait for a really big problem to arise before you learn to problem-solve — practise on less critical difficulties. See how the above method works for you, and if necessary modify it to suit your style.

Assertiveness training

Many anxious people have developed unassertive ways of dealing with other people that create anxiety about asking for what they want and saying 'No' to what they don't want. If you are such a person, learning the principles and skills of assertiveness could be useful (after you have begun to gain some control over your anxiety). You can learn assertiveness techniques from books (see page 304), training courses or an appropriately trained counsellor.

Coping plans

If you fear you won't be able to cope with a particular situation, adopt strategies that prepare you for dealing with it. There are two main types of strategy:

1. *Coping techniques* such as relaxation, postponing a worry and rational self-analysis. Develop a number of these so you have the flexibility of choice.
2. *Distractions* for taking your mind off the thing that is making you anxious. Carry out, and concentrate on, specific tasks, such as mowing the lawn or painting the house, and/or indulge in pleasant activities, such as soaking in the bath, telephoning a friend, reading a novel or watching a video. List 10–20 such tasks and activities.

Write down the strategies before you need to use them. Be clear as to exactly what you are to do in each case, and be sure you choose strategies that will actually help you reduce your anxiety. Remember that the purpose of adopting these strategies is to *cope* with the situation about which you are anxious, not to be especially skilful. You can record your strategies as follows:

	What I can do when I am alone	What I can do with others
During the day		
During the evening		
If I wake in the night		

Positive self-instruction

People often tell themselves what *not* to do, e.g. 'Don't get out of control' or 'Don't mess this up.' *Negative* instructions like these tend to increase anxiety by focusing attention on potential dangers.

Try using *positive* self-instruction instead, e.g. 'Be concerned' or 'Be careful.' Make sure your instructions are realistic: avoid impracticable affirmations like 'Everything's going to be fine' or 'I'm totally in control', which won't necessarily be true and are likely to be ineffective or to help only in the short term. Realistic self-instruction will work better in the long run.

Twelve strategies for stress management

General stress management is a huge topic in its own right and as such is beyond the scope of this book. But below is a list of strategies for managing stress that are especially relevant to coping with anxiety:

1. Be able to relax your body and mind.
2. Know how to solve problems.
3. Sleep well.
4. Have clear and realistic goals. Knowing what you want out of life will help you make wise day-to-day decisions in keeping with your goals and values.
5. Care for your body. Eat a balanced diet; use caffeine and alcohol in moderation, avoid harmful drugs, and maintain a regular exercise programme appropriate to your health, age and level of fitness.
6. Maintain a helpful support system that includes family and friends.
7. Be able to act assertively in your dealings with other people.
8. Keep stimulation and variety in your life.
9. Manage your time effectively.
10. Manage your financial and material resources in ways that minimise stress and help you achieve your goals.
11. Manage change in your life.
12. Be able to ask for help when you need it.

Some of these strategies are described elsewhere in this book, and all are dealt with in depth in my earlier book *GoodStress*.[1] While stress management alone is unlikely to be enough to deal with problem anxiety, reducing unneeded pressure in your life will almost certainly help.

Part III
Managing specific types of anxiety

18 Worry

It is wise to be concerned about the chance of things going wrong in your life. Concern can keep you alert and motivate you to fix things. For some people, though, concern gets out of hand. They think obsessively about their problems, while doing little to solve them. Or they simply feel anxious 'about everything'. For these people, concern has turned into worry.

People can worry about almost anything. The most common worries are over finances, performance at work, coping in social situations and the possibility of an illness or accident. For some, the symptoms of worry can cause significant distress, disrupting their work, social or personal lives.

Worrying may involve avoidance behaviour. While this is usually less focused than with other types of problem anxiety, it is still disruptive and reinforces the problem because it gets in the way of action. Severe worrying may be referred to as *generalised anxiety disorder* (GAD).

Most people who worry would rather not, but find it hard to stop the flow of unwanted thoughts. Some even worry about not worrying, fearing that bad things will creep up on them if they are not constantly on the alert. In this chapter, you will learn why human beings worry, why you don't need to and how to stop if you do.

Let's return to Paul, the worrier we met in chapter 1. He was a 46-year-old self-employed builder. His business was successful and his home life stable — but this didn't stop him worrying. He had worried since childhood, the tendency worsening as he grew older. He worried about money, the security of his business, the health of his wife and children, whether he would still have friends in the future, anything that might possibly go wrong with his car, work that needed doing on his house — in fact, just about anything he put his mind to was a potential subject for apprehension.

Worrying gave him stomach pains and cost him sleep, his productivity declined because he worried instead of doing, and his wife was tired of constantly hearing about what might go wrong in the future. Unfortunately, Paul found it next to impossible to control his worrying thoughts.

What is worry?

Worry is a chain, or stream, of negative thoughts and images about concerns, usually related to the future. It involves a combination of *obsessive thinking* about how to solve or avoid problems, and *catastrophising* about the possible consequences of those problems. Put another way, you are worrying when you obsessively think about your problems, fear what they might lead to, but do little about them. Worrying is a way of *thinking*. It leads to the set of *feelings* we call *anxiety*: tension, apprehensiveness, frustration, upset stomach, and so on.

Anxiety is a natural 'warning bell'. The feelings of which it is composed are designed to alert us to possible danger and, ideally, to motivate us to take action to deal with the danger. Worrying, however, while *seemingly* aimed at finding solutions to problems usually produces the opposite result. When people worry, they foresee bad things happening and feel anxious; but instead of doing something about their worries, they keep ruminating — mulling them over and over in their minds. Whereas *appropriate* anxiety leads to action — after which the symptoms subside — *worry* just goes on and on.

This was Denise's experience. A hard-working mother of two (Liam and Joanna) and homemaker in her late thirties, Denise also worked as a receptionist–typist for a large medical practice. Her husband, Nigel, was a senior manager with a software manufacturers.

Denise was thinking about a message from Joan, the practice manager, signalling some changes to her conditions of employment. She was unhappy with the changes, but instead of clarifying what she wanted, she just kept turning over in her mind what might happen if she disagreed with Joan, which made her feel increasingly tense and upset.

Why do people worry?

Worry originates in the natural — and quite rational — human tendency to reflect on problems and dangers in order to solve or avoid them. But, like many other human tendencies, this one can become exaggerated and take on a life of its own, causing a person to keep thinking about a problem but do nothing to deal with it.

Perhaps the main reason many people keep worrying is this: *they think it somehow protects them from danger*. They hold beliefs such as 'I must always be prepared for danger', 'If I don't worry, bad things might creep up on me' and 'If I worry, I can stop bad things from happening.'

Worry also becomes a *habit*, which makes it hard to stop. The belief that worry 'stops bad things happening' is reinforced because, usually, nothing does happen — which leads the worrier to assume, superstitiously, that this was because they worried!

Emotional reasoning plays a part — thinking that because you *feel* anxious, this somehow *proves* that something bad is likely to happen. Worrying, because it creates fearful images in the mind, feeds the idea that danger really does exist.

Worrying is often fuelled by *demands for safety* — that life must be completely safe, certain things must be guaranteed, one's marriage, home, money, job, etc. must be totally protected. If you view anything as an absolute *need* rather than as a *preference*, you are going to worry about it. And if you believe 'There *must* be a perfect solution to every problem', whenever you are faced with a situation that doesn't have an obvious 'best' choice, you are likely to put off doing anything about it.

Self-image issues may be involved. Some people think it is 'caring' or 'responsible' to worry, believing 'If I don't worry, that will show I'm an uncaring/irresponsible person.' And a person who is overly concerned about disapproval or criticism from other people will tend to worry about making mistakes, looking foolish or saying or doing 'the wrong thing'. Similarly, someone who lacks confidence in their ability to cope with life's demands and stresses is more likely to worry about the chance of them happening.

For Denise, worrying had been a lifetime habit. She felt uncomfortable when she was not worrying, believing it somehow protected her from danger catching her unawares. Underlying this tendency were internal demands, self-taught during childhood, such as 'Life must be safe' and 'I must ensure that nothing bad happens to me or my family unless I am prepared for it.' She also believed she would be an irresponsible person if she didn't worry about the possibility of danger to her family.

The vicious circle of worrying

Worrying, like other anxiety-related problems, involves a vicious circle. An activating event — a problem experience — triggers an underlying predisposition to worry. This stimulates the symptoms of anxiety. The symptoms are interpreted as a warning of danger. This increases the anxiety. A loop is thus established: by focusing on the worrying and its symptoms, a person effectively takes their attention off the original problem. Here is a graphical representation of the process using the *ABC* model introduced on page 28 (*A* = activating event, *B* = beliefs/thinking about *A*, *C* = consequence of *B*):

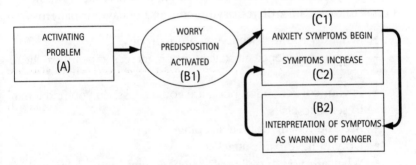

What you can do about it

The usual aims of a self-treatment programme for worrying, and the strategies for achieving them, are as follows:

- To *restrain obsessive worrying*, using rethinking and problem-solving techniques.

- To *control physical symptoms* with relaxation and breathing control.
- To *reduce avoidance behaviour* by using graduated exposure.
- To *solve problems more effectively* using new skills.
- To *develop a lifestyle that minimises worrying* by changing self-defeating behaviours.

Start by clarifying the problem

Is worrying a feature of your life in general? Or has it only begun recently, or does it occur only under certain circumstances? If either of the latter, there may be some other issues to check out:

- Depression (see page 45).
- Medical disorders, e.g. hyperthyroidism or diabetes (see your medical advisor if you are in any doubt).
- Substance-induced anxiety (you will need to do something about the substance use before anything else).
- Anxiety resulting from trauma (see page 236).

When you are ready to begin work on the worrying itself, the first step is to make a list of your symptoms and behaviour patterns:

- What do you feel while you are worrying?
- Do you experience muscular tension, increased heartbeat, headaches?
- Is your concentration poor, are you restless, do you find it hard to settle to tasks?
- Are you having trouble sleeping?
- Do you have panic attacks?
- What are you avoiding? Do you procrastinate, delay making decisions, neglect everyday tasks (such as paying bills) or fail to check out concerns (such as getting a lump examined by a doctor)?

You may find it helpful to record some of this information in a diary for clarifying your worry patterns, as described next.

Identify your worry patterns

Keep a log of your worrying thoughts and avoidance behaviour for a month or so. Ask yourself:

- *What do I typically worry about?* This might include such things as dealing with financial matters, tackling tasks about which you lack confidence, acting assertively with others, you or a loved one becoming ill, making mistakes, upsetting others.
- *What do I typically avoid?* Recording this will provide additional clues to what you worry about. If you avoid balancing your chequebook or paying bills, this may reflect the fact that you worry about money; putting things off at work may suggest you worry about your performance.

Identify any lifestyle factors that could increase anxiety

- Are you overusing caffeine, alcohol or unhealthy food?
- Are you using any drugs, including cannabis?
- Do you get adequate exercise?

Develop your plan

Clarify your goals

List the goals of your self-treatment plan. As far as possible, state them in specific, behavioural terms. For example:

- To reduce my episodes of worry to 30 minutes maximum.
- To know how to solve difficult problems.
- To balance my chequebook within one week of receiving my monthly bank statement.
- To wean myself off tranquillisers.

Aim to minimise your worrying as far as possible, but not to eliminate it entirely — otherwise you will set yourself up to be disillusioned. Striving for management rather than cure will almost certainly increase your chance of success.

Draw up your treatment plan

Next, draw up your self-treatment plan. This will be based on the information you have gathered about the nature of your problem — its symptoms and patterns. List the various strategies and techniques you will use to achieve your treatment goals. These might include any of the following:

- Self-education about the nature of worrying and anxiety in general.
- Rethinking strategies to reduce worrying, e.g. reality-checking, stimulus control. (The *six-step worry plan*, outlined on the next page, may be the most effective strategy.)
- Relaxation training or breathing control to reduce tension and other physical symptoms.
- Exposure to any activities and situations you have been avoiding.
- Changing any dysfunctional core beliefs.
- Learning to use problem-solving or assertiveness training to deal with issues that need attention.
- Appropriate lifestyle changes.

The basics of overcoming worry

Accept that worrying is not helpful

Worrying has *no* positive benefits. It does not help you avoid danger. Bad things happen to people no matter how much they worry. Worrying just adds a further layer of emotional pain. Nor does worrying solve problems. In fact, it gets in the way of problem-solving. It is unproductive, because it leads to procrastination rather than action. It affects the body, creating stomach ulcers, muscular tension and headaches. It stops people enjoying the present moment by keeping them focused on what might happen in the future. And the longer you worry about something, the worse it seems.

The first step, then, is to remind yourself that worrying is both unnecessary and bad for you. Using the *worry calculator* on page 68 is a good way to begin getting your worrying in perspective.

Have a replacement for worry

Simply telling yourself to 'stop worrying' is unlikely to be enough, because usually there are matters that require specific attention. What you need is a realistic replacement for worry. The best alternative is to be 'concerned'. How does concern differ from worry? It is still a negative emotion, but not as draining, and it leads to action rather than rumination. Make concern your aim.

Have an anti-worry procedure

Finally, have some kind of procedure you can follow when you realise you have slipped into worrying again, e.g. the *six-step worry plan*.

The six-step worry plan

Worrying is a hard habit to break. The six-step plan provides a well-structured procedure for beating it. Here is a summary of what is involved:

1. *Pause* when you catch yourself worrying. To combat worrying, you need to recognise when you are doing it.
2. *Identify the real issue.* Ask yourself: 'What am I really concerned about?'
3. *Do a reality check.* Ask yourself: 'How likely is it that what I fear will happen?' and 'How bad would it be if it did?'
4. *Decide whether action is required.* Ask yourself: 'Do I need to do anything about this? Or is it something that is unlikely to happen, or about which I can't do anything anyway?'
5. *Take action* to *solve* the problem when the thing you fear *is* likely to happen.
6. *Let the worry go* when you decide it *isn't* really an issue, using psychological strategies.

Let's look at these steps in greater detail.

1. Pause

Catch yourself worrying

Pick up on the early signs of worrying. Worrying, and its attendant

145

anxiety, is much easier to inhibit at an early stage, before it begins to spiral. Learn to self-monitor. Note any signs that may indicate you are starting to worry:

- You feel uncomfortable, anxious, tense or unhappy.
- You are mulling something over but doing little about it.
- You are predicting catastrophic consequences.
- You are engaging in avoidance behaviour.

Also note whatever triggers these responses. Acknowledge that you are worrying rather than problem-solving, and that this not only feels bad but is unproductive. *Stop drifting* — consciously stop and *take action*. You might find it helpful to keep a diary for a few weeks to help identify what signs to watch for.

Denise eventually realised that her tension, upset stomach and poor concentration indicated she was worrying again, so she decided to sit down with pen and paper to analyse what was going on in her mind.

Decide what to do with the worry

With some worries, it is helpful to go through all the steps in the worry plan; with others, you can skip some steps:

- If you are already clear in your mind as to what you are really worried about, go straight to step 3.
- If you think the issue is not worth worrying about at all, go straight to step 6.
- If the issue seems important but you don't have time to deal with it immediately, make a commitment to revisit it at a specific time — then let go of the worry for the interim. If letting go is difficult, see the strategies under step 6.

2. Identify the real issue

Sometimes you will be quite certain what the real issue is, in which case you can proceed straight to step 3. At other times, though, you will only feel vague discomfort, or you will have identified the trigger to your worries but not the underlying issue.

List your concerns and select the main one

Start by asking yourself questions such as 'What am I bothered about?' or 'What is the issue?' Write down the answers. You may well have more than one thing on your mind — list them.

If this is difficult because the worrying seems to be unfocused, it may help to pause, sit down, be aware of the feelings of discomfort in your body and focus your mind on them. Then ask the questions again.

Denise listed four things that were on her mind to a greater or lesser degree:

1. The message from Joan.
2. Liam complained of toothache before school this morning.
3. Received a larger-than-usual electricity bill a week ago.
4. Nigel has begun talking about leaving his secure job and setting up a business of his own.

If you have a list of more than one, ask yourself: 'Which of these things am I most worried about? Which is contributing most to my feelings of discomfort?' You will usually answer intuitively. (Refocusing on the physical sensations of discomfort may help you do this.) Whichever item you choose is the 'key issue'.

Denise relaxed herself, cleared her mind and concentrated on her feelings of anxiety. Before long, an image of her manager sitting at her desk floated into her mind. She deduced from this that the issue with Joan was the key concern on which to work.

List your thoughts and select the main one

What are you telling yourself about this issue? What is it about it that most bothers you? List your thoughts about it, like you listed your concerns.

Denise listed three thoughts:

1. The changes could mean less flexibility in my hours.
2. If I don't say anything, I'll become resentful.
3. If I disagree with Joan, she'll think I'm being difficult.

147

Now choose the 'key thought' — the one you intuitively sense is most associated with your feeling of anxiety. Denise decided that her key thought was: 'If I disagree with Joan, she'll think I'm being difficult.'

Follow the thought chain

Expand on the key thought in order to identify the main underlying issue. You are seeking to answer questions like the following: 'What am I ultimately anxious about?', What exactly am I predicting will happen?' and 'What is the crucial issue with that?'

Do this by *chaining* (first introduced on page 59). Worrying thoughts usually run in chains, one 'link' leading to another. For example:

> If Nigel goes into business we'll be even more short of money ⇒ We'll have to cut back ⇒ The kids will go without ⇒ My mother will criticise me for not caring for them properly ⇒ I'll feel bad about myself ⇒ and so on.

Move down the chain asking yourself questions like 'What really bothers me about that?', 'What is worrying about that' or 'If that were true, what would that mean to me?' Denise began like this:

Thought:	If I disagree with Joan, she'll think I'm being difficult.
Question:	Assuming she does, what will that mean to me?
Thought:	She'll think less of me.
Question:	And if she thinks less of me?
Thought:	1. She'll be less keen to help me develop my career.
	2. She'll tell other people I'm difficult.

Denise then considered which of these two last thoughts was the most significant and decided it was (1). She continued:

Question:	What will bother me about that?
Thought:	My career will suffer; I won't advance.
Question:	What is worrying about that?
Thought:	My mother will think I'm a failure.
Question:	What would that mean to me?
Thought:	I couldn't stand it; it would be unbearable.

Identify your evaluation-thinking

Note that Denise is engaged in two types of worrying thinking. First, most of her thoughts are *inferences*, i.e. statements about what she *thinks* will happen, such as 'My mother will think I'm a failure.' Second, she *evaluates* her inferences, e.g. '. . . it would be *unbearable*.' It is usually evaluative thoughts that create distress, and most thinking chains end with one.

As we have already seen, there are four main types of evaluative thinking that are likely to cause people trouble (see page 31 for more information):

- *Demanding* — putting 'shoulds' and 'musts' on ourselves (and sometimes on others). Ask yourself: 'What demands are involved? What am I telling myself *should* or *must* be; or *should not* or *must not* happen? Am I thinking I *must* worry, otherwise (a) something bad will happen, or (b) it'll mean I'm uncaring?'
- *Awfulising* — evaluating something as catastrophic or as the worst thing that could happen. Ask yourself: 'What am I thinking would be awful/terrible/horrible?'
- *Can't-stand-it-itis* — viewing something as 'unbearable' or 'intolerable'. Ask yourself: 'What threat to my comfort do I fear? What would be *unbearable* if it occurred?'
- *Self-rating* — evaluating one's total self on the basis of one or a few characteristics or behaviours. Ask yourself: 'What threat to my self-image do I fear? What do I think such and such would *prove about me as a person* if it were to happen?'

What kind of evaluative thinking was Denise engaging in? She identified *can't-stand-it-itis* at the end of her thought chain: '. . . it would be unbearable'. On reflection, she realised she was evaluating her mother's criticism as 'unbearable' because, subconsciously, she believed that if she were to fail at something important it would somehow prove she was a failure as a person. On further reflection, she realised that underlying this self-rating belief was a demand: 'To be OK as a person I must achieve and succeed at whatever I do, and never fail at anything that is important to me.'

Step 2 may seem rather long and laborious at first glance, but it is worth the time and effort. Face it — you're already using up a lot of time and energy by worrying! Combat it now and you'll save a lot of time in the future.

3. Do a reality check

Having identified the real issue, it's time to check it out. There are three key questions to ask about it:

1. 'How does this thought affect me?'
2. 'What evidence is there?'
3. 'Does it follow?'

How does this thought affect me?
'Is it helpful or harmful to believe this?' Ask this question about any worrying thought. Weigh up the benefits and costs of *worrying* against the benefits and costs of being *concerned*.

Denise decided that her underlying demand — to achieve, succeed and never fail — far from helping her achieve, often blocked her from getting on when success was not guaranteed, thereby causing her unnecessary anguish and anxiety.

What evidence is there?
'What evidence is there that x will occur (and in the way I predict) and what evidence is there that it won't?' These questions are most relevant to inferential thoughts. Consider in particular:

- What is (a) the worst that could happen, (b) the best that could happen, and (c) the most likely to happen?
- What are the chances (use a 0–100% scale) that these things will happen, and what are the chances that they won't?
- What does the evidence suggest?
- How often in the past have your worries actually come to pass, and how often have they not?

You might find it helpful to test the soundness of your predictions;

see *hypothesis testing* on page 67.

Denise realised that her chain of inferences about what her boss Joan would think was not supported by the evidence. In fact, past experience showed that Joan usually listened and took a reasonable position with her staff when they disagreed with her. Denise did consider it likely, though, that if her career suffered for some reason, her mother probably *would* criticise her — but challenged the idea that her mother's views somehow proved something about her.

Does it follow?

'Does it logically follow that if *x* happened, *y* would be the result?' This question is particularly useful with evaluative thoughts.

Denise challenged her underlying demand that she *must* succeed, asking herself: 'Does it logically follow that because it would be *desirable* to achieve, I absolutely *must*? And how does it follow that when I fail at something, I go from being OK as a person to not OK?' The answer, of course, is neither one of these follows.

Summary of the disputation process

There is more information about disputing self-defeating beliefs on page 63. Here is a summary of the questions to consider:

- 'What is the *evidence*? What is the likelihood that what I fear really will happen?'
- 'Where is it written that because I *prefer* bad things not to happen, they *must* not?'
- 'If it did happen, would it really be *awful* or *unbearable* — or simply *unpleasant* but survivable?'
- 'Would such and such an event really prove something about the kind of *person* I am?'

4. Decide whether action is required

Decide what, if anything, to do about the issue bothering you:

- Does the issue need attention? If so, either get on to it immediately, or make a concrete plan to attend to it later. Be very specific about what actions you will take and when you will take them (see step 5).

- If you decide the issue is not really important after all, let it go. If you find letting go difficult, as most people who worry do, see the strategies described in step 6.

5. Problem-solve and take action

For issues that require action, structured problem-solving will help you plan it. Follow these steps:

1. Gather information. What are the facts?
2. Clarify exactly what the problem is.
3. Identify the cause(s).
4. List all the options for action available.
5. Decide on the most appropriate option(s).
6. Carry out the action(s) you have decided on.

Ask yourself: 'Can I sort this out on my own? Or would it be better to obtain some help? If the latter, who can I ask, and what is stopping me from asking them?' See page 129 for more on problem-solving.

6. Let the worry go

What do you do when you have checked out a worry and either problem-solved or decided that it doesn't need attention, but you still can't get it out of your mind? The answer is to apply letting-go strategies.

Break the connection between your worry and its triggers

If the conditions under which worrying happens are restricted, it gradually becomes associated with fewer and fewer triggers or stimuli. With this in mind, Thomas Borkovec and his associates at Pennsylvania State University developed a technique known as *stimulus control*. It involves interrupting worry whenever it is triggered, postponing it till a set time each day. The idea of postponing worry may sound a bit strange at first, but people find it surprisingly effective once they try it. Postponing breaks the connection between a worry and its trigger. The procedure is as follows:

1. Schedule a 15–30 minute 'worry period' at the same time each day (the evening is usually best).
2. Postpone all worrying till that time. Tell yourself you will focus on the issue then. Do the same if you wake in the night and find yourself worrying. To help get the worry out of your mind in the meantime, do one or more of the following:
   - Write down the worry in a notebook. (Carry this around with you, and keep it by your bed.)
   - Use *distraction*, *thought-stopping* (p. 108) or the *breathing focus* technique (p. 126).
   - Work out the anxiety with physical exercise — walking, jogging, swimming, etc.
   - Talk it over with someone else.
3. When you come to the worry period:
   - Go through the concerns you have postponed and decide which of them are still issues (many will not be).
   - Use problem-solving on those that you decide need action.
   - Let go of the others.

Distract your mind

Once you have decided that a particular worry is not justified, you can inhibit the obsessive thinking involved by distracting yourself in any number of ways. For example:

- Entertainment: watching TV, listening to music.
- Physical activity: gardening, home maintenance, household tasks, walking, jogging, swimming.
- Mental activities: using a computer, reading, arts and crafts, doing a puzzle.
- Relaxation: the *breathing focus* technique (p. 126), which not only relaxes the body but also clears the mind.

Begin by making your own list of suitable distractions. Keep this list where you know you can find it when you are worrying.

NB: Don't use distraction to put off problem-solving when there is something that really needs attention. Such avoidance may only lead to more serious worrying later on.

Interrupt the worrying
Use *thought-stopping* (p. 108) to cut an episode of worrying. Like distraction, it will help only temporarily, but can be useful for breaking patterns of obsessive thinking.

Rational cards
On a pocket-sized card write down the key *worrying* thought, or old belief, and a *rational alternative*, or new belief, and read them repeatedly every day. See page 87 for further guidance.

Release your tension
Learn how to reduce the tension in your body. Two ways to do this are the *breathing-focus* technique (p. 126) and *three-stage relaxation training* (p.114). The breathing focus technique is an excellent way to clear the mind as well as relax the body. Relaxation training can relieve sleep-preventing tension, as well as generally reduce the 'alarm signals' that a tense body sends to the mind.

Project your worry into the future
Time projection (p. 72) is a simple yet effective technique for combating catastrophising and getting a feared event into perspective:

- Visualise the feared event, then imagine going forward in time one day, a week, a month, six months, a year, and so on.
- Consider how you are likely to be feeling at each of these points in time.

What usually happens is that people envisage feeling better the further in time they get from the event. Time projection will help you see that if a bad event did occur, life would go on, even though you might need to make some adjustments.

Talk it over

Talking through a worry with someone else can help sort fact from fiction and aid problem-solving. Even if the other person does little more than listen, expressing a worry can help reduce the pressure.

A note to helpers: Mainly listen — don't judge, interrupt or give advice except when the worried person indicates they would like to hear your views.

Putting it all together

Denise, whose worrying tendency was a lifetime problem, decided that stimulus control would be a useful technique to develop. She set aside 7.00–7.30 p.m. as her worry period. Whenever she found herself worrying rather than acting, she wrote down what she was worrying about in a notebook she kept with her. Then, if the worrying thought reintruded, she combated it with a technique appropriate for the situation she was in at the time. At work, she read a rational card and then occupied herself with an absorbing task. Walking home, she distracted herself from worrying thoughts by closely observing the view. At home she used the breathing-focus technique. She sometimes used thought-stopping for especially intrusive thoughts. At 7.00 p.m., she opened her notebook and looked through her worry list. Many items seemed unimportant by then and she simply crossed them off. If an item merited attention, she analysed it in more detail, using problem-solving where appropriate. As time went by, she found she needed to record items in her notebook less and less, because her brain began to internalise the message that worrying served no useful purpose.

Dealing with a resistant worry

When a worry seems especially difficult to deal with, ask yourself three questions:

1. 'What is it about this worry that makes it hard to let go?'
   - 'What are the possibilities?' (Brainstorm ideas.)
   - 'What is the worst that could happen? What do I really fear?'

- 'Am I afraid that the consequences will reflect on my self-image, or affect how I live my life, or both?'
- 'What could there be that might actually need attending to? Is my concern exaggerated?'
- 'Is there some reason why I may be hanging on to this worry? Am I afraid of what will happen if I act?'

2. 'What is the outcome that I would really prefer to see?'
   - 'How would I like to see this concern resolved?'

3. 'What strategies and techniques could I be using here?'
   - 'What have I tried that hasn't worked? Why might it have failed?'
   - 'What haven't I tried yet? Why not?'
   - 'Have I done a rational self-analysis of this worry? Would it be helpful to do one?'
   - 'Could I be using stimulus control or distraction or some other technique?'
   - 'Would it help to talk it over with someone? Who could I talk with?'
   - 'What could I do right now to ease the worry?'

Confront what you fear

The more you avoid situations you fear, the larger they will loom in your mind. Conversely, if you repeatedly face your fears, you will discover that they rarely come to pass. As a result, you will eventually extinguish them. *Real-life exposure* (p. 94) is crucial to overcoming anxiety. It is usually most effective when undertaken in a graduated way, and only after you have developed rethinking skills, learnt how to relax and developed other coping strategies to use during exposure.

Identify your avoidance behaviour

Draw up two lists. In the first, write any major things you have been avoiding, such as going to the doctor to have something checked, tackling a contentious issue with another person, seeing an accountant about your debts, or starting an academic assignment. These may have accumulated if you have been worrying more than usual.

In the second, write the things you typically avoid in your every-day life. These may be harder to identify because they are more routine. Procrastination is a common avoidance behaviour: look for tendencies such as putting bills aside, delaying decisions, neglecting to balance your chequebook, putting off tasks for which you lack confidence, or failing to act assertively with other people. It will probably help to keep a *diary* (p. 47) for a month or two to identify these subtle types of avoidance behaviour.

Major avoidance: undertake graduated exposure

Select several items from the first list, develop *exposure hierarchies* for each and get started on the first step. See page 96 for how to do this.

Routine avoidance: act or postpone

Tackle the items on the second list either by acting on them immediately or by putting them off until a specific time. With the latter approach, be alert for two unhelpful outcomes: you continue to worry, or — at the other extreme — you simply forget to deal with the issue.

If you continue to worry, repeat steps 3 and 4 of the six-step plan. If the issue needs attention now rather than later, proceed with step 5.

If you tend to forget to deal with the issue at the set time, reflect on why that may be. You may need to develop a more efficient reminder system. Or the issue may be so anxiety-provoking that you are suppressing the anxiety and subconsciously forgetting as a way to avoid dealing with it. If the latter, make yourself confront the issue. You could do this by completing a full *rational self-analysis* (p. 52) and then doing some exposure work to tackle it directly.

Beyond letting go

Analysing a worry and letting it go is only part of the picture. There are other things you can do to reduce your tendency to worry in the long term.

Take preventative action

As you start to get a grip on your worry, begin developing strategies that will reduce the likelihood of it happening in the first place.

Could you make helpful changes to your lifestyle? Do you worry about such matters as overspending, debt, your health or your job? Do you do things that increase your feelings of anxiety, such as overusing stimulants like sugar or caffeine, taking insufficient exercise or abusing substances? If so, list them. Keep a diary for a month or two of all the things you worry about, then summarise the themes that emerge. Use *problem-solving* (p. 129) to help make changes. If motivation is an issue, see page 285 for guidance on enhancing it.

Plan ahead. Identify the things you typically worry about, then develop strategies to handle them more effectively. For example, if you worry about being on time, you could buy a second alarm clock to wake you in the morning, or a digital organiser to remind you of appointments. Plan in advance for major activities and developments, such as maintaining your car, studying, moving house, giving birth, growing old and looking after your health. If you worry about it, plan for it — although ensure your planning does not itself become an obsession or a source of worry, and don't *overplan* for things that are unlikely to happen.

Develop confidence in your ability to cope with life

If you think you lack the ability to cope with life's demands and stresses, you are likely to worry about them. See page 79 for guidance on developing *ability confidence*. If there are things you frequently worry about, learn as much as you can about them. Understanding the things you fear will give you more power over them and build your confidence in your ability to cope.

Deal with perfectionism

Do you have perfectionist expectations? Watch for absolutist beliefs like 'Every problem has a perfect solution and I must find it.' Perfection is impossible, and expecting it will keep you tense and anxious and make you less productive. Accept that there is never one 'right' solution — only solutions that are better or worse than each other.[1]

158

Work towards self-acceptance

Do you worry about criticism and disapproval from other people, or fear that if such and such occurs you will be shown to be deficient as a human being? Much worrying is of this nature. The solution is to develop self-acceptance. This involves uncovering and changing any *demand* that you be something other than what you are. See page 79 for guidance on developing self-acceptance.

Accept what you can't change

What if you can't change something you dislike? This is where acceptance of reality comes in. Acceptance is a way of coping with the realities of life when things don't happen as we would wish — as is often the case. To accept something is to do three things:

1. *Acknowledge that it exists.* See it as inevitable that many things will not be to your liking, and view uncertainty, frustration and disappointment as aspects of normal life.
2. *Understand that there is no reason why it should not exist.* You may *prefer* people or things to be different from how they are, and you may even work at changing them, but remind yourself there is no 'Law of the Universe' that says they *should* or *must* be different.
3. *See it as bearable.* Acknowledge that you dislike some things and find them unpleasant, but without catastrophising them as 'horrible' or 'unbearable'.

Some people have trouble with the idea of acceptance. They think that to accept something means they have to like it, agree with it, justify it, be indifferent to it, or resign themselves to it. But acceptance is none of these things. You can dislike something, see it as unjustified and continue to prefer that it not exist. You can be concerned about it. You can take action to change it, if change is possible. But you can still accept it by rejecting the notion that it *should* not exist and that it absolutely *must* be changed.

Acceptance can be summed up by a paraphrase of an old saying: 'Have the courage to change the things you can, the serenity to accept the things you can't — and the wisdom to know the difference.'

159

From worry to concern

Finally, the most important aspect of all: changing the self-defeating beliefs that maintain the worrying habit. Here are some typical irrational worry-causing beliefs, with rational alternatives:

Worry beliefs	Concern beliefs
If I worry about things that might be dangerous, unpleasant or frightening, I can stop them happening.	Worrying about things that might go wrong won't stop them happening, but will upset me now. Better to do what I can about the future, and then get on with living in the present.
There are certain things in life that I just can't stand.	Certain things are uncomfortable or unpleasant, but it's wrong to say I 'can't stand' them. If that were true, I wouldn't be here to tell the tale.
I should worry when other people have problems or feel unhappy.	I can't change other people's problems and bad feelings by getting myself upset.
It is caring to worry. If I didn't worry, it would mean I was an uncaring person.	Worrying has nothing to do with caring. Better I demonstrate caring in *action* rather than rumination.
If I feel anxious, this proves something bad is likely to happen.	I feel because of what I *think*. Assuming that a feeling proves something about reality is 'emotional reasoning'.
Life must be safe: my marriage, home, money, job, etc. must be guaranteed.	Safety is desirable, but in real life there are no guarantees. Making safety a 'must' rather than a preference will just keep me worrying about it.
Because I can't stand discomfort and pain, I must avoid them at all costs.	Total avoidance would mean a restricted life. Although I don't like discomfort and pain, I can bear them.
Every problem has an ideal solution, and I should not relax until I find it.	Problems usually have many possible solutions. The wisest thing is to select the best available and get on with it, and accept reality when I can't have the ideal.

The end of therapy

Your self-therapy will probably end when you have reduced your worrying to a manageable level and are facing all the things you were previously avoiding. Bear in mind, though, that some worries are almost certain to recur, especially at times of stress. Anticipating this is the best protection against slipping back into your old ways, because you will be ready to brush up your coping skills. Worrying need never take control of your life again.

Both Denise and Paul got their worrying under control. Paul accepted that it would take considerable effort to overcome a lifetime of anticipating disaster, and that he would probably never stop worrying completely. But reducing his apprehensiveness by 80 per cent made him and his family much happier. Whenever they find themselves worrying, Denise and Paul dust off their worry diaries and stop their fear before it takes over.

The effort has proved invaluable for both of them. It can be the same for you, so don't delay — start getting on top of your worrying now.

19 Panic attacks and avoidance behaviour

To have a panic attack is to experience a huge paradox. You feel overwhelming terror in the face of what appears to be extreme danger; yet, in reality, the danger is practically nil. A panic attack is a graphic demonstration of how fearful thinking can lead to escalating anxiety.

Panic attacks involve intense fear and discomfort. They are often unpredictable and usually lead to fear of future attacks. They begin suddenly, usually peak within 10 minutes and last less than 30 minutes. They may occur on a daily basis or only now and then. Many people wake at night with an attack.

If a person fears further attacks, they may avoid situations where panic symptoms are likely to occur, where they think escape may be difficult or embarrassing, or where help may not be readily available. If they do enter a feared situation, they may take someone with them, or ensure in advance that help is nearby.

Linda was like this. She engaged in avoidance behaviour to minimise the chance of having an attack. When her youngest child started high school and she took up work again as a clerical assistant, the discomfort she had felt for many years on entering public places such as supermarkets and theatres grew more intense. Matters came to a head when she began making excuses to avoid meetings or dealing with members of the public.

Not everyone who has panic attacks engages in avoidance behaviour, however. Take Wendy, the other sufferer we met in chapter 1. A legal receptionist, Wendy planned to marry her boyfriend of three years' standing. She admitted to being rather perfectionist, and overconcerned since childhood with self-control and behaving 'correctly'. She'd had a short depressive episode several years previously and been successfully treated with medication but without psychotherapy. Since then she had experienced occasional anxiety about getting depressed again, and strongly believed that she 'must never slip back'.

Wendy drank heavily at an office party and woke up the next day feeling low. Shortly after getting up she had a panic attack — her first. It soon passed, but from then on she increasingly feared further attacks — which, inevitably, triggered them. Eventually she was having attacks on an almost daily basis. While going ahead with her wedding, she was anxious about the possibility of having an attack in front of the guests.

Soon we'll see how Wendy and Linda dealt with their problem anxiety. First, let's look at the causes of panic and avoidance behaviour.

Vulnerability

There is increasing evidence that panic attacks, and associated avoidance behaviour, are the result of an underlying vulnerability coupled with particular ways of thinking.

As we have seen, if you suffer from excessive anxiety you probably have a *biologically based* or *inherited* propensity to become highly anxious in reaction to potential danger, which, over time, has led to a tendency to overfocus on potential danger. Why this manifests itself in panic as opposed to some other type of problem anxiety may be due, at least partly, to *learning* experiences. Linda's anxiety dated back to her earliest years, when the key influence in her life was her excessively safety-conscious mother. This suggests her being prone to panic attacks was the result not only of biological inheritance but also of parental influence.

Certain *personality factors* appear to predominate in people with a panic disorder, in particular perfectionism, self-imposed demands to perform well, overconcern with the approval and disapproval of others, and a belief that one's emotions are controlled by external factors. Wendy's lifelong perfectionism illustrates how a facet of personality can predispose a person to problem anxiety.

The exact influence of childhood learning on behaviour has yet to be established. What we know is that whatever the balance between biology and learning, some people appear more vulnerable to anxiety. They escalate feelings of anxiety into panic by interpreting them as omens of extreme danger, then catastrophising about the discomfort involved.

Causes of panic

Physiological factors

The fight-or-flight response involves an increase in the breathing rate, which can lead to overbreathing, also known as hyperventilation. Hyperventilation reduces the amount of carbon dioxide in the blood, causing dizziness, light-headedness, raised heartbeat, confusion and other symptoms. While the reduction is harmless in itself and has no long-term effect, the temporary sensations to which it gives rise can be frightening.

External or internal triggers

Panic attacks usually have an obvious trigger. Some are anticipated; for example, you go to a supermarket worrying you will have an attack there. Others are unexpected; for example, you are asked to speak at a gathering without prior warning.

A smaller percentage of attacks have no obvious trigger and appear to be totally spontaneous. However, it is likely these have a trigger that isn't consciously perceived; for example, internal bodily changes such as the heart missing a beat.

Many people report waking with night-time panic attacks. It appears we remain aware of our breathing and other bodily changes while we are asleep, and that detection of such changes may trigger panic. It is commonly observed that the initial sensations of panic on waking are quickly followed by catastrophising, which leads to an escalation of the anxiety.

Circular thinking

Your first panic attack may have one or more causes, e.g. surgery, illness, childbirth, miscarriage, loss, an accident, or even a drinking binge. It may be impossible to identify the initial trigger, but, fortunately, it isn't necessary to do so. Since your first, you will have been worrying about further attacks, and this worry will have brought them on thus creating a *panic cycle* (see below).

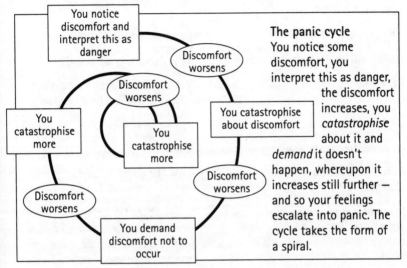

The panic cycle
You notice some discomfort, you interpret this as danger, the discomfort increases, you *catastrophise* about it and *demand* it doesn't happen, whereupon it increases still further — and so your feelings escalate into panic. The cycle takes the form of a spiral.

If you find that avoiding certain situations helps you avert panic attacks, you may also find yourself in an *avoidance cycle*. This builds on the panic cycle: you anticipate panicking if you enter a certain situation, which makes you anxious, so you decide to avoid or leave the situation, which makes you feel less anxious, and this reinforces the belief that 'Because it is unbearable to feel panic, I must avoid any situation where it might occur', a belief that is repetitively reinforced by subsequent avoidance, which makes you even more likely to avoid the situation in future — and so it goes on.

Panic attacks followed by avoidance behaviour graphically illustrate how, through circular thinking, moderate emotions can escalate into extreme reactions that are reinforced by repetition.

Panic beliefs

The panic and avoidance cycles both have two major components: *misinterpretations* of what is happening in the body, followed by *negative evaluations*.

Misinterpreting your body

The following is a list of typical physical sensations and their most common misinterpretations:[1]

Physical sensation	Misinterpretation
Abdominal or chest pain, faintness	'I'm having a *heart attack*.'
Faintness	'I'm about to *die*' or 'I'll *pass out in public*, which will be a disgrace.'
Difficulty breathing	'I'm about to *die*.'
Freezing, tremor, muscular weakness	'I'm having a *stroke*.'
Difficulty focusing and other cognitive changes	'I may be going *insane*.'
Sense of loss of control over internal sensations	'I may *go insane*' or 'I may *commit antisocial acts* (e.g. cause harm to others, commit suicide, engage in inappropriate sexual behaviour).'

Negative evaluations

Self-defeating evaluations of misinterpretations of the body may take the form of *catastrophising*, e.g. 'That would be the worst thing that could ever happen', *self-rating*, e.g. 'That would show I was crazy', or *demanding*, e.g. 'This must not happen.'

Panic sufferers also evaluate the *feeling* of panic itself, e.g. 'I can't stand it', 'Having this problem shows I'm a weak person', 'I must avoid this feeling, or any situation that might trigger it, at all costs.'

Control, discomfort and the fear of death

Most panic thinking seems to focus on three things:

- *Loss of control* that is usually taken for granted. You become aware that you have difficulty focusing, concentrating, thinking straight and controlling your actions. You may feel you are losing consciousness (although you rarely, if ever, do). Wendy felt like this, and found it especially frightening, having been overconcerned with self-control for most of her life. Loss of control may also involve *self-image anxiety*: 'I'm losing my mind/going mad', 'I may lose control and do things that will be embarrassing', 'Others may criticise me for having this problem' or 'I will feel bad about myself if I lose control.'

- *Fear of being overwhelmed by anxiety.* You are afraid of the feeling of panic itself — more than you fear whatever it was that triggered it. Typical thoughts behind such *discomfort anxiety* are usually along the lines of 'It's awful to feel this way', 'I can't stand these feelings' or 'I must avoid any situation where these feelings might occur.'

- *Fear of dying.* You misinterpret symptoms such as choking, a racing heart and breaking into a sweat as signs that you are about to die.

Core beliefs

Underlying these ways of thinking are core beliefs such as 'I can't stand discomfort or pain and must avoid them at all costs', 'I must avoid any danger to my physical or psychological wellbeing', 'I must be in total control of myself and/or my behaviour at all times' and 'Others must see me as a totally rational person who has complete self-control.'

An introduction to self-treatment

To overcome panic and avoidance behaviour, there are two things to do. First, develop skills to take rapid control of the symptoms. Most panic sufferers can learn to do this and so gain a degree of immediate relief. Second, change self-defeating beliefs to increase tolerance for anxious feelings in the longer term.

Avoidance behaviour may take longer to address than panic, especially if it has been going on for a long time. The most effective approach is graduated exposure to the situations commonly avoided (after learning coping skills to help do this), followed by work on the underlying core beliefs. This usually takes between six and 18 months.

Before going any further, a note on the use of medication for panic.

Some antidepressants may aid treatment by reducing the severity both of panic attacks and of baseline anxiety. On the negative side, benzodiazepine tranquillisers may provide short-term results at the cost of physical dependency and relapse when they are discontinued. They can also interfere with exposure work, because tolerance for anxious feelings in feared situations is unlikely to develop when those feelings are temporarily sedated.

The following is a summary of treatment for panic and avoidance behaviour:

1. *Assess* the problem; look at its history and identify any current contributing factors.
2. Establish *baselines*.
3. *Educate* yourself about the problem.
4. Develop a *self-treatment plan*.
5. Learn *relaxation* and *breathing control*.
6. Develop *rethinking* skills to combat catastrophising and other self-defeating thinking about panic.
7. Plan and carry out *graduated exposure*.
8. Deal with any *underlying issues*, such as self-acceptance.

1. Assess the problem

Clarify the nature of your panic problem.

Check for related problems
Check whether you have any other problems that may need attention in their own right:

- Do you have any other anxiety problems, especially generalised anxiety?
- Do you suffer from *depression* at all (p. 45)?
- Are you misusing alcohol, cannabis or any other substances that might complicate a self-treatment programme?
- Do you have any physical condition of special concern?

List your symptoms and behaviour patterns

- What exactly do you experience when having a panic attack?
- What do you do to deal with an attack? In particular, identify any avoidance behaviours in which you engage, and any substances, such as alcohol and cannabis, or drugs, such as tranquillisers, that you use.

Consider the history of your problem

- Does your *family* have a history of anxiety or other mental health problems?
- What has been *your own experience* of anxiety and any other difficulties throughout your life?
- What is the *history* of your panic problem, from your first attack to the present? Can you identify any *triggers?*
- When did you *begin to engage* in avoidance behaviour, and what was happening in your life at that time?
- Have you had any *previous treatment* and how did you view it?

Identify any contributing factors

- Are there any *lifestyle issues* that might be contributing to your anxiety, such as lack of exercise, poor diet, difficulty sleeping or stress arising from relationship or financial problems?
- Are you using any *substances* that might be contributing to your anxiety, such as caffeine, cannabis, alcohol or drugs?

Is there a secondary emotional problem?

- Do you feel *hopelessness* about overcoming the problem?
- Are you *downing yourself* for having a problem?
- Do you *fear disapproval* from others for having a problem?

2. Establish baselines

So you can measure the progress of your treatment, you need to establish the *frequency* and *intensity* of your panic attacks, i.e. the

169

baseline. To develop an effective self-treatment plan you also need to record what happens in an attack, where attacks take place and the thoughts involved. Probably the best way to establish baselines is to keep a *log* of attacks (p. 47), noting the following (roughly in order of importance):

- The date and time.
- How quickly the attack came on, and how long it lasted.
- The specific physical symptoms you experienced during the attack, and how severe they were (using the scale on page 95).

Once you have established the baseline, add the following to your log. They will help you understand more fully what the causes are and whether there is anything about your reactions that may be contributing to the problem:

- The situation where the attack took place, and who was there.
- What you were thinking immediately before, during and after the attack.
- What you did to try to cope. For example, did you leave the situation, take medication or use alcohol?

Finally, list the situations you avoid. If you have been engaged in avoidance behaviour for a long time, you may have become so used to not going to certain places that you will find it hard to recall them. A family member or friend may be able to jog your memory.

3. Educate yourself about the problem

Understanding what is happening to you, and why, will increase your sense of personal control. It will also normalise the experience of panic and thus reduce your fear of it.

Refresh your understanding of the nature of anxiety generally as described in Part I, especially of the fight-flight-or-freeze response and how a reaction designed to protect you can get out of hand. The following information is about panic attacks in particular:

- Panic arises from a normal physical reaction — the fight-or-flight response, designed to prepare the body for action — that occurs out of context and is exaggerated.
- Panic attacks involve a circular process: feeling ⇒ thinking ⇒ feeling ⇒ thinking, etc.
- Physical symptoms, such as tension and hyperventilation, can be misconstrued as dangerous, which can create anxiety about them, which can result in their intensification — and so a vicious circle is set up.
- There is a good prognosis for panic attacks: while distressing, they can be effectively overcome with the application of learning and effort.

Avoidance behaviour is self-reinforcing. If you are engaged in this type of behaviour, examine the costs and keep in mind how important it is to face feared situations rather than keep away from them.

4. Develop a self-treatment plan

List your self-treatment goals; for example, 'To manage my panic by increasing my tolerance for anxiety', or 'To face situations I've been avoiding.' Keep in mind that your goal is to manage your panic, not totally get rid of it. Make sure you state your goals in specific terms so you are able to measure how successful you are at achieving them.

Linda's goals were:

1. To manage my panic so that attacks remain below 4 on the anxiety scale.
2. To enter supermarkets, theatres and all other public places I'd like to go to while maintaining my anxiety at level 3/10.

Next, plan the steps you will take to reach your goals. The following sections describe the various components of treatment you will need to consider to do this.

Finally, enhance your motivation for change by reminding yourself that facing short-term discomfort is to your long-term advantage. The *benefits calculation* (p. 65) can help you do this.

5. Learn relaxation and breathing control

To reduce your panic symptoms, learn to use *deep, slow breathing* (p. 126). Note that at the time of writing, breathing control is widely regarded as the most useful technique for managing panic. To relieve muscle tension, use *relaxation training* (p. 114). As you learn to control your symptoms your confidence will increase.

Ensure you are well-practised in these techniques before applying them in anxiety-triggering situations.

6. Develop rethinking skills

Rethinking skills will help you get your panic into perspective and cope with the discomfort of exposure work.

Deal with self-defeating thoughts about panic

What are you telling yourself about your panic attacks? Identify any *misinterpretations* of your physical symptoms (p. 166). Adjust any *overestimations* of the 'danger' posed by your panic, e.g. 'I'll have a heart attack/die', and of the consequences of panic, e.g. 'I'll faint/lose control.'

Next, examine your fear of panic attacks. There are two ways to approach this. One is to consider how likely it is that a feared outcome will eventuate. The other is to explore what a feared outcome would *mean* to you, using *rational self-analysis* (p. 52).

Below is a list of commonly held fears about panic and how you can deal with them using one or both of these approaches:

- *Going mad.* Either: (1) learn about the significant differences between symptoms of anxiety and symptoms of psychosis; or (2) explore the meaning that 'going mad' has for you. Is it a self-image issue, e.g. 'If I go mad it will show I'm a hopeless person', or is it a discomfort issue, e.g. 'If I go mad I will spend the rest of my life in a hospital and that would be unbearable'? See page 211 for more details.
- *Losing control.* Clarify exactly what you mean by 'losing control'. (1) How likely is it that you will completely lose control? What

evidence are you using? (2) Explore what *meanings* you attach to 'losing control'. Do you believe that if you lose control it will prove you are a 'weak person'?

- *Embarrassment.* In the unlikely event of a panic attack and subsequent avoidance behaviour attracting notice and even criticism, embarrassment is a normal and appropriate human reaction. Decatastrophise the embarrassment — see it as uncomfortable but bearable.

- *Fainting.* The light-headedness associated with panic might lead you to believe you are about to faint. This is most unlikely, except in rare circumstances in which there is something else that may cause this to happen. You can usually ease the feeling by breathing deeply and slowly and moving around. It may also be helpful to go deeper and explore your fears about the *consequences* of fainting and the meanings it has for you. You may have *self-image* issues, e.g. 'If I faint, other people will think I'm neurotic and that will prove I am', or discomfort issues, e.g. 'I couldn't stand the feeling of fainting.'

- *Choking or stopping breathing.* Choking is caused by a tightening of the neck and chest muscles — and will pass. The body has a reflex mechanism that forces it to breathe when it is getting short of oxygen.

- *Having a heart attack.* Learn to distinguish a heart attack from a panic attack. The pain of a heart attack is a crushing sensation, usually in the centre of the chest, and is made worse by exertion and eased by resting. The pain of a panic attack tends to be sharp and is located in the upper left of the chest; staying still makes it worse, activity eases it. You could also explore the meaning for you of having a heart attack. Is it a discomfort issue, e.g. 'I couldn't stand the pain/being disabled', or are you afraid of dying?

- *Dying.* The research literature, as far as this writer has been able to ascertain, does not contain a single report of anyone dying from a panic attack. If this reassurance is not enough for you, it may be helpful to carry out an in-depth exploration of your issues around dying. This can be a complex matter, as there are a variety of reasons why people are excessively afraid of death. See page 213 for more information.

Raising your tolerance for discomfort

Raising your tolerance for the discomfort of panic, and of anxiety symptoms in general, will make you less sensitive to it. Paradoxically, as you become more able to live with your anxiety, so it will diminish. Here are some ways to increase your tolerance:

- Reframe the symptoms of panic as 'uncomfortable' as opposed to 'dangerous' or 'unbearable'.
- Challenge catastrophising thoughts about danger, discomfort and having a panic attack.
- Change your 'shoulds' and 'musts' about avoiding discomfort and danger to preferences.
- Decatastrophise the discomfort you think exposure work will involve.
- Adopt the attitude of 'going with' panic rather than fighting it. Resisting panic symptoms actually makes them worse; and avoiding the symptoms only reinforces the idea that they are unbearable. Doing the opposite — letting panic run its course — shows that it is bearable, and that feared consequences do not come to pass. Develop some succinct reminders for when panic strikes, along the lines of 'Just accept what my body is doing', 'Float with the wave of panic' and 'Allow it to pass over.'[2]

Rethinking techniques

The following are aids to rethinking:

- *Education* — reading about panic, carrying out research on the internet, obtaining information from appropriate professionals, etc.
- The *benefits calculation* (p. 65) — for increasing your motivation to face fears.
- *Rational self-analysis* (p. 52) — for analysing panic episodes. Alternatively, you use a simpler process, like the following:

Physical symptom	Interpretation (what I fear will happen)	Evaluation (how I rate this)	New interpretation	New evaluation
Dizziness	I'm going to faint and look foolish	That would be unbearable	This is just anxiety — it will lead to nothing	Looking foolish is uncomfortable, not fatal.

- *Rational cards* (p. 87) — displaying coping statements, or old, irrational beliefs contrasted with new, rational alternatives. Use these before undertaking exposure, and then take them into your exposure situations. Keep them handy for when panic strikes unexpectedly. Here are some typical coping statements:
    * 'The feeling is uncomfortable, not awful.'
    * 'I don't like it, but I can stand it, as I have stood it in the past.'
    * 'I can go with it; I'll just let my body do what it's going to do.'
    * 'This feeling is unpleasant, but it won't do anything to me — it's just anxiety.'

A variation of this is to write some key questions on a card, and then, when panic strikes, read the card and answer the questions.[3] For example:
    * 'Are these symptoms really dangerous?'
    * 'What is the worst that could happen?'
    * 'What am I telling myself that is making me feel worse?'
    * 'What is the most useful thing I could do to help myself right now?'

- The *catastrophe scale* (p. 70) and *reframing* (p. 71) — for getting your various fears, and the panic itself, into perspective.
- *Imagery* (p. 73) — for replacing old, catastrophising fantasies with new, coping ones, and for practising coping before undertaking exposure.
- *Distraction* (p. 108) — for handling panic (as long as it doesn't become a form of avoidance behaviour or a replacement for

175

dealing with underlying issues). You can distract yourself by talking to another person, walking around the house, doing chores, exercising, focusing on a specific object (such as a food display in the supermarket), or in any number of other ways.

- *Time projection* (p. 72) — for reducing fears about future events and consequences. Think of a fear — for example, that you might collapse in public and look foolish in front of others — then consider how you would feel (or what others might think of you) the day after, a week later, a month later, a year later, and so on.

7. Plan and carry out graduated exposure

When you are confident about using your coping skills, it is time to begin confronting your fears in a graduated, step-by-step fashion. Before you begin, ensure you have practised combating dysfunctional thoughts and reducing physical symptoms. Finally, keep in mind that your real fear is not of situations and places, but of panic itself. Consequently, exposure ultimately means experiencing panic, albeit under *controlled* conditions.

Symptom induction
This involves using physical behaviours to bring on the very thing you are desperately keen to avoid — a panic attack (see page 91 for details).

Inducing the symptoms of panic can be helpful in several ways. First, it allows you to practise your self-help techniques on panic while it is actually happening. Second, as you experience panic under *controlled* conditions, you will become less sensitised to it and the attacks will affect you less. Third, it is a chance to practise coping with panic before you engage in real-life exposure.

Wendy found symptom induction particularly helpful, as she experienced quite severe panic but did little in the way of avoidance behaviour.

Exposure via imagery

One way to prepare for real-life exposure is to practise in your imagination (see page 72 for details). This involves vividly envisaging a feared situation until you experience the early symptoms of panic, whereupon you employ your new relaxation and rethinking skills. Linda, who engaged in considerable avoidance behaviour, found this helpful.

Real-life exposure

Entering the actual situations you fear is the final stage of exposure. It is essential for panic sufferers who engage in avoidance behaviour. See page 94 for details of planning and implementing a real-life exposure programme. If you have not been engaging in avoidance behaviour you can skip this section.

One of Linda's objectives was to be able to enter a supermarket and stay long enough to buy the groceries, for which she used the exposure hierarchy on page 96, with her husband Peter as helper.

Michael was a computer salesman who had become afraid of being too far from home in case he had a car accident and couldn't get help. His fear had gradually developed after a minor accident in which nobody had been hurt but which had shaken him up. His exposure hierarchy was designed to help him achieve the objective of being able to drive to the next city:

Step	Item	Anxiety level
1.	Travel to halfway point as a passenger with Jenny driving. Have coffee at the café as a reward.	4
2.	Drive to halfway point with Jenny as passenger.	5
3.	Travel right through to city with Jenny driving.	6
4.	Drive right through to city with Jenny as passenger.	7
5.	Drive alone to halfway point.	8
6.	Drive alone to city, return straight home.	9
7.	Drive alone to city, stay and have coffee.	10

8. Deal with any underlying issues

As you gain control over your panic and avoidance behaviour, you can begin looking at any underlying or subsidiary issues. Most of this work will involve the use of rethinking strategies; some might also involve skills training or additional specialist counselling.

Self-acceptance

If you have had your problem for a while, especially if you been engaging in a lot of avoidance behaviour, you may be downing yourself and worrying about how others view you. Try the following:

- *Acknowledge* your problem but *accept* your 'self' unconditionally (p. 78). This is probably the most useful thing you can do.
- Use *shame attacking* (p. 99) to confront your fear of disapproval.
- *Dispute* any perfectionistic performance demands you are placing on yourself. See Further Reading (p. 303) for sources of ideas on beating perfectionism.

Emotional responsibility

Do you believe your emotions are caused by external factors and are therefore out of your control? Reread page 81, where the issue of external versus internal control is addressed.

Assertiveness

Do you have trouble asking for what you want and saying 'No' to what you don't? See Further Reading (p. 303) for sources of ideas on developing assertiveness, and consider joining an assertiveness training group.

Relationship problems

Whether a relationship difficulty is a trigger for or an effect of your problem anxiety, you would be wise to reduce the chance of relapse. Is your partner afraid that as you get better you might 'need' them less? Is he/she subconsciously subverting your treatment process? If you are not confident you can deal with a relationship issue yourself, consider professional counselling.

From panic to calm

Here are the more common panic-causing beliefs, with rational alternatives:

Panic beliefs	*High discomfort-tolerance beliefs*
I can't stand the feeling of panic.	I don't like the feeling, but I can stand it. I have been panicky many times, and I am still here to talk about it.
I might die.	People don't die from panic attacks. Anyway, being excessively afraid of dying won't allow me to enjoy living.
I must avoid the feeling of panic, or any situation that might trigger it, at all costs.	The more I avoid panic, the more I fear it. Better to face my fears using my new coping skills.
I must be in total control of myself at all times.	Self-control is important, but demanding total control (which is impossible for anyone) will, paradoxically, make me so anxious that I'll be more likely to lose control.
I'll lose control and do things that will be embarrassing, which will be awful.	I may lose control, but, judging by the evidence I have to date, how likely is that? And if it *did* happen, it would be uncomfortable, not horrific.
Others must see me as a totally rational person who has complete self-control.	It would be *desirable* for others to see me as totally rational, but I can live with the fact that some people may see me as less than perfect.
Having this problem shows I'm a weak person.	Having this problem simply shows I'm a person with a problem — nothing more.
I'm losing my mind and going mad.	I'm overreacting to my feelings of panic.
I can't stand discomfort and pain, so I must avoid them at all costs.	Total avoidance would mean a restricted life. Although I don't like discomfort and pain, I can bear them.

179

The end of therapy

Your self-therapy will probably end when several things occur. First, you are able to recognise the early symptoms of a panic attack and take action to keep them from escalating. Second, you can enter all previously avoided situations with manageable anxiety.

Prepare to manage relapse. Remember that further panic attacks are likely, especially at times of stress, and may strike after a long period of absence. If you keep it in mind that you will need to use your coping skills at such times, you will almost certainly find that panic and avoidance behaviour will have little effect on the rest of your life.

How did Wendy, Linda and Michael get on? Wendy learned to manage her panic attacks fairly quickly. Her underlying demand for perfect control, because she'd held it all her life, took longer to deal with, but now when it returns she is able to challenge it quickly. Each time she does so, it loses a little more of its power.

Linda also overcame her panic attacks. Her longstanding avoidance behaviour took about 18 months to deal with. She became discouraged by what she considered slow progress, but her determination eventually led to success. She still has twinges of fear about going to some places, but as she continues to challenge her self-defeating thinking and make herself confront her fears, they intrude less and less frequently.

Michael dealt with his avoidance behaviour somewhat faster. He took longer to deal with some of his underlying issues, especially his workaholic tendencies and excessive performance demands, but he wanted to minimise the risk of relapse and this enabled him to make the necessary changes to his lifestyle. Has taking better care of himself reduced his work performance? Not at all. Overcoming his fears has made him more efficient than ever. In fact, he is now an ex-salesman — he owns the business.

You, too, can overcome panic and avoidance behaviour. It may happen quickly, it may take a while. But if you faithfully learn and apply the strategies and techniques that others have used so effectively time and again before you, it will happen.

20 Social anxiety

Human beings are, by nature, social creatures. With few exceptions, our day-to-day lives involve numerous contacts with other humans, at work, at home and during recreation. It is not uncommon to feel shy, to a greater or lesser degree, in some social situations. Most of us prefer to avoid the risk that others might see us in a negative light.

For some people, though, social interaction is fraught with anxiety. They have an excessive fear of what others think of them. They imagine they are being constantly observed when in the presence of other people. They believe this will lead to disapproval or rejection, and that they will feel humiliated or embarrassed. Catastrophising about these possibilities leads to performance anxiety and, in turn, to avoidance of social situations.

Dennis had been excessively shy all his life. A problem when he was at school, his shyness became an even greater issue when he started work as a mechanic with a large car dealership. At age 20, single and living at home with his parents, he was marked out for ribbing by his fellow mechanics, who soon noted his reluctance to eat lunch with them or go drinking at the end of the week.

It wasn't that Dennis didn't wish to mix with other people — in fact, he desired this very much. He longed to have a girlfriend. He frequently forced himself to go to social functions, believing that he must not give in to his fears. But these brave forays into the world of social contact inevitably followed the same negative pattern: he went only after drinking several cans of beer to give himself courage, and while there he would hardly ever approach anyone to talk to. Afterwards he would be highly self-critical, calling himself 'weak', 'cowardly' and 'a loser'.

People with social anxiety can find it impairs many aspects of their life, including work, education and social activity. Here are the most common social fears:

- Performing or speaking in public.
- Speaking with a member of the opposite sex.
- Interacting with an authority figure.
- Eating in the presence of others.
- Writing in the presence of others.
- Urinating in public toilets.
- Communicating at social functions.

In its most severe form social anxiety is generalised, affecting almost every social situation, but it may be restricted to specific situations, such as sitting examinations, sexual encounters or public speaking.

What causes social anxiety?

Biochemistry

There is some evidence that social anxiety has a genetic component.[1] Shyness can be observed in young infants before environmental factors are likely to have had a significant impact. No doubt general hyperarousability (p. 25) is also involved.

It is likely, too, that an evolutionary process is involved in the way some people interpret the behaviour of others and respond with submission or withdrawal. Shyness has survival value — it protects one from doing things that might lead to dangerous responses from other people.[2]

Whatever the explanation, it appears some people have an inborn tendency to fear certain triggers in their environment, such as angry, critical or rejecting faces or being the centre of attention.

Development

Most people with social anxiety were notably shy as children and cannot remember when the problem began. If your parents overprotected you or criticised you a lot, this and other early learning experiences may have added to the effects of genetic inheritance. On a more encouraging note, it is also possible that favourable learning experiences, especially those that build tolerance to discomfort, can to some extent compensate for a child's genetic predisposition.[3]

In adolescence, acceptance by peers becomes especially important. There is also the need to develop a sexual identity and achieve intimacy outside the family. As a result, concerns about social evaluation and the possibility of rejection can loom particularly large.

Crises in adulthood, such as the break-up of a marriage or career failure, may also lead to increased social fears.

Personality

Sufferers of social anxiety tend to have high, self-imposed performance and social standards. If you believe you must perform perfectly to be accepted by others, you are more likely to worry about whether your personal qualities and behaviours are acceptable to them.

Socially anxious people tend to be highly self-conscious. If you have an intense self-focus that makes it hard for you to look outwards, you are more likely to jump to the conclusion that other people are always examining your behaviour.

Social skills

Some sufferers of social anxiety have poor social skills, but, contrary to what one might expect, most possess perfectly adequate skills — they just have trouble exercising them because of their anxiety.

Beliefs and attitudes

The combination of biochemical inheritance and developmental factors can lead to ways of thinking that maintain social anxiety. There are three common patterns — check which rings a bell for you:

1. Do you tend to overestimate the likelihood that other people will disapprove of and reject you?
2. Do you have exaggerated fears about how others will respond if your anxiety shows?
3. Do you have doubts about your ability to make a favourable social impression?

Let's break these down into the three levels of thinking introduced in chapter 4: inferences, evaluations and core beliefs.

Mis-inferring what is going on

There are a number of ways in which socially anxious people make erroneous inferences about what is happening in social situations:

- *Jumping to conclusions.* Do you see criticism where there no evidence it is intended? Where a social situation is ambiguous, do you tend to view it as unpleasant?
- *Fortune-telling.* Do you frequently predict that people will be watching and criticising you? Do you fear this will lead to disapproval and rejection?
- *Personalisation.* Do you tend to interpret other peoples' upset, e.g. anger, as meaning that you personally have fallen short in some way?
- *Mind-reading.* Are you prone to assuming that other people are thinking about you?
- *Emotional reasoning.* Do you believe that because you *feel* you are being criticised, you really *are* being?
- *Overgeneralisation.* Do you tend to view your real or perceived social difficulties as demonstrating that you are socially dysfunctional through and through?

Distressing evaluations

Inferential errors lead to distressing evaluations:

- *Demanding.* Do you believe that you 'should' or 'must' avoid social failure, criticism and embarrassment?
- *Awfulising.* Do you find yourself exaggerating the badness of criticism or disapproval?
- *Can't-stand-it-itis.* Do you view social difficulties as 'unbearable'?
- *Self-rating.* Do you tend to label yourself 'stupid', 'hopeless', 'socially incompetent', etc.?

Core beliefs

Underlying faulty inferences and evaluations are irrational core beliefs:

- *Self-image anxiety.* 'I must perform well, get approval from others and avoid disapproval.'

- *Discomfort anxiety.* 'I can't stand emotional discomfort and must avoid it at all costs.'

Summary

To summarise, social anxiety involves thinking like this:

- One or more of your core beliefs is activated in a social situation, or when you are thinking about such a situation.
- As a result you make distorted inferences, misinterpreting what is happening, e.g. you think everyone is looking at you when they aren't, and that they disapprove when they don't.
- You evaluate these inferences as catastrophic, as things that must not happen, or as proving something negative about your entire 'self'.
- These highly negative evaluations make you anxious, as a result of which you engage in avoidance behaviour.

Typical beliefs about specific social situations

The beliefs typically associated with the most common social fears are as follows:

Performing or speaking in public

1. 'It would be unbearable to make a mistake and look foolish in front of other people.'
2. 'I'll get anxious, and it will show.'
3. 'They'll think I'm incompetent and reject me.'
4. 'That would prove I was useless.'

Speaking with a member of the opposite sex

1. 'It's awful to be rejected.'
2. 'If I try to talk to a man/woman I don't know, I'll get confused and come across badly.'
3. 'They'll think I'm stupid and probably reject me.'
4. 'Then I'll feel stupid — and that would be unbearable.'

Interacting with an authority figure

1. 'People who have more power than me will see my short-comings.'
2. 'They will look down on me.'
3. 'I'll feel shame.'
4. 'That would be unbearable, so I'm better off avoiding contact with people in authority.'

Eating in the presence of others

1. 'Any normal person is able to eat in front of others without feel-ing uncomfortable or making any mess, so I should be able to.'
2. 'Other people will be watching to see how I eat and they'll notice if I'm noisy, drop any crumbs or make a mess — and they'll then think I'm a slob and reject me.'
3. 'It would be awful if people thought badly of my eating habits.'
4. 'I mustn't be seen to be a slob, so I must avoid any situation where I have to eat in front of others.'

Writing in the presence of others

1. 'Everyone else is able to write perfectly and naturally wherever they are or no matter who is watching, so I should be able to do so.'
2. 'It would be awful if other people thought I couldn't manage such a basic everyday task.'
3. 'They'll reject me, and that would be unbearable.'

Urinating in public toilets

1. 'Normal people can urinate quickly and easily wherever they are, so I should be able to.'
2. 'It would be awful if other people thought I couldn't manage such a basic function.'
3. 'If they did think that, it would prove I was hopeless.'
4. 'I mustn't be seen or heard urinating in case people think I'm too slow or get angry because I'm keeping them waiting.'

Communicating at social functions

1. 'I should be able to perform with perfect confidence in every social situation.'
2. 'I won't know what to say and I'll look conspicuous by being alone; and if anyone speaks to me there'll be long silences.'
3. 'People will then think I'm stupid and won't want anything to do with me.'
4. 'That will prove I'm stupid.'
5. 'I couldn't bear the discomfort I would feel in that situation.'
6. 'I must avoid any situation where I might not cope perfectly with social conversation.'

The basics of self-treatment

If you are a socially anxious person, reducing your fear of negative evaluation by other people offers the best route to long-term improvement. Develop a self-therapy programme with the following aims:

- To change any demands for perfect performance and approval into preferences.
- To reduce catastrophising about negative evaluation by others (which will help reduce demands for performance and approval).
- To increase your self-acceptance.
- To increase your tolerance for discomfort in social situations.

The process of self-treatment for social anxiety is as follows:

1. *Assessment* of the problem.
2. *Education* — increasing your understanding of social anxiety and how avoidance behaviour reinforces the problem.
3. *Planning* — developing a self-treatment programme
4. *Learning coping skills* — relaxation, rethinking techniques, etc.
5. *Graded exposure* — confronting your social fears using imagery and real-life exposure. This allows you to practise and consolidate new ways of thinking.

6. *Changing core beliefs* — replacing the irrational, self-defeating thoughts that create anxiety and avoidance behaviour with rational alternatives. This will lead progressively to long-term change in the underlying belief system that maintains your social fears.

Supplementary strategies

You can adopt a number of additional strategies.

Medication may be appropriate. Some research evidence supports the use of antidepressants, especially where depression is present. The use of benzodiazepine tranquillisers, however, is not recommended: while they provide temporary relief, they interfere with exposure, and symptom relief does not continue when drug therapy ceases.

Some people may benefit from *social skills training*. This might include learning such behaviours as making eye contact, talking more loudly and more slowly, greeting and leave-taking, asking for what one wants, saying 'No', and responding to criticism.

1. Assess the problem

To develop an appropriate self-treatment plan you need to know what you are dealing with.

Consider the history of your problem

Does your family have any history of emotional problems, including social anxiety? How has your shyness manifested itself over the years and what effect has it had on your relationships with peers, on your schooling, on your work, on intimate adult relationships, and on your dealings with other people in general?

What difficulties have you had in handling social situations? Have you had any traumatic social experiences? Have you engaged in any avoidance behaviour?

At what stage did you become aware you had a problem? What previous treatment have you had, and what was your experience of it?

Do you have any secondary emotional problems?

Do you down yourself for being socially anxious? Do you ever feel hopeless about overcoming the problem? The two often feed each other: if you believe you are 'weak', you are likely to believe you are unable to effect change.

How are you functioning?

How do you see your weaknesses and strengths in social interaction? What social situations do you tend to avoid? What behaviours do you adopt to avoid social interaction, e.g. using alcohol or drugs, making excuses?

Identify your typical thinking styles

Do you hold perfectionist beliefs? In particular, do you demand that you perform adequately in social situations? Do you tend to rate your total 'self'? Do you awfulise or engage in can't-stand-it-itis about disapproval?

Keep a log

A useful way to clarify your thoughts, behaviours and difficulties is to keep an *ABC diary* (p. 57) of social situations about which you are anxious, recording the following:

- The events or occasions that trigger your anxiety (*A*).
- Your thoughts before, during and after the event (*B*).
- How you feel, the avoidance behaviours you engage in, and the degree to which you tend to focus on yourself (*C*).

2. Educate yourself about your problem

Ensure you have read the material at the beginning of this chapter. This will give you an understanding of how social anxiety is maintained by highly negative thinking about how (you assume) other people view you. In particular, ensure you understand how avoidance behaviour can perpetuate the problem. Also check out the subheadings relating to specific fears (pp. 185–187). Read any sections that deal with your own fears and reflect on the extent to which you identify with the thoughts presented.

3. Develop a self-treatment plan

Check your motivation

How much do you want to overcome your fears? How prepared are you to carry out exposure work? There are several strategies for increasing motivation:

- The *benefits calculation* (p. 65). List the advantages and disadvantages of staying the same and of facing the short-term discomfort of changing.
- *Time projection* (p. 72). Visualise the future (1) if you avoid the short-term discomfort of change and remain socially anxious, and (2) if you face the discomfort of change and overcome your anxiety in the long term.

Set your goals

What do you want to change about the way you feel and behave? Be specific, and ensure your goals are such that you can measure your progress against them. For example, 'To be able to eat around other people' is too vague; 'To eat lunch in the cafeteria with my colleagues each day' is better.

Decide on your strategies and techniques

See steps 4 and 5 for the most commonly used strategies and techniques for dealing with social anxiety.

4. Learn appropriate coping skills

Relaxation

If, like many people, you feel tense in social situations, a good starting point is to learn how to release tension. The *three-stage relaxation training* procedure (p. 114) will teach you to release tension instantly, in any situation, even when you are with other people.

Breathing

If you feel panicky, or find breathing difficult, when you are anxious, you will probably find it helpful to learn *breathing control* (p. 126).

5. Rethinking

You have probably already been forcing yourself to enter social situations. But if you do so while thinking in the old, irrational ways, it will do you no good; in fact, it is quite likely to make your anxiety worse. Consequently, it is essential to develop new ways of thinking before you engage in exposure.

Correct inferential errors

Tackle any possible misinterpretations about what is happening around you; for example, the idea that other people can see your anxiety and will judge you for it. Strategies such as the following will help you do this:

- *Disputation.* Ask *pragmatic*, *empirical* and *logical* questions (p. 63). For example:
    * 'What effect does it have on me when I jump to the conclusion that someone thinks I'm pathetic?' (pragmatic)
    * 'What evidence do I have that they are thinking this way about me?' (empirical)
    * 'How does if follow that, because they only talked to me for 10 minutes, they thought I was inadequate?' (logical)
- *Correcting probability estimates* (p. 67). This can help you see when you are overestimating the likelihood of negative social experiences.
- *Behavioural experiments.* Test your predictions by entering situations you fear. For example, test an inference like 'Saying the wrong thing would lead to total rejection by everyone' by deliberately saying something incorrect to a group, then observing what happens.
- *Decentering.* Challenge the belief that you are the centre of everyone's attention by putting yourself in other people's shoes.

Next time you are in a social situation, be aware of how intensely you are focusing on yourself; then reflect on the possibility that other people are most likely just as inward-looking, rather than focused on you.

Correct evaluative errors

Inferences are followed by evaluations, e.g. if you *infer* that rejection will occur, then you may *evaluate* such a prospect as 'awful' or 'unbearable'. It is evaluative thinking that creates unpleasant emotional states and leads to self-defeating behaviour. Evaluative beliefs also point to *core* beliefs. Thus, it is wise to spend most of your self-therapy time working on this level of thinking. Some recommendations for doing this follow, but first let's look at the two kinds of psychological disturbance that can result from faulty evaluative thinking.

Deal with discomfort anxiety

Increase your tolerance for the discomfort of being in social situations:

- Accept that *some* unpleasant social experiences are inevitable for everyone.
- *Prefer* rather than *demand* that such events not occur.
- View negative social encounters, and the feelings to which they give rise, as *unpleasant* rather than horrible and *uncomfortable* rather than unbearable.
- Appreciate that you can have a happy life overall, in spite of any negative social experiences.
- Learn to be less afraid of expressions of anger by other people (see page 197 for details).
- Decatastrophise any panic attacks (see page 172).

Deal with self-image anxiety

Reduce the anxiety you feel when you consciously or subconsciously perceive a threat to your self-image:

- Understand that having a problem doesn't mean you are weak or stupid by definition; negative social experiences prove nothing about your total 'self'.

- View criticism, disapproval and rejection as *unpleasant* or *inconvenient*, rather than awful or unbearable.
- Get rid of the idea that you absolutely *must* be seen (by yourself as well as others) as totally competent in all respects. See it as *desirable* to have approval and to avoid disapproval rather than as absolutely necessary.
- Work, ultimately, towards unconditional self-acceptance. This may well be the key to effective long-term management of your social anxiety. Understand the principle of *self-acceptance*.

Correct evaluative errors

The following techniques can help you deal with discomfort and self-image issues:

- The *catastrophe scale* (p. 70) will help you combat awfulising about disapproval or the risk of rejection.
- The *benefits calculation* (p. 65) will help you compare the advantages of confronting discomfort with the disadvantages of remaining socially anxious.
- *Rational-emotive imagery* (p. 73) and *coping rehearsal* (p. 74) will help you change your thoughts by visualising yourself in feared social situations.
- The *blow-up technique* (p. 72) will help you get feared events into perspective by using humour.
- *Time projection* (p. 72) will help you see that even if the worst happens you will ultimately adapt to it.
- *Rational cards* (p. 87) will help you combat irrational thinking prior to and during social situations.

6. Graded exposure

The purpose of exposure is to develop your tolerance for feelings of anxiety and to reduce your fear of social encounters by repeatedly confronting the situations you fear while using a variety of coping skills. Exposure strategies and techniques for social anxiety are similar to those for other types of problem anxiety:

- *Real-life desensitisation* (p. 94) is the basic exposure strategy. It involves entering social situations you have previously avoided.
- *Shame attacking* (p. 99) will help you practise coping with your fear of what others may think of you by deliberately doing things you think might attract moderate disapproval. For example, if you fear disaster should you get someone's name wrong, you could introduce or refer to someone incorrectly. Other exercises might involve wearing 'inappropriate' clothing in public, going out with your hair not done properly, disagreeing with someone in a group setting, and so on.
- *Risk-taking* (p. 99) will help you see that taking reasonable risks does not usually lead to social disaster.
- *Response-prevention* (p. 99) involves refraining from unhelpful ways of avoiding discomfort, such as taking alcohol or tranquillisers before a social event, or using distraction during it (when you need to be focused on what is happening).

Exposure situations

Here are some examples of exposure assignments for confronting social fears:

- Contact a telephone information service.
- Start a short conversation with a shop assistant while paying for goods.
- Make eye contact and smile at people.
- Compliment someone.
- Tell a joke to a group of people.
- Ask someone to dance.
- Ask for a date.
- Eat in the presence of other people.
- Ask someone how they like their job, the bowling alley, a particular movie, etc.
- Sign up for a night-school class, join a club, take up a team sport.

An exposure hierarchy

Here is the hierarchy that Dennis developed. His objective was 'To eat in the presence of other people at work.' He decided to start small and gradually work his way up to more anxiety-provoking experiences, and to include in his plans a young woman who had captured his interest:

Step	Item	Anxiety level
1.	Go to the staff cafeteria, buy lunch and take it away.	3
2.	Go to the cafeteria, buy lunch, stop and say hello to at least one person before leaving.	4
3.	Have a cup of coffee in the cafeteria alone.	5
4.	Eat lunch in the cafeteria alone.	6
5.	Arrange to meet one of the guys in the cafeteria for lunch.	7
6.	Get a coffee and sit and drink it at a table with a group of the boys.	8
7.	Eat lunch at a table with a group of the boys.	9
8.	Drink coffee at the same table as Cherie, the receptionist.	9.5
9.	Eat lunch at the same table as Cherie.	10

Dennis took about six weeks to work through these steps. You can insert intermediate steps at any point of a hierarchy like this, and modify it for different goals.

Enhancing exposure

- Exposure needs to be repeated — briefly but frequently. As far as possible, repeat tasks on a daily basis until you can do them with minimal anxiety.
- Exposure via *imagery* (p. 92) can prepare you for real-life situations. Likewise *role-playing*; for example a friend could play the part of a disapproving observer while you practise your rethinking techniques.
- Before undertaking exposure, it is important to identify and change your self-defeating beliefs. Many socially anxious people

force themselves to enter feared situations anyway, but while still thinking in their old negative way. Consequently, they don't benefit; in fact, they may become more anxious. They may even interpret successful social interactions negatively — for example, as meaning that more will be expected of them in future. The solution is to ensure that you carry out your exposure exercises using new thinking: challenging internal demands for perfect social performance, decatastrophising failure, and accepting yourself when you are rejected or make mistakes.

- You can build your confidence by preparing for certain exposure situations. Before starting a conversation, for example, make a short list of possible topics culled from the newspaper.
- Try to focus on the present moment rather than on some feared outcome.
- Remember that the purpose of exposure is deliberately to provoke your anxiety symptoms in order to increase your tolerance for them. Avoid unhelpful ways of dodging anxiety, such as drinking alcohol or engaging in distraction.

7. Related fears and core beliefs

As your exposure work starts to take effect and you find yourself coping better with social situations, orient more of your time to addressing the underlying beliefs that until now have maintained your anxiety: how you rate your 'self'; beliefs about how what other people think somehow proves something about you; self-imposed demands for perfect performance in every situation; your 'need' for approval; etc. Some of these, e.g. self-image issues, have been touched on earlier. Here, let's look at some additional key underlying issues.

Dealing with specific social fears

Here are some suggestions for dealing with the more common problems associated with social anxiety that involve core beliefs about discomfort and self-image:

- *Fear of your own panic.* Panic attacks can reinforce social anxiety. See pages 162–180 for how to deal with panic.

- *Fear of others' anger.* If you are concerned about maintaining emotional control when facing an angry person:
    * Resist the temptation to be defensive or to counterattack.
    * Accept the other person's anger, rather than tell yourself they 'have no right' to be angry or 'shouldn't' be angry.
    * Keep in mind that the other person is largely creating their own anger (although, if appropriate, acknowledge any contribution you have made to the problem).
    * Remember that someone else's anger doesn't prove anything about you as a person.
    * Remind yourself that the other person's approval is *desirable* but not *necessary.*

    If you are concerned about how to *react appropriately* to an angry person:
    * Concentrate on listening to them.
    * When you are in the wrong, acknowledge the fact and consider apologising.
    * Undertake *problem-solving* (p. 129) where appropriate.

    You could also practise coping with angry responses from other people using *rational-emotive imagery* (p. 73).

- *Fear of disapproval.* To combat the fear of what other people may think of you, *dispute* the idea that you 'need' approval and that disapproval is 'awful' or 'unbearable'.[4] *Shame attacking* and *risk-taking* (p. 99) are also useful for confronting the fear of disapproval.

From social anxiety to social concern

Here are the more common irrational beliefs that lead to social anxiety, with rational alternatives:

Social-anxiety beliefs	*Concern beliefs*
Everyone else is able to perform perfectly and cope confidently in social situations.	Most people feel a degree of anxiety around others, but they usually cover it up. There is no evidence that I am the only one who has difficulty.

Social-anxiety beliefs	Concern beliefs
Other people are watching me and will be critical of how I'm behaving.	How do I know they're watching me? Some might be, but most people will be more concerned with how they themselves are doing.
I should be able to perform with perfect confidence in every social situation.	It is *desirable* to be confident in social situations, but there is no 'Law of the Universe' that says I 'should' be.
I must always make the right impression on other people.	It is desirable to make a good impression, but demanding I come across perfectly will only make me anxious and therefore more likely to behave clumsily.
I couldn't stand it if people thought I was clumsy, stupid or incompetent.	It would be unpleasant if people viewed me like that, but I'd still be alive. And their opinion would hardly damage my life irreparably.
I'm totally incompetent in social situations.	I have difficulty in many social situations, but I can learn to manage my anxiety and cope better in the future.
I must always get approval from others and avoid disapproval.	I certainly prefer to get approval and avoid disapproval, but this is not always possible, and demanding the impossible will only make social situations a misery.
I can't stand feeling bad and must avoid it at all costs.	I don't like feeling bad, but I can — and do — stand it. And I will stand it better if I accept my feelings rather than demand they not happen.
Having this problem shows I'm a weak person.	Having this problem simply shows I'm a person with a problem.

The end of therapy

Your self-therapy will end when you are able to face all the day-to-day social situations you previously avoided with a manageable level of anxiety. As with all types of problem anxiety, it is important to prepare for relapse. Plan what to do should social anxiety strike again so you are ready for it. It is only natural to slip back into the old ways from time to time, but if you can quickly dust off your coping skills you will soon be back on track.

How did Dennis get on? His was a long road with many adventures. He is still somewhat shy, but can now handle most social situations without becoming excessively anxious. He owns his own garage and employs two other mechanics — with whom he eats lunch. And guess who helps out as receptionist and book-keeper during the week when her two children are at school.

21 Specific fears

Dogs, heights, flying, spiders, thunderstorms, injection needles —
what do they have in common? Nothing except that they are ordinary
objects or experiences that for some people are the focus of inordi-
nate dread. Do you have a persistent fear of a specific thing or situation
and a strong desire to avoid it? When exposed to it, do you immediately feel anxious, perhaps even panicky; and try to get away from it?
Do your distress and avoidance behaviour interfere with your life? If
so, you may have a *specific phobia*.

Usually, the closer a phobic person is to the trigger of their phobia, or the more difficult it is to escape from it, the worse they feel.
When not thinking about it or not exposed to it, they don't tend to
feel anxious. Many deal with their phobia by simply staying away
from the trigger. They usually recognise that their fear is irrational or
excessive, but find it hard to ignore.

There are five main types of specific phobia:

1. *Situational*, e.g. air travel, confined spaces.
2. *Natural environment*, e.g. thunderstorms, heights.
3. *Blood–injection–injury*
4. *Animal*, e.g. spiders, dogs, snakes.
5. Situations that might lead to *illness, choking* or *vomiting*.

Phobias are common. About 10 per cent of people experience
specific phobias, although not all are recognised; for example, someone who lives in New Zealand may hardly be aware they have a fear
of snakes because they are unlikely to encounter one outside a zoo
or reptile collection. A person may have more than one phobia. Phobias about animals and darkness usually begin in childhood, fear of
blood or injury in adolescence, and fear of driving, enclosed spaces,
air travel and heights at 30–40 years of age.

Childhood phobias usually pass as adulthood is attained. Phobias that develop later in life tend to be more lasting. Most phobias are not sufficiently disruptive to warrant seeking treatment, as it is usually easy to avoid the objects or situations that trigger them.

We first met Susan, the woman with an extreme fear of dogs, in chapter 1. At the age of 33, she was married and had two children, the youngest of whom had recently started school. She worked part time as a nurse. Her fear of dogs dated back many years but had become much worse following a bout of post-natal depression following the birth of her youngest child.

Susan became anxious at the thought of being in any situation where there might be a dog. On the rare occasions when she was actually near one, her anxiety escalated into panic. She tried to avoid any situation where there was a chance of meeting a dog. If she wished to visit someone who owned a dog, or who might have friends there with a dog, she would try to arrange for it to be locked away. Consequently, her lifestyle became increasingly restricted.

What causes a specific phobia?

Predisposition

Like other types of problem anxiety, it is most likely that a phobia begins with some kind of predisposition composed of various elements:

- *Genetic inheritance.* Most human beings alive today are descendants of people who survived to reproduce only because they had the ability to quickly recognise and react to environmental threats — poisonous insects and reptiles, other wild animals, a lack of air, the possibility of falling from a height or of being trapped or crushed, and so on. As a result we possess an inherited caution regarding such dangers.
- *High arousability.* This leads to higher-than-normal levels of anxiety, thereby confusing the brain into thinking that a feared object is more dangerous than it is.
- *Early learning.* If you are predisposed by biology and personality, you may learn to fear a specific object through direct

experience (e.g. through being bitten by a dog), through indirect experience (e.g. by observing another person being bitten by a dog), or vicariously (e.g. through reading or hearing about someone being bitten by a dog).

Susan's story illustrates a typical combination of inheritance and developmental learning. Her father, to whom she had been very close, was an anxious man who showed fear in many situations. Susan observed this from her earliest years. He also constantly warned her about the absolute necessity of being able to recognise danger and keep oneself safe at all costs.

Thinking habits

Whatever mix of predisposing factors is involved, specific phobias, like all anxiety problems, are maintained by thoughts and beliefs concerning discomfort and self-image:

- *Discomfort anxiety* is a key factor.[1] If you catastrophise about confronting a feared object or situation, you are likely to develop the belief that it 'must' be avoided. You may fear the *physical danger* associated with it, or the *discomfort* you would feel if confronted by it, or both. A vicious circle usually operates here: 'It's awful, so I must avoid it, and because I must avoid it I couldn't stand to be exposed to it, which proves it's awful, so I absolutely must avoid it' — and so on.
- *Self-image anxiety* can exacerbate the problem. You may worry that other people will see your fear and judge you for it; or that you will end up feeling bad about yourself should you react to the thing you fear in a 'weak' or 'crazy' fashion.

The main issue for Susan with her fear of dogs was discomfort; but this was complicated by concern for the effect on her self-image should other people notice her dread and think badly of her. Faced with this double fear, Susan found it simplest to avoid dogs altogether.

Core beliefs

Underlying habitual thought patterns about feared objects or situations are core beliefs like the following:

- 'Strong emotional discomfort is unbearable, and I must avoid exposure to objects or situations that may trigger it.'
- 'I must not, at all costs, expose myself to any significant risk of physical danger, because I would find it unbearable.'
- 'I must be able to keep myself safe and avoid significant danger at all times.'
- 'If I were to experience high levels of anxiety and lose control over myself, it would show I was weak/neurotic/hopeless/etc.'
- 'I must always maintain complete control over my emotions and behaviour.'
- 'The best way to cope with danger or high levels of discomfort is simply to avoid certain objects or situations.'

If you hold core beliefs like these, they will create a bias in your thinking. This will cause you to interpret vague information as implying something threatening rather than neutral or even encouraging, and overestimate the likelihood that a threatening experience will occur. It will also cause you to evaluate such an experience as 'terrible' or 'unbearable'.

One of Susan's core beliefs was 'Large dogs are always dangerous and must be avoided at all costs.' She developed this as a child and carried it into adulthood. Underlying it was an even more general core belief in the 'need' to keep oneself perfectly safe and free of danger at all times, which she had learned directly from her father's many statements to that effect and from observing his behaviour.

To sum up

Let's put all this together. Like all human beings, you fear dangers both real and perceived. But unlike some, you also have a tendency to become excessively anxious — a predisposition that has the potential to exacerbate your common fears. At some stage in your life, direct or indirect learning experiences have probably triggered this predisposition, causing you to develop some particularly strong fears. You have reinforced these by (1) catastrophising about the discomfort they cause, and (2) demanding that this be avoided. As a result you engage in avoidance behaviour intended to keep the danger or discomfort at bay; paradoxically, however, this simply reinforces your belief that the thing or situation you fear is dangerous and the discomfort unbearable. The vicious circle common to all problem anxiety continuously reinforces your fears: you feel anxious, which sets off your alarm; you then avoid the thing or situation you fear, and feel relieved (temporarily); this 'proves' you were indeed in danger, and that you will be wise to engage in the same avoidance behaviour next time you are threatened.

How to deal with specific fears

To overcome your specific fear(s), work towards two goals. First, aim to experience a manageable level of anxiety whenever you are confronted by what you fear. Second, aim to cut out any inappropriate avoidance behaviour. The key approach to overcoming your fear is deliberately to confront it while managing your anxiety with skills learned especially for that purpose. The steps of self-treatment are as follows:

1. *Assess* the problem.
2. *Plan* a self-treatment programme.
3. *Educate* yourself about the causes of specific fears and how avoidance behaviour reinforces them.
4. Learn appropriate *coping skills*, especially relaxation and re-thinking.
5. Undertake *graduated exposure* to the feared object or situation, using the coping skills you have learned.
6. Deal with any self-defeating *core beliefs* that predispose you towards excessive fears.

1. Assess your fears

Clarify the problem

What exactly are you afraid of? Do you have any co-existing problems, e.g. *depression* (p. 45) or another type of problem anxiety? Are you using any substances, including prescribed medication, in a way that may be contributing to your anxiety or might complicate your self-therapy programme?

Historical factors

Does your family have a history of anxiety, particularly of specific fears? For how long have you had the fear? When did it begin? What might have been the original triggers? Have you had any previous treatment, and how helpful was it?

Secondary problems

Identify any secondary problem(s) that might need attention before you start work on the phobia itself. Do you down yourself for having the fear? Do you get depressed in response to it? Do you have an excessive fear of the discomfort likely to be involved in overcoming your fear? Are you using any substances to relieve your anxiety?

Establish baselines

Keep a *log* (p. 47) for 2–4 weeks in which you record the occasions when your phobia has some effect on your day-to-day life. Make an entry whenever you experience anxiety either because you have been exposed to the object or situation you fear, or because you have been thinking about it. Record the following items:

- Where you were and what was happening.
- The degree of anxiety you experienced (on a scale of 0–10).
- How you behaved — in particular, any avoidance behaviour.
- Your thoughts.

If you are successfully avoiding the thing you fear, this may not be practical, in which case proceed directly to the next step.

2. Educate yourself about your problem

Learn something about the nature of anxiety in general and the origins of specific fears in particular. Both problem anxiety and phobias are protective mechanisms that have become exaggerated and are maintained by certain ways of thinking.

Identify the thoughts you have when you are confronted by, or imagine being confronted by, the object or situation you fear. This will help you clarify what you are really afraid of. What do you think will happen? That you will faint, panic, lose control or be judged by others? Are you afraid of your *reaction* as well as the thing that triggers it?

One way to identify your thoughts is to keep an *ABC diary* (p. 57). Another is to use *imagery* (p. 48): imagine being exposed to the thing you fear and note the emotions and thoughts this prompts.

3. Plan your self-therapy

Set your goals

Set your self-treatment goals. What would you like to be able to do that you avoid doing now? How would you prefer to feel when thinking about or confronted by the object or situation you fear. Make sure your goals are clear, specific, and stated in behavioural terms so that you can measure your progress towards them. Susan's goals were:

1. To go to all the places that I wish to, even when a dog may be present.
2. To have an anxiety level of about 3 out of 10 in the presence of dogs.

Check your motivation

How motivated are you to overcome your fear? Why do you want to deal with it? What will you gain by confronting the discomfort it causes you? Be clear in your mind about the relationship between short-term pain and long-term gain. You might find it helpful to do a *benefits calculation* (p. 65).

Decide on your strategies and techniques

Choose strategies and techniques for achieving your goals. See the following steps for ideas.

4. Learn appropriate coping skills

The first step in implementing your self-treatment plan is to develop skills for managing your anxiety as you engage in exposure work.

Relaxation

Relaxation training (p.114) and *breathing control* (p. 126) are especially useful techniques. When you relax, this interrupts the feedback loop whereby your mind observes your body tensing for action and concludes that danger is threatening.

Adopt rethinking techniques

Rethinking techniques will help you get your perceptions of danger into perspective and decatastrophise the discomfort involved in facing your fears.

Combat negative self-rating

Do you down yourself for having a phobia, labelling yourself 'weak', 'hopeless', etc.? This is detrimental to progress: if you believe you are weak by definition, you are effectively saying you can never change. Self-rating represents an illogical leap from recognising you have a problem to defining your entire 'self' in terms of the problem. Fight this tendency with *rational self-analysis* (p. 52) and other techniques for dealing with self-downing (p. 79).

Check the real level of danger

To check the likelihood of a feared event occurring, or the level of danger involved, use a technique like *correcting probability estimates* (p. 67) to examine the evidence. Tackle any catastrophising with techniques such as the *catastrophe scale* (p. 70), *rational cards* (p. 87) and *rational-emotive imagery* (p. 73).

Rehearse for exposure

You can practise coping with exposure by using *coping rehearsal* (p. 74). You can also use this technique as a type of exposure in its own right.

Deal with fear talk

Here are some examples of typical fear talk with rational alternatives:

Fear talk	Rational talk
I can't do it.	I can most likely do it.
I'll faint.	I'm unlikely to faint, but even if I did it would hardly be the end of the world.
It's awful.	It's uncomfortable.
I'm a weak person.	I have a problem with . . .
It's not worth the discomfort.	Short-term pain will mean long-term gain.
I don't have what it takes to make it.	I'll beat this like I've beaten many other things in my life.

Internalise new ways of thinking by using *rational cards* (p. 87).

Begin addressing your core beliefs

Begin analysing your core beliefs while you are carrying out your exposure programme (see step 5), especially any that contribute to low discomfort-tolerance. See page 211 for ideas on addressing the beliefs that typically contribute to particular types of fear.

5. Graduated exposure

Exposure is essential to overcoming specific fears. It can be carried out via *flooding* (p. 100), which entails confronting the feared object or situation directly; however, it is more common to use *graduated* exposure. This usually proceeds as follows:

1. Choose an objective.
2. Set your target anxiety level.
3. Plan a hierarchy of steps for reaching your objective.
4. Carry out each step on the hierarchy, using your relaxation and rational thinking skills to manage your anxiety.

Exposure hierarchies

The following sample hierarchies will give you ideas for developing your own:[2]

Specific fear: Spiders

Objective: To be able to handle a common spider with manageable anxiety.

Steps:
1. Look at pictures of spiders.
2. Touch the pictures.
3. Look at spiders in jars.
4. Handle a rubber spider.
5. Touch a jar containing a live spider.
6. Imagine how it feels to touch a real spider.
7. Briefly touch a real spider.
8. Allow a spider to remain in the palm of my hand.

Specific fear: Heights

Objective: To be able to stand at the top of a tall building and keep my anxiety level at 3/10 or below.

Steps:
1. Look out of a ground-floor window alone.
2. Look out of a second-floor window with a helper.
3. Look out of a second-floor window alone.
4. Look out a third-floor window with a helper.

Carry on for as many floors as necessary, then:

5. Look out from a high open space on a multistorey building with a helper.
6. Look out from a high open space on a multistorey building alone.

Each step can be repeated and the time increased — one minute the first time, three minutes the second time, five the third, etc.).

Specific fear: Needles/injections

This example uses *imagery exposure* (p. 92). Read the section about blood–injury phobia on page 211.

Objective: To be able to have a blood test or injection with manageable anxiety.

Steps:

Visualise the following images:

1. Talking to a friend about their immunisation injection.
2. Travelling to a laboratory to have a blood test.
3. Entering the waiting room.
4. Sitting in the waiting room and thinking about the test.
5. The nurse calling your name.
6. Following the nurse into the test room.
7. The nurse binding your arm.
8. Seeing the test equipment on a table next to you.
9. Smelling the alcohol and feeling it being rubbed onto your arm.
10. Seeing the hypodermic needle in the nurse's hand.
11. Feeling the needle being inserted.
12. Seeing the blood being drawn off.

As a practice exercise, try designing a hierarchy for Susan to achieve one of her goals in relation to her fear of dogs.

Basic exposure principles

Keep the following in mind as you design and carry out your hierarchies:

- Exposure works best when each session is prolonged, at least till your anxiety reaches the lower *target level* (p. 95). You may retreat from the situation if your anxiety rises above the upper target level, provided you return as soon as it falls back. Gradually work towards being able to remain in the situation until your fear subsides.

- As an aid to imagery exposure, *tape-record* the instructions (p. 92). The tape could open with some relaxation training.

- Use imagery exposure as *preparation* for real-life exposure rather than a *substitute*. (NOTE: With some phobias, such as fear of flying, it may be necessary to rely largely on imagery because actual exposure is too inconvenient or expensive.)

- You may find it helpful, especially early on, to take a helper with you when carrying out real-life exposure (see p. 102).

Particular types of fear

Some specific fears are particularly complicated. Suggestions for dealing with the more common of these follow:

- *Blood or injury.* Blood–injury phobias are associated with visiting the dentist, having injections and undergoing other medical procedures. Because someone with a phobia of this sort is likely to faint when exposed to the object or situation they fear, the standard phobia treatment requires modification.

  It helps to understand how blood–injury phobia works. Sight of an injection needle, for example, can activate a freeze response, causing a decrease in heart rate and blood pressure that leads to fainting. In some situations this is an entirely normal and automatic response to physical damage, its purpose being to reduce further damage (lower blood pressure means less loss of blood). In a doctor's surgery, however, it serves no useful purpose.

  To deal with fear of blood or injury, plan a standard programme of graduated exposure but with the following additional measures to prevent yourself from fainting: either lie down while carrying out your exposure exercises, or, at the first sign of fainting, consciously *tense* your various muscle groups instead of relaxing them.

- *Going mad.* Psychologist Susan Walen has analysed phrenophobia — the fear of going mad — as follows:[3]
  1. You *observe* your own behaviour, e.g. 'I cry a lot'; then you *compare* yourself to others, e.g. 'Other people don't do that'; then you *judge* your behaviour, e.g. 'I shouldn't be doing this.'
  2. You make a *self-diagnosis*, e.g. 'I cry all day without reason. Only mad people cry all day, therefore I'm mad.'

211

3. You *catastrophise* about what you think is happening, e.g. 'I'll get depressed again, then end up in hospital and never get out, and that would be unbearable.'

Remember: if you worry about going or being mad, you probably aren't. If this assurance isn't enough, consult a mental health professional who can carry out a full assessment and put your mind at rest. If you are still unhappy, try the following:

* Uncover your underlying fears using *inference-chaining* (p. 59).

* *Check out the reality.* How much time do you actually spend crying? Clarify what is *really* happening by keeping a *log* (p. 47). And ask yourself this: is it really true other people hardly ever cry?

* *Consider alternative conclusions.* For example, is your crying a symptom of depression, which is extremely common and very treatable? Or is how you feel a normal reaction to current problems in your life, such as an unhappy relationship or a stressful job?

6. Changing core beliefs

Now it's time to tackle the core beliefs that underlie your specific fears: exaggerated ideas about the dangerousness of certain things; the demand for total safety or complete control over yourself; the fear of fear itself; and so on. Two common fears illustrate the importance of 'getting beneath the surface':

Flying

Fear of flying embraces a number of distinct fears. The real issue varies from person to person. The more common fears are crashing, being high up, being in a confined space, and panicking and losing control. Identify what the key issue is for you and develop an appropriate self-treatment programme.[4]

Death

Fear of death isn't really a phobia in itself, rather it is a reflection of fears about the *consequences of being dead* or what may be involved in the *process of dying*. Some of these are phobic — for example, the fear of being buried alive when mistaken as dead. Others are more existential, such as the fear of not completing the things one has set out to do.[5]

Overcoming blocks to treatment

- *Low discomfort-tolerance during exposure.* Are you resistant to exposure work because of low discomfort-tolerance? It may be necessary to re-examine your motivation. Think again about what you stand to gain in the long term by tolerating short-term discomfort. Do a *benefits calculation* (p. 65) of the costs and benefits of exposure work.
- *Disengaging during exposure.* If you confront the object of your fear but use distraction or sedation to avoid discomfort, the exposure will serve little purpose. It is important to focus on what you are doing and to avoid sedative medication.
- *Depression.* Any significant depression — whether a result of having a phobia or of unrelated factors — usually requires attention before a phobia is addressed. Depression may result from low discomfort-tolerance, and thoughts like 'It's too hard', 'I shouldn't have to face this discomfort' and 'I can't stand the discomfort involved in this treatment', in which case this should be the focus of your self-therapy. Severe depression may require professional assistance — consult your doctor or an appropriate health professional if you think you are significantly depressed.
- *Doubt about the effectiveness of exposure.* Do you have trouble seeing how exposure can help? If so, return to step 2 of the procedure — the self-education phase:
  * Note how phobias are developed and maintained by unrealistic fears and can't-stand-it-itis.
  * See how exposure can help you both to check out your fearful predictions and to raise your tolerance for discomfort.

- *Lack of confidence in your own ability.* If you doubt you are capable of getting on top of your fear, reflect on the other problems in your life you have overcome even though you initially thought you wouldn't be able to. Then get started! If necessary, read again about enhancing your motivation (p. 285).

From fear to tolerance

Here are some common irrational beliefs that underlie phobias, with rational alternatives:

Phobic beliefs	Tolerance beliefs
I couldn't stand to be faced with the thing I fear.	I'd feel uncomfortable but I wouldn't die. And if I stopped catastrophising, I'd cope better.
To feel very afraid is unbearable, and I must avoid exposure to objects or situations that may trigger such discomfort.	I don't like the feeling of fear, but I can — and do — stand it. Avoidance behaviour just reinforces it so better I face my fears in order to master them.
I must not, at all costs, expose myself to any significant risk of physical danger, which I would find unbearable.	It makes sense to avoid any significant risk of danger, but demanding total safety is unrealistic and will only lead to a fearful and restricted life.
I must be able to keep myself safe and to avoid significant danger at all times.	Keeping myself safe is wise as long as I don't overdo it to the point where life becomes miserable — which negates the point of keeping myself safe.
If I were to experience high levels of anxiety and lose control over myself, it would show I was weak/neurotic/hopeless/etc.	It I lost control it would show I sometimes lose control, not that I'm weak/neurotic/hopeless/etc. by nature.
I must always maintain complete control over my emotions and behaviours.	Self-control is generally desirable, but the unrealistic demand for total control will make me anxious and, paradoxically, more likely to lose control.

Phobic beliefs	Tolerance beliefs
The best solution for coping with danger or high levels of discomfort is simply to avoid certain objects or situations.	It is wise to avoid some things, but too much avoidance behaviour restricts one's life and, paradoxically, maintains fear.
Having this problem shows that I'm a weak person.	Having this problem simply shows I'm a person with a problem.

The end of therapy

Your therapy will be over when you are able to face the things you fear with a tolerable level of anxiety. As with other types of problem anxiety, your fears may return in the future, but if you confront them without delay, they won't regain their hold. Best of all, do some preventative work and reinforce your gains by taking every reasonable opportunity to confront the objects and/or situations you used to fear and avoid. As you increase your control over your anxiety, your fears will diminish.

How did Susan get on? She enlisted the help of several dog-owning friends to help her with graduated exposure. She also learned as much as she could about dogs, including how to know when they might be dangerous and how to deal with them if they were. She took only a few months to overcome her fear. She is still wary when around dogs, but no more so than most people.

You may master your fear as quickly as Susan, or you may take longer. But with a structured plan and a bit of determination, you can free yourself from the prison of your fear.

22 Obsessions and compulsions

Most people, from time to time, experience thoughts that are repugnant to their value system, such as being contaminated, their house burning down, or causing harm to others. Such thoughts may be a protective device, a warning against danger, but are usually recognised as unnecessary and quickly dismissed.

Some people, though, overreact to them. They become extremely anxious and seek to neutralise them with 'rituals', such as repeated washing or checking or complicated thought patterns. But defensive rituals become disabling; paradoxically, they end up reinforcing the unwanted thoughts. Sometimes the thought–ritual cycle develops into what is known as *obsessive-compulsive disorder* (OCD).

The unwanted thoughts are known as *obsessions* and the defensive rituals as *compulsions*. Understanding the difference between the two, and how one relates to the other, is essential to effective treatment.

Obsessions

Obsessions are recurrent thoughts, ideas, images or impulses that a person sees as senseless or repugnant and about which they feel anxious. They are unintentional. The person knows they are a product of their mind but is unable to stop them. The most common obsessions involve:

- Fears of contamination.
- Doubts, usually about safety.
- Fear of harming others via contamination, fire, use of a motor vehicle, etc.
- Thoughts, usually of a religious nature, that are seen as blasphemous.
- Thoughts about violence or sex.

Compulsions

Compulsions are things a person does to try to suppress their unwelcome thoughts. They are rituals designed to reduce the anxiety that results from the obsessions.

A compulsive person may regard their compulsions as unreasonable or excessive but finds it hard to resist doing them, even though, unlike obsessions, they are essentially voluntary.

Behavioural rituals are the more common kind of compulsion. Examples include:

- Repetitive washing and cleaning.
- Repeatedly checking locks, electrical appliances, the road, etc.
- Endlessly counting or rearranging things.
- Carrying out everyday activities in a rigid, unvarying order.

Cognitive rituals usually involve complicated and detailed thoughts and images that the thinker believes they must complete in a certain order, leaving nothing out.

Compulsions relieve the anxiety that arises from obsessions, but only temporarily. If a person believes they have not executed them perfectly, they feel compelled to repeat them again and again. This can be very time-consuming and significantly affect day-to-day life.

Varieties of obsessive–compulsiveness

Let's revisit some of the people we met at the beginning of the book.

Richard, the taxi driver, had a strong fear of contamination. For some years he had engaged in excessive hand-washing, which his wife and children found annoying but otherwise didn't interfere with his daily life. But following the serious illness of his son, he began to develop additional symptoms. He insisted on handling money only while wearing plastic gloves and on wiping down the passenger seats in his taxi after each use.

Janet was a bank officer who had recently returned to the workforce after giving birth to her second child. She experienced repetitive thoughts about her parents dying, and feared that if they died it would be her fault for thinking of it. Consequently, she telephoned them up to a dozen times daily to check on them. Her parents were concerned about this behaviour, but as Janet had been overly fussy since childhood, they tolerated her calls. Janet also feared causing the death of her children by fire, so repeatedly checked and rechecked the oven, heaters and other appliances in the house.

Marie had recently been widowed. Her two adult children lived in other cities. She hoarded just about every piece of paper she received, including letters, newspapers, magazines and even junk mail. Her fear was that she might throw out something important. This problem had been partially controlled while her husband had been alive, but following his accidental death her house had begun to fill with paper and was becoming a fire risk. She believed, as she put it, that 'It would be terrible to throw out something I may need in the future, so I can't allow any risk of this happening.' Things came to a head when one of her daughters visited and, alarmed at the condition of the house, began throwing out some of the papers.

We'll meet these people again shortly. First, though, to see the variety of ways in which obsessive-compulsiveness may manifest itself, let's meet some others. Beryl worried that nine years before, when she was aged 14, she may have accidentally harmed an infant she was babysitting. She had only been temporarily concerned at the time, but, following a period of stress with her university studies, she had resumed thinking about it. Whenever the thoughts came to mind, she would telephone her parents to enquire after the welfare of the then 10-year-old child; she sometimes did this five or six times a week. At other times she alleviated her anxiety by rereading a particular chapter of a book on child development that was part of her study curriculum. This temporarily reassured her that the child was progressing more or less normally.

Simon, brought up in a strongly religious environment, experienced images of himself committing sexual acts in a church building. He found these abhorrent and deeply upsetting. Whenever they occurred, he would stop whatever he was doing and engage in a complicated mental ritual, in which he imagined himself undertaking a series of pious actions to 'undo' the images. The ritual was always the same and took over an hour to complete. If he believed he might have missed out part of the ritual, he felt obliged to start all over again. While his job as a lawyer allowed him some freedom to hide in his office to carry out the ritual, his frequent delays in attending to clients and his generally poor productivity had come to the notice of his senior partners.

Sophie was afraid that when out driving she might hit a pedestrian or cyclist. Whenever she went over a bump in the road or the car vibrated while turning a corner, she feared she might have hit someone. She would then stop the car and walk back along the road to check. Not only was this very time-consuming, but Sophie had also begun to avoid certain streets that were especially bumpy, any areas unfamiliar to her and driving after dark.

Although these cases are very different, the underlying causes — and the procedures for treating them — are fairly similar.

What causes obsessions and compulsions?

Obsessive-compulsiveness, like other types of problem anxiety, has its roots in a biological susceptibility. On top of this foundation come childhood learning experiences, whereby one finds out what kinds of thoughts are acceptable and unacceptable. Stressful life events — inevitable for everyone, but for the anxiety-prone person a breeding ground for unwanted thoughts — lead to the development of the obsessive-compulsive cycle:

1. The person responds to intrusive thoughts by thinking 'I should not be having these thoughts', 'These thoughts are dangerous' and 'Having these thoughts will cause bad things to happen, and I will be responsible'. This makes them anxious.
2. The person discovers that certain behaviours, such as checking, counting or hand-washing, temporarily alleviate their anxiety.
3. The person gradually develops behavioural — or, sometimes, cognitive — rituals to avoid the intrusive thoughts that create anxiety.

4. The person begins watching out for the unwanted thoughts —
which, paradoxically, brings them on.

This cycle is repeated time and again, so developing into a disorder. Here is a graphical representation:

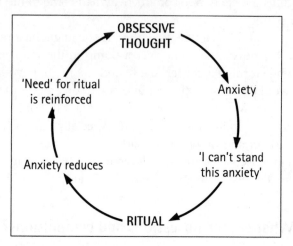

Sometimes there are complicating factors. It is not unusual for sufferers to become *depressed* in response to their condition. *Secondary emotional problems* are common, such as awfulising about the problem, the belief that obsessions and compulsions must be avoided, and self-downing for having a problem.

The basics of self-treatment

As with all types of anxiety, the goal of self-treatment is to *minimise* obsessive-compulsive behaviour rather than eliminate it — in other words, *management* rather than *cure*. If you believe you should become totally free of your symptoms for ever, you will simply hinder progress, because total freedom is an impossible goal. You will eventually become disillusioned and give up. If, on the other hand, you aim to minimise and manage your symptoms, you will stand a much better chance of success.

A key aim of self-therapy is to *increase your tolerance* for the discomfort that results from your unwanted thoughts, thereby becoming less focused on the thoughts so they gradually diminish. To do this you need to stop carrying out the rituals, for while these temporarily ease the anxiety, they paradoxically reinforce the obsessive thoughts. The main steps of self-treatment are as follows:

1. *Assess* your problem.
2. *Educate* yourself about obsessive-compulsiveness.
3. *Plan* a self-therapy programme.
4. Learn some *coping skills* to reduce your anxiety and help you cope with exposure.
5. Plan and carry out *exposure with response-prevention*.
6. Change the *core beliefs* that maintain obsessive thinking and compulsive behaviour.

Certain antidepressant medications, taken as an addition to the treatment strategies outlined here, may help some people with obsessions and compulsions. See your doctor or other health professional for further information and advice on whether medication may be appropriate for you.

1. Assess your problem

See page 44 for guidance on assessment. In particular:

- Trace the history of your problem. Have you always had obsessions and compulsions, or did they begin at a certain point in your life? Does your family have a history of obsessive thinking and compulsive behaviour?
- Check for any related problems that may also need attention; for example, depression, other types of problem anxiety, or habit disorders such as overeating, compulsive spending or hair-pulling. Consider whether these need to be addressed first, or if they require professional help.
- Do you have any secondary emotional problems? Look for self-downing, anxiety about the discomfort of facing your fears, and any sense of hopelessness about getting better.

Gather baseline data

Establishing baselines is most important. Start by recording the situations in which you feel anxious. The best way to do this is to keep a *diary* (p. 47) in which you note:

- The *triggers* of your anxiety: objects, situations, circumstances, activities (such as touching certain things), thoughts or images (e.g. 'There's dirt on my hands' or 'There'll be a fire') that make you feel anxious.
- The *rituals* you engage in to try to reduce your anxiety.

2. Self-education

Make sure you have read the early part of this chapter so you are clear about the nature of your problem, in particular the difference between obsessions and compulsions. Understanding how these develop and are maintained will make it easier for you to see why the suggested treatment steps are necessary and help you develop an appropriate self-treatment plan.

3. Plan a self-therapy programme

Set your goals

Your overall goals will be to moderate all rituals to the point where they have minimal effect on your life, and to reduce your anxiety to manageable levels. Remember that a total cure is an unrealistic goal, as the biological component cannot be eliminated, but it can be mediated so it has a minimal effect on your life.

Make sure your targets are concrete and specific. For example, 'To be able to check heaters carefully once, and then leave them' is better than 'To overcome my compulsive behaviour.'

To deal effectively with one's own obsessions and compulsions usually takes nine to 18 months, depending on how long-standing the problem is, how bad it is, whether there are any complicating problems, and how much time per week can be put towards self-treatment.

Enhance your motivation to work on the problem

You can prepare yourself for successful self-treatment by maximising your motivation and anticipating potential blocks:

- List the advantages and disadvantages of changing. Ensure you record the real practical disadvantages of obsessive-compulsiveness, e.g. 'It is putting strain on my marriage', not just the 'moral' objections, e.g. 'I shouldn't have this problem.' You might find the *benefits calculation* helpful (p. 65).
- Consider the effect of a long-term reduction in your obsessive-compulsive symptoms on the other people in your life. For example, how will your family react to your being less fussy about cleanliness or safety?
- Remind yourself that while your rituals provide short-term relief, in the long term they reinforce and intensify your obsessive, anxiety-provoking thinking. Adopt the idea of 'Short-term pain to achieve long-term gain.'

Deal with any secondary problems

Do you down yourself for having a problem? Self-acceptance is particularly important for sufferers of obsessive-compulsiveness, as they tend to denigrate themselves for what they frequently consider to be repugnant thoughts and for behaving in what they see as bizarre ways. For help with self-acceptance see page 79.

Are you anxious about the treatment programme itself? Techniques that can help with this include *rational self-analysis* (p. 52), *time projection* (p. 72) and *coping rehearsal* (p. 74).

4. Develop coping skills

Soon you will be confronting your fears and deliberately inhibiting your rituals. You are most likely to succeed if, first, you develop coping skills for managing the discomfort this will entail. Here are some suggestions:

- *Rational self-analysis* (p. 52) will help you identify and change self-defeating thinking in response to obsessions.

- Use the *catastrophe scale* (p. 70) to deal with any awfulising about the discomfort involved in resisting rituals, or about the consequences you fear will result. Also check the likelihood of these consequences with techniques such as *empirical disputing* (p. 63), *correcting probability estimates* and *hypothesis testing* (p.67).
- *Rational-emotive imagery* (p. 73) and *coping rehearsal* (p. 74) will enable you to practise coping in advance of exposure.
- Use *rational cards* (p. 87) and *self-recorded tapes* (p. 88) during exposure.
- If you are tense, try *relaxation training* (p. 114). If you have panic attacks, learn *breathing control* (p. 126 and chapter 19 (pages 162–180)).

5. Graded exposure with response-prevention

To overcome obsessions and compulsions you need to resist the latter. These are the defensive rituals that reinforce anxiety. 'Exposure with response-prevention' (ERP) is the key strategy. This involves deliberately exposing yourself to obsessive thoughts at the same time as inhibiting compulsive rituals. For example:

Problem	Exposure	Response-prevention
Fear of contamination leads to excessive hand-washing.	Deliberately put dirt on hands.	Refrain from washing for gradually increasing periods of time.
Fear of violent burglary leads to excessive checking of locks.	Unlock then relock all doors at night.	Check locks a set number of times and no more.
Fear of being gassed leads to excessive checking of oven.	Turn oven on then off.	Leave kitchen and don't check oven for a set period of time.

You may wonder why it is necessary *deliberately* to bring on your obsessive thoughts; after all, don't you have them too much already? Yes, you do — but under conditions in which you have little control.

With planned exposure you set up a situation, prepare for it and go in ready to use your coping skills, which means you can influence your response.

Inhibiting your usual compulsive response to anxiety serves several purposes. By using your new coping skills instead of giving in to the rituals you will build up confidence in your own self-control. And the more you experience obsessive thoughts while preventing the compulsions they have prompted for so long, the more you will discover that the disasters you have feared are unlikely to occur.

Plan your exposure programme

1. List your rituals.
2. Using your baseline diary, identify activities or situations that trigger anxiety and the urge to perform each ritual.
3. Rate these activities and situations according to the amount of discomfort you would feel if you didn't perform the ritual.
4. Arrange the activities and situations in order, from least to most anxiety-provoking. This will give you an exposure hierarchy for each ritual.
5. Choose a hierarchy with which to begin.

Decide how you will avoid ritualising
Here are some strategies with which to combat the urge to ritualise:

- Use *distraction* techniques (p. 108).
- Listen to a prepared *disputation tape* (p. 88).
- Self-administer *reward and punishment*.
- Use *relaxation* to let go of any tension (p. 114).
- Have *a helper* restrain you from engaging in rituals.

Set up a recording system
Keep a log in which you record:

- The date.
- The exposure activity.
- The response-prevention activity.

- Your thoughts.
- Your anxiety level before, during and after practice.

Carry out exposure

- Undertake the exposure activity that provokes least anxiety. Resist the compulsion to carry out the ritual in which you would normally engage. In the case of excessive hand-washing, for example, you might dirty your hands (exposure) and avoid washing for one to two hours (response-prevention). Afterwards, fill in your log for that activity.
- Practise daily for a week or so, or until the exposure causes only minimal anxiety.
- Repeat the exercise with the next exposure activity in the hierarchy.
- Continue until you have systematically worked through all the exposure activities in the hierarchy.
- Move on to the hierarchy of a different obsession-compulsion (assuming you have more than one).

Tips for exposure with response-prevention

- Regular daily practice is important.
- Exposure can be carried out wherever the things that trigger obsessions are present — your home, your workplace, etc.
- Sessions need to last as long as it takes for the discomfort to be reduced without rituals. This may be anything from 30 minutes to two hours.
- As soon as you master a particular step, move on to the next without delay. Conversely, if you have trouble with a particular step, stay with it for as long as necessary.
- Once you have mastered a particular step, maintain the new behaviour in all situations, not just when doing exposure work.
- Compromise may be needed. You are unlikely to undertake activities that make you overwhelmingly anxious; on the other hand, undertaking activities that provoke little or no anxiety will be of minimal benefit as it will simply reinforce low discomfort-

tolerance. The answer is to undertake activities that are challenging but not overwhelming.

Exposure examples

The following hierarchies will give you ideas for developing your own. First, one developed by Janet:

Obsession: Causing a fire
Compulsion: Excessive checking of electrical appliances

Strategy and techniques
Carry out each step once daily for about a week using the following procedure:
- Reread a rational self analysis completed earlier.
- Read a rational card whenever tempted to check an appliance.
- Except for the two final steps, listen on a portable player to a recording in my own voice that disputes my irrational anxiety-causing beliefs about not ritualising.

Steps
1. Run all heaters for at least 10 minutes, turn them off, return to each heater and check it once, then stay outside in the garden for two hours (anxiety rating 5/10).
2. Use the iron, turn it off and go to another part of the house for two hours (6/10).
3. Use the oven, switch off the elements but leave the wall switch on and stay out of the kitchen for two hours (7/10).
4. Get ready to go out, check all appliances once according to a preprepared list, then leave the house for two hours (8/10).
5. Turn on the iron, oven and heaters for 10 minutes, then switch them all off and spend an hour with Alice across the road (9/10).
6. As per step 5, but leave the neighbourhood and go shopping for half a day (9/10).

Now one developed by Richard:

Obsession: Contamination from handling money
Compulsion: Repetitive hand-washing

Steps
1. Dirty hands by handling old bank notes; wash with warm water and soap for five minutes.

2. Repeat step 1, but wash for four minutes only.
3. Repeat, but wash for three minutes only.
4. Wash for two minutes only.
5. Wash for one minute only.
6. Wash with *cold* water and soap for two minutes.
7. Wash with cold water and soap for one minute only.
8. Repeat, but delay wash for 15 minutes.
9. Delay wash for 15 minutes and wash for 30 seconds only.
10. Delay wash for one hour while carrying out normal activities around the house and wash for 30 seconds only.

Different types of obsessive-compulsions

Here are some examples of exposure and response-prevention tasks for different types of obsessive-compulsive behaviour. Exposure should be graduated in all instances:

- *Excessive cleaning.* Rub butter on the kitchen taps or whatever other objects feature in your compulsions, then delay cleaning them for a set period.
- *Repetitive checking of locks.* Before going to bed, unlock all the doors in your house, then return to lock them, allowing yourself a preset number of checks.
- *Repeated checking to see if you have hit a pedestrian or cyclist while driving.* Deliberately drive on a road where you know there are many bumps; drive at night; take an unfamiliar route.
- *Repeating actions to prevent some 'catastrophe' from occurring,* e.g. saying particular words, phrases or sentences over and over again, or recounting things in your mind. Imagine the catastrophe you fear using increasing levels of vividness, at the same time as inhibiting your ritual.
- *Repeatedly arranging objects in a particular order.* Place the items out of order, or have someone do this for you. Progressively increase the extent of the disorder or the length of time you allow the items to remain out of order.
- *Hoarding things because you think you may need them sometime in the future.* Rank items according to the degree of anxiety associated with them, then throw them out, starting with the least anxiety-provoking.

- *Repeatedly seeking reassurance from others that you have not said or done something inappropriate.* Say or do something you think might be inappropriate, then resist the compulsion to ask for reassurance that it wasn't.

When using exposure to combat excessive behaviour, don't go to the opposite extreme and become excessively lax. Just get your compulsion down to a manageable level.

Cognitive rituals

Sometimes people try to neutralise obsessive thoughts with further thoughts, i.e. with *cognitive* rather than *behavioural* rituals. Simon's complicated mental ritual, in which he imagined himself engaging in a series of pious acts to 'undo' the images of sexual acts he found so repugnant, is an example.

Cognitive rituals are an especial challenge, because it is possible to engage in them almost anywhere; and because their triggers are less predictable, the rituals are harder to inhibit. Treatment consists of *exposure* to the anxiety-provoking *obsessive* thought, and *response-prevention* of the neutralising *compulsive* thought. For this to work, you need to be clear which thought is the obsession and which is the compulsion. In Simon's case, the images of sexual acts were the obsession, and the images of pious acts were the compulsion.

- *Exposure to the obsessive thought.* Here are some ways to expose yourself to an obsessive thought:
  * Deliberately evoke the thought. Hold it in your mind for as long as it takes to make you feel anxious. Pause. Repeat.
  * Write down the thought repeatedly.
  * Record the thought on a loop tape.
- *Response-prevention of the compulsive thought.* Here are some ways to inhibit a compulsive thought:
  * *Thought-stopping.* Hold the obsessive thought in your mind; then, when the compulsive thought comes, shout 'Stop!' Eventually you will be able to shout subvocally — that is, in your mind. Note that you are trying to stop the compulsive thought, not the obsessive one.[1]

* *Distraction.* Hold the obsessive thought; then, when the compulsive thought comes, distract from that either by thinking a prearranged, pleasant thought or by engaging in some pleasant, interesting activity.

- *Using a loop tape.* This is probably the most effective technique,[2] as it allows presentation of the obsessive thought under controlled conditions. Make a loop tape of the obsessive thought in your own voice. (Loop tapes, usually about 30 seconds long, are often sold by commercial stationers for use in telephone answering machines.) For example: 'I may contaminate my children's food and they will die slowly and in agony.' Ensure you record the obsessive thought only, without the neutralising compulsive thought. Then:

  * Listen to the tape twice or more daily for at least one hour — preferably till your anxiety has reduced by about 50 per cent.
  * While listening to the tape, resist the urge to use compulsive thoughts. Instead, practise the coping strategies you have prepared.

When you can listen to the tape without neutralising and with only minimal anxiety, repeat the procedure with a new obsessive thought (if you have more than one).

Note that it is essential to discriminate between (1) intrusive, *involuntary* thoughts (your obsessions), and (2) thoughts initiated by *deliberate* effort (the compulsions that make up your anxiety-reducing ritual). The latter are the focus of response-prevention. Don't fall into the trap of trying to apply blocking procedures to your *obsessions*; rather, block the cognitive *rituals*.

Also, a *ritual* thought may be the same as an *obsessive* thought, e.g. your compulsion may be to repeat the obsessive thought a certain number of times. To deal with this, *expose yourself to the involuntary thinking* but *prevent the deliberate repetition*.

It will be obvious from this that cognitive rituals can be difficult to deal with. If the procedures described here don't work for you, don't give up — a professional therapist can almost certainly help you.

6. Changing fearful thinking and core beliefs

As your exposure with response-prevention progresses, begin to tackle the underlying beliefs that maintain your obsessive thinking and compulsive behaviours. Confront your exaggerated fears of causing harm, your demands for total safety, and any self-downing for having a problem.

Fear of causing harm

If you worry about the risk of harm to yourself or others and tend to overestimate your responsibility for that harm, here are some strategies to help you get the danger into perspective:

- *Review the evidence.* Write down all the information you are using as evidence for your belief that what you fear is likely to happen. Review what you have written, then ask yourself: 'Given the evidence, does it make sense for me to think that such and such will happen?' Do some reality testing on your belief (see hypothesis testing, page 67).

- *Reassign responsibility.* Give a percentage value to how much responsibility you think you would bear if the feared outcome were to occur. Then ask yourself: 'If the harm I fear were to occur, what would make it happen?' List all the possible causative factors. Follow this with a second question: 'Exactly how much control do I have over each of these factors?' Assign values to each one and compare them with your starting value.

- *Define 'causing harm'.* Use rational self-analysis (p. 52) to identify the underlying meaning that causing harm has for you. A common issue is self-image anxiety, rooted in the idea that causing harm, i.e. a bad act, would make one a bad person.

Get the risk of danger into perspective

Whereas most people assume situations are safe unless there is evidence of danger, obsessive-compulsive sufferers tend to think the other way round — that things are dangerous until proven safe. They *demand* a guarantee of safety, which leads to indecisiveness, doubt, and reliance on rituals to ensure safety. Here is a strategy to deal with this:

1. List the advantages and disadvantages of applying the rule that everything in life is dangerous until proven safe.
2. Use *imagery* (p. 73) to practise applying the rule that everything is safe until proven dangerous. Imagine being in a feared situation, thinking it's dangerous, then disputing that thought and replacing it with the thought that the situation is safe.
3. Practise the more rational style of reasoning during real-life exposure, perhaps with supporting techniques such as *rational cards* (p. 87) or *tape-recorded disputation* (p. 88).

Deal with the fear of anxiety

Do you fear that if your anxiety were to increase you would be unable to work, function or cope with the tasks of daily life? Challenge this by disputing the prediction that anxiety and discomfort will continue indefinitely unless you ritualise, and that the anxiety will lead to incapacity.

Purposely expose yourself to anxiety-provoking triggers without the comfort of ritualising. While you wait for the discomfort to subside, practise appropriate functioning, e.g. housework, reading, gardening, walking. This will help you see that you continue to function in spite of obsessive thoughts.

Reject self-downing

Like many sufferers, you may regard your obsessions as abhorrent and your rituals as abnormal, and feel ashamed of your symptoms, seeing yourself as stupid, weak or bad. Because of this, you may be secretive about your problems and reluctant to reveal them. Here are some ways to combat such self-downing:

- Dislike the problem but *accept yourself* as a person (p. 79). Remember that obsessive-compulsiveness is not what you *are* — it is a problem you *have*. Use the *double-standard dispute* (p. 74). Ask yourself if you would condemn a friend if it came out they suffered from the same problem.
- Challenge your fearful perceptions about how others might view you, e.g. that because of your obsessions and compulsions you will be universally rejected, that what other people think of you

determines what you are, or that you could not bear to be disapproved of because of your problem. Use *rational-emotive imagery* (p. 73) to reduce your anxiety, guilt or shame while imagining you are being criticised.

- Understand that if you behave in ways that seem bizarre and out of control it doesn't mean you are crazy or weak.
- Put the problem into perspective by studying the causes of obsessive-compulsiveness, especially its biological roots.
- Undertake structured exposure to the risk of disapproval; for example, tell selected people about your problem (see *shame attacks*, page 99).

From obsessive-compulsiveness to moderation

Here are some common irrational beliefs that keep people locked into obsessive thinking and compulsive behaviours, with rational alternatives:

Obsessive-compulsive beliefs	*Moderation beliefs*
I must never run any risk of being responsible for harm to others.	It makes sense to avoid significant risk of causing harm, but demanding a total guarantee is unrealistic and will only cause me to live in fear.
If I were responsible for harming others, it would mean I was a bad person.	I will certainly aim to avoid harming others; but if I were ever responsible it wouldn't make me a bad person — just a person who sometimes behaves badly.
I must be able to keep myself safe and avoid significant danger at all times.	Keeping myself safe is wise as long as I don't overdo it to the point where life becomes miserable, which would negate the point of keeping myself safe.
I must never have thoughts that are obnoxious or offensive or that conflict in any way with my values.	I would prefer not to have such thoughts, but most people do from time to time. Why should I alone be flawless?
Having bad thoughts shows I'm a bad person.	Having bad thoughts shows I'm a person who sometimes has bad thoughts.

Obsessive-compulsive beliefs	Moderation beliefs
I can't bear obsessive thoughts and must get rid of them no matter what the cost.	Obsessive thoughts are uncomfortable, not unbearable. And if I don't catastrophise about them, they'll bother me less.
Having this problem shows I'm a weak person.	Having this problem shows I'm simply a person with a problem.

The end of therapy

Therapy ends when you have eliminated all of your rituals and you know what to do if your obsessions return. Prepare for this eventuality. Obsessive-compulsive symptoms will reappear periodically, especially at times of stress, but if you have learned the right strategies you will be able to stop them taking control again. If you *expect* the occasional recurrence, you will be less likely to give up and fall back into your old ways. Make sure you can recognise the early signs of relapse and that you know what to do.

There are a number of ways in which you can reduce the likelihood and impact of slipping back. For example, consider asking family members or friends to provide ongoing reinforcement of nonritualistic behaviour. Develop avenues of social support, like other people with obsessive-compulsive difficulties who successfully maintain moderate thoughts and behaviours. And, last but not least, look to the longer-term future. Clarify your life goals and plan ways to achieve them so you have things to look forward to. Continue to develop a rational philosophy of life that will help you cope with a range of events and circumstances.

Richard, Janet and Marie have managed to do this. Richard is still fussy about cleanliness but not much more than many people. When he feels the urge to wash excessively, he plays a tape-recorded disputation if he's in his taxi or distracts himself with a pleasurable activity if he's at home. The plastic gloves are long gone. His relapses are increasingly less frequent — currently he has one just every couple of years — and last for only a short time before his coping skills take over.

Janet rarely phones her parents more than once a week, and has made an agreement with them never to ask how they are. (If they are unwell or need any assistance from her, they will ask.) She is still more careful than most people about checking ovens and other household appliances, but she and her family are comfortable with her level of checking. Like Richard's, her relapses are becoming less and less frequent and are quickly overcome.

Marie's house burned down. Authorities suspect loose papers fell on a heater and ignited. The large amount of paper in the house meant the fire was out of control in no time. Marie almost died in the conflagration but was rescued, unconscious due to smoke inhalation, by an alert neighbour. Until then, she had resisted treatment for her obsessive-compulsive problem, but she realised it was time to change when her demand for total safety — her belief that she must not risk throwing out anything important — had led to the loss of her home and almost her life.

Marie went to live with one of her daughters while the insurance was sorted out. While she was there, the family helped with her therapy and monitored any hoarding behaviours. After purchasing a new flat, she committed herself to keeping paper for limited periods only; for example, newspapers were to be thrown out after no more than two days. At the end of each week, she gave herself a reward for sticking to her programme. Now when she feels the urge to break her commitment, she reminds herself that demanding total security once compromised her safety, and that reasonable risk-taking is a safer way to go.

Hopefully you won't need anything so dramatic to get started on your obsessive-compulsive problem. The real message from the stories of all three people is that overcoming obsessions and compulsions is both desirable and possible. Why not start changing your story now?

23 Post-trauma anxiety

Human beings possess enormous resilience. Every person, during their life, will bounce back from a great variety of negative experiences. Sometimes, though, resilience is stretched too far. This happens when a severe experience, or a series of such experiences, befalls a person who may already be vulnerable in some way. The result can be repeated reliving of the experience, excessive vigilance, emotional numbness, social withdrawal and avoidance of any reminders of the experience.

It is not uncommon for people to have symptoms like these after a traumatic experience, and most recover before long. But if the symptoms are severe and persist for more than a month, they may indicate what is known as *post-traumatic stress disorder* (PTSD).[1] PTSD is most common among survivors of combat, floods, earthquakes, rape, repeated childhood abuse, abduction, kidnapping, hostage-takings and aeroplane crashes. It may also affect people who witness such events or who learn about severe trauma suffered by others to whom they are close.

Martin's story illustrates the nature of trauma-based anxiety. A landscape gardener in his early thirties, married with three children, Martin generally enjoyed life. His work provided him with the satisfaction of creating beauty while being outdoors and keeping fit. His successful business seemed to have a good future and he was able to provide his family with the kind of lifestyle he had always wanted. He'd always had a tendency to worry overmuch, but financial security and a happy family life kept this under control.

All this changed one summer evening. While walking to his local post office, Martin was viciously assaulted by three youths in a passing car. There was no apparent reason for the assault. In fact, Martin couldn't remember much at all about the incident. The youths were never identified.

Martin spent several weeks in hospital. Fortunately he'd suffered no permanent damage, his income was maintained through sickness insurance so finance wasn't a concern, and eventually he was pronounced fit for work. However, all was not well. He was easily distressed when reminded of the assault — for example, by news reports of violence. His sleep was disturbed and he had frequent dreams of being attacked. Gradually he became depressed and socially withdrawn. His increasing avoidance of any situation where he might be left alone began to create difficulties with his work.

What causes the trauma reaction?

Post-trauma anxiety results when a pre-existing susceptibility is triggered by a severe experience, or a series of such experiences. It differs from other types of problem anxiety in that the nature of the trigger is more significant, incorporating an experience that most people would regard as unusual and excessively disturbing. It might involve the threat of loss of life, participation in intensive combat, physical harm, rape, torture, sudden significant loss or multiple losses, injury, surgery, violent displacement, natural disaster, or multiple events that have a cumulative effect, such as sexual or physical abuse over a period of time.

As we shall see, a person's *view* of the event is just as important as its actual severity. You are more likely to overreact to trauma when three conditions exist. First, you initially believed that the location or circumstances were safe. Second, you perceived a threat to your own or someone else's life. Third, you regarded the event as unpredictable and uncontrollable and experienced an intense feeling of helplessness as a result.

Following a traumatic event, avoidance behaviour that succeeds in reducing anxiety can become self-reinforcing and thus promote the development of post-trauma anxiety. This is the pattern we see with all types of problem anxiety — avoiding anxiety perpetuates it.

Vulnerability
Most people will experience trauma at some time in their lives, but

not everyone who does will develop post-trauma anxiety. The disorder is unlikely to develop in the absence of a pre-existing susceptibility.

Biochemistry may be a factor. Cortisol, a hormone secreted by the adrenal gland when a person is stressed, is possibly involved. It has been found that post-trauma anxiety sufferers have lower-than-average levels of cortisol in their blood.[2]

Previous experience, such as childhood abuse or a series of bereavements, may leave a person vulnerable to post-traumatic stress.

Personality may also be involved. A person who finds it hard to tolerate discomfort will react more strongly to both trauma and its aftereffects, and will be more likely to engage in avoidance. Failure to accept oneself can lead to fear of disapproval from others, either for having experienced a trauma, or for having difficulty coping with its aftermath.[3] And believing that one's reactions are controlled by external events can lead to an attitude of helplessness in the face of traumatic experiences.

Martin, happy though he was before the assault, was vulnerable through his lifelong tendency to worry. Without that, his distress may have been shorter-lived. And, as we shall see next, some aspects of his belief system also put him at risk.

Core beliefs

Vulnerability to trauma is closely associated with certain ways of viewing the world and oneself. You are more likely to react severely to trauma if you hold one, or both, of two key belief patterns: *just-world* beliefs, and *vulnerability, safety and comfort* beliefs:[4]

Type of belief	Assumptions	Corresponding rules
Just-world	The world is a just and fair place. People get what they deserve and deserve what they get. Bad things do not happen to good people.	The world should be a just and fair place. Bad things should not happen to good people. If bad things do happen to me, it must be because I am a bad person.

Type of belief	Assumptions	Corresponding rules
Vulnerability, safety and comfort	It can't happen to me. (The illusion that somehow one is uniquely invulnerable to victimisation.)	The world should be a safe place. I must not experience emotional pain. Bad things must not happen to me.

If you hold beliefs like these, you are less likely to accept any traumatic events that befall you as part of life. Trauma, in effect, will shatter your basic view of how the world is supposed to be. Absolute demands such as 'The world *must* be a safe place', when contradicted by events, result in greater emotional pain than beliefs that are preferential in nature, such as 'I *prefer* the world to be a safe place.'

Martin knew that violence occurred in the world, even in his own community, but he believed it only happened to people who were careless or who were themselves engaged in antisocial activities. The apparently motiveless nature of the assault added to his confusion as to how it could have happened to him.

Current thinking

Core beliefs such as the above lead to current ways of thinking that create post-trauma anxiety:

- *Thoughts related to guilt*, e.g. 'I should have been able to prevent it happening. Because I didn't, I must be a bad/weak/etc. person', or 'I shouldn't have survived when others died.'
- *Demands about how others should react*, e.g. 'They should be understanding and supportive.' These will make you angry, which may alienate others and deter them from providing support.
- *Demands about those perceived as responsible* for the event, e.g. 'People must not do such things' may lead to *demonising* of those concerned ('They are bad people'), and possibly to overgeneralisations ('All people are bad and no one can be trusted').
- *Catastrophising about reminders* of the event. Objects and

events in the present may remind you of the traumatic experi-ence. But your emotional responses are not conditioned — how you react depends on how you view these triggers. You can overreact to reminders by *awfulising*, e.g. 'It is terrible to have these flashbacks/bad dreams', succumbing to *can't-stand-it-itis*, e.g. 'The feelings I get when I'm reminded are unbearable', and *demanding*, e.g. 'I must not experience these feelings.'

• *Secondary problems*. If you catastrophise about the post-trauma anxiety itself, or down yourself for not being able to control it (e.g. 'I'm weak/stupid/pathetic/etc.'), this may perpetuate the problem by creating a sense of hopelessness.

The three 'solutions'

Traumatic experiences may contradict deeply held beliefs. If you hold absolutist core beliefs about justice and invulnerability, you will find it hard to integrate negative experiences with your beliefs. Con-sequently, thoughts of a traumatic event will continue to intrude into your consciousness and create distress. There are three ways a per-son may try to resolve this conflict between belief and reality: *assimilation, overaccommodation* and *accommodation*. A descrip-tion of each follows, with an example of typical thinking:

Trauma solution 1	*Trauma solution 2*	*Trauma solution 3*
Assimilation	**Overaccommodation**	**Accommodation**
You alter information about the *event* to make it conform to your pre-existing belief system.	You alter your pre-existing *belief system* to accommodate the event, swinging to the opposite extreme in the process.	You alter your *belief system* to bring it into line with the reality of the event.
The world is a totally safe place — it is me that is the problem.	*The world is a totally dangerous place.*	*The world is not after all a totally safe place — there are some dangers of which I need to be aware.*

Martin initially tried assimilation. He blamed himself for the assault, told himself it had happened because of his carelessness and clung to the belief that the world was still a safe place. As time went by and he realised the world was in fact not altogether safe, he gradually overaccommodated, switching to the opposite view and coming to see the world outside his house as a thoroughly violent and unpredictable place. This marked the onset of his fear and avoidance behaviour.

The most functional solution is to avoid either of these extremes. The aim of post-trauma anxiety treatment is accommodation: to see the world as a mixture of good and bad, of safe and unsafe.

To sum up

Let's put all this together. Post-trauma anxiety appears to result from:

1. A *severe experience*, or a series of such experiences — the trigger.
2. The person who has the experience is predisposed to post-trauma anxiety by virtue of:
   * biological make-up/previous experiences/personality characteristics, and
   * just-world and/or vulnerability, safety and comfort beliefs, which are contradicted by the experience.
3. This leads to self-defeating thinking about:
   * the extent of danger
   * responsibility for the event
   * the symptoms experienced
   * oneself for having difficulties and being unable to control the symptoms.
4. This maintains negative emotions and leads to avoidance behaviour, thus turning an otherwise acute stress reaction into chronic post-trauma anxiety.

An introduction to self-treatment

As we have seen, the main aim of self-treatment for post-trauma anxiety is accommodation. Many people cope with an experience that

241

contradicts their world-view by altering their perception of the event itself. In other words, they assimilate a view of the event into their existing belief system. They may adopt a number of strategies to do this, such as avoiding reminders of the event (e.g. by staying away from situations that act as cues), reframing the event (e.g. redefining an assault as their own fault), or seeing what happened as justified (e.g. 'I must have done something to deserve it).

Assimilation is unhelpful because it denies reality, thereby leaving you at risk. Your belief system could be contradicted again in the future. You may also fail to learn from your experience and take note of dangers that do exist in your environment.

Accommodation, on the other hand, involves changing your beliefs about the world so they are more consistent with reality. For example:

Old belief	New belief
The world is, and must be, a totally safe place.	The world is, and always has been, a place that contains some dangers. It is better to acknowledge this rather than demand that reality not exist.
I must be immune from danger.	There is no law that says I should be immune from the dangers faced by the rest of humankind.

Be on the alert for *over*accommodation, which entails swinging from one extreme, e.g. 'The world is a totally safe place where everyone can be trusted', to the other, e.g. 'The world is a totally dangerous place and no one at all can be trusted.' This also represents a distortion of reality, and a damaging one, because total lack of trust can lead to a negative and restricted life.

To achieve realistic accommodation it may be necessary to revise some basic assumptions about yourself, others and the world in general, so that your recollections of the traumatic event become integrated and tolerable.

Treatment strategies and steps

How do you revise basic assumptions? By applying the following key interlocking strategies:

- *Develop appropriate copying skills*, in particular *rethinking* (p. 65) and *relaxation* (p. 174). You can use these to relieve your symptoms, build confidence in your ability to cope and prepare for exposure work.
- *Exposure work*. Exposure for post-trauma anxiety is carried out using *new information* that alters the world-view that has been contradicted by the trauma. It usually takes two forms: imagery exposure and real-life exposure.
- *Change self-defeating beliefs about the world*. Address any underlying safe-world or just-world beliefs, along with any self-downing or discomfort issues that may be stopping you from moving on. To do this you can draw on the usual range of cognitive, emotive and imagery techniques.

Additional strategies may include:

- Attending to any safety issues.
- Linking in with your support systems.
- Any of the following: sleep management, anger management, problem-solving, relationship counselling, medication.

The main steps of self-treatment are as follows:

1. *Assess* your anxiety.
2. *Educate* yourself about post-trauma anxiety.
3. *Plan* your self-treatment programme.
4. Develop appropriate *coping skills*.
5. Undertake *exposure*.
6. Change your *self-defeating beliefs*.

1. Assess your anxiety

Clarify your problem and establish baselines

Start by listing your symptoms. You may find it helpful to categorise them as follows:

- *Intrusive thoughts, images or dreams* that are unwanted and unpleasant.
- *Anxiety* when exposed to reminders of the traumatic event.
- *Physical symptoms*, such as tension, panic, sleeplessness, irritability, jumpiness and difficulty concentrating.
- *Avoidance behaviour*, such as emotional numbing, social detachment, difficulty recalling significant aspects of the event, staying away from situations or places that act as reminders of the event.
- *Situations you are currently avoiding.*

Use this information to establish the baselines from which you will measure your progress. The best way to gather it is to keep a diary in which you record the following:

- Your symptoms, i.e. what you experience, including the content of any dreams or images.
- The triggers to these symptoms.
- Your thoughts.
- Daily ratings of your general anxiety level.

Identify any related problems

- If you are suffering significant *depression* (p. 45), this may need treating before your anxiety. See your health professional for advice.
- Do you practise any *substance abuse*? This, too, will usually require attention before you proceed further. The discomfort involved in self-treatment may prompt you to increase the abuse, and exposure will be pointless if you are in an altered state of consciousness.
- Do you have a history of *repetitive self-harming*? The discomfort involved in self-treatment may prompt you to inflict greater

self-harm. Work on increasing your tolerance for *emotional discomfort* (p. 80) and be free of any self-harming tendency before beginning exposure.

- How are your current relationships affected by your post-trauma anxiety?

Consider the history of your problem

- How was your mental health prior to the trauma?
- Have there been previous traumatic experiences?

Identify any secondary emotional problems

Look for any thinking that suggests you may have developed a problem about having a problem. For example:

- 'I'll never get over this' or 'I'm going crazy.'
- 'Other people are handling it better — I shouldn't be this way' or 'I should be able to handle my feelings.'
- 'I'm weak/stupid/hopeless/etc. because I can't handle this.'
- 'I can't stand the flashbacks/intrusive thoughts/bad dreams/ etc.'

If you identify thoughts like these, use standard rethinking techniques to deal with them, such as *rational self-analysis* (p. 52).

2. Educate yourself about post-trauma anxiety

Ensure you have read the early sections of this chapter. They will help you understand how post-trauma anxiety is caused and maintained, which in turn will help you make sense of the self-treatment recommendations that follow. In particular, ensure you are clear about the three solutions to the problem, and why only one of these is helpful.

3. Plan your self-treatment programme

Set the goals for your self-therapy and the strategies you will use to achieve them.

FearLess

Your overall aim will be to reduce your anxiety and avoidance behaviour, but there is a potential problem here: some people with post-trauma anxiety want to keep their anxiety, because it motivates them to undertake avoidance behaviour, which, they believe, protects them from a recurrence of the traumatic event. If this is how you think, you will need to start with some work to convince yourself that change is in your long-term interests. The *benefits calculation* (p. 65) can help you with this.

Address any secondary emotional problems
If you think there is little hope of your getting better, or you see yourself as 'useless' for having anxiety symptoms, you will find it hard to do the work necessary to recover. Consequently, you need to address these issues first. Use *time-projection* (p. 72) to work on the belief that you have no hope of getting better, and see page 252 for techniques to help you tackle the tendency to down yourself.

4. Develop coping skills

Learning techniques for managing your anxiety will give you some control over your symptoms and prepare you for exposure work.

Relaxation training
Letting go of rising tension inhibits the feedback loop whereby the mind observes the body tensing and interprets this as a signal that danger threatens. If physical tension is one of your symptoms, carry out *relaxation training* (p. 114).

Rethinking
While relaxation training is in progress, begin learning some techniques to deal with the self-defeating thinking that feeds your anxious reactions:

- Start with an *ABC diary* (p. 57). Record your anxiety-producing thoughts (*B*), their triggers (*A*) and the symptoms that follow (*C*).

- After a week or so, go to the next step. Dispute and replace the thoughts you identify, using *rational self-analysis* (p. 52) for a comprehensive approach or a *daily thought record* (p. 57) as a simpler alternative.
- Use *reframing* (p. 71) to label your anxious feelings 'uncomfortable' rather than 'unbearable'.
- Record old and new beliefs on *rational cards* (p. 87) to use whenever your symptoms occur and to prepare for and cope with exposure.
- *Self-instruction*[5] involves repeating to yourself phrases that summarise self-help concepts you have developed, e.g. 'Stay with it — it's worth having pain now to feel better later', 'Anxiety is uncomfortable, not terminal' or 'I don't like it, but I can stand it.' Write these down on small cards that you can keep in your pocket during exposure and look at quickly if necessary. Beware of superficial or unrealistic affirmations that are unlikely to stand up in the real world. Make sure your statements are realistic and believable.

5. Undertake exposure

Begin with imagery exposure

Imagery exposure involves consciously confronting your memories of the traumatic event (a) in a graduated manner, and (b) under conditions controlled by you. As you employ rethinking and other coping skills, your anxiety will progressively diminish.[6]

Imagery exposure can be carried out in several ways:

- *Writing.* Write an account of the traumatic event, describing in particular your sensations, emotions and thoughts at the time. Reread this daily until you can get all the way through with significantly reduced anxiety. You might also choose to read it to a helper, such as a trusted family member or friend.
- *Talking.* Describe the event verbally to a helper, recording what you are saying on a tape cassette. Listen to the tape alone every day until you can get all the way through with significantly

reduced anxiety. Alternatively record the tape alone, then play it to your helper. You might prefer this if having someone else hear your story the first time you tell it is itself anxiety-provoking. Other options are to dispense with the tape and simply tell your story every day to a helper (who is able to make the time available), or to dispense with a helper and record the tape and listen to it alone.

Choose the approach that you think will work best for you, then carry out the following steps.

Prepare for exposure

Acknowledge that your anxiety will temporarily increase as you recall the traumatic event, but remind yourself that it is important to stay with this until it reduces. Be clear in your own mind what the point of telling your story is, painful though it may be, and how it will help you.

Be sure to have developed some coping skills beforehand. When you are ready to begin, decide on your upper and lower *target levels* of anxiety (p. 95).

Carry out the exposure

Exposure is usually carried out in a graduated fashion, along the following lines:

1. At the first level write or talk about the *effects* of the traumatic experience on the way you think about yourself, others and the world in general. While doing this, use relaxation, breathing control and rethinking to manage your anxiety. Reread your account or listen to the tape-recording as often as it takes to reduce your anxiety to a tolerable level.

2. When you are ready, move to the next level. Prepare a detailed account of *the event itself*, covering (a) what happened, and (b) the thoughts and emotions you experienced at the time. Either write this down or relate it verbally into a tape recorder. Again, reread or listen repeatedly until your anxiety is tolerable.

3. Gradually increase the level of detail about the experience, and eventually add to the record your *current* thoughts and feelings about it.

At each level of exposure:

- Carry out your reading or listening daily, using your coping strategies.
- Allow yourself to experience whatever emotions surface — don't try to suppress them. Use your coping skills to manage any anxiety. If your anxiety rises above your upper target level, return to a lower level of exposure. Continue to bring out the story, and, gradually, to complete it.
- Begin to challenge self-defeating thinking as it becomes apparent (more on this below).
- As you proceed, take note of (1) any additional anxiety symptoms that become apparent, (2) any difficulty you have relating particular parts of the story (are there some things you avoid), and (3) any anxiety-producing ways of thinking. Deal with these using rethinking, relaxation or other coping skills.
- Take every opportunity to give yourself credit for any helpful thoughts and emotions of which you become aware.

Work at your own pace
This may be the first time you have really told your story. You may not want to relate the whole account straightaway. Use a graduated approach, allowing the level of emotion involved to rise at your own pace as you gradually provide more detail. Make your exposure challenging but not overwhelming.

When desirable, several steps can be condensed into just one or two sessions, or, conversely, a single step can be spread over several sessions.

Gradually start work on your core beliefs
As you undertake exposure, you will become aware of the core beliefs that underlie your anxiety. Begin tackling these as they come up. Watch especially for thoughts about the following:

- Your responsibility for what happened.
- The kind of person you think you are.
- Your hopes for recovery.
- Your perception of personal vulnerability.
- Assumptions that are contradicted by the traumatic event.
- How you view your symptoms — intrusive thoughts, flash-backs, bad dreams, etc. Especially note any awfulising about these, any demands that they not occur, and any self-downing for not being able to control them.

Move to real-life exposure

When you are ready, move from imagery to real-life exposure. See page 94 for guidance. Specific areas to address might include the following:

- Situations that you are currently avoiding.
- Fear of what others might think of you. Use *shame attacking* (p. 99).
- Aspects of your lifestyle that have become overly restricted. Carry out appropriate *risk-taking* (p. 99).

Introduce additional strategies as appropriate

- *Increasing self-control.* In addition to the strategies described above, there are others that may enhance your sense of self-control:
    * You can use *thought-stopping* (p. 108) to inhibit intrusive recollections and obsessive thoughts that remain *after* you have completed deeper-level analysis.
    * Do some *sleep management training* (p. 272) if you aren't sleeping well.
    * If anger is a complicating factor, do some *anger management training* (p. 253).
    * If you need to resolve any difficulties in your circumstances, use *problem-solving* (p. 129).
    * *Rational self-analysis* (p. 52) is a tool you can use with difficult emotions you experience at any time in your life.

- *Using help.* You might find it easier to deal with your anxiety if you have support from family, friends or a community support group. This will be most effective if you have realistic expectations of what others can do for you, and, if necessary, you use rethinking skills to deal with any fear of criticism or disapproval from others.
- If you are in a relationship that has been under strain because of your post-trauma anxiety, a relationship counsellor may be able to help.
- *Medication.* Antidepressant medication will help some people, especially those with symptoms of depression. However, as with other anxiety disorders, benzodiazepines are usually unhelpful: they may contribute to the avoidance behaviour that promotes post-trauma anxiety, meaning any relief gained will only be temporary.

6. Deal with specific issues and self-defeating beliefs

As exposure work progresses, extend the work on your core beliefs until this becomes the primary focus. Deal with any safe-world beliefs, beliefs about personal invulnerability, and beliefs about negative self-image. Focus especially on assumptions that are contradicted by the traumatic event.

Don't fall into the trap of disputing how bad the traumatic event itself was. For example, challenging a belief such as 'What happened was awful' will simply direct attention away from the cause of your pain in the present. It is more useful to deal with the thoughts behind your *current* distress, e.g. 'I can't stand these flashbacks I keep having', and the core beliefs that existed *prior* to the event, e.g. 'The world should be a totally safe place for me.'

Safe-world beliefs
Are you clinging to a belief that the world is a safe place? A traumatic experience will contradict this and may lead you to think that what happened was your fault. To deal with this, first make sure you understand that the safe-world belief is unrealistic. Then develop an

alternative, rational belief about the world by considering the reality, which is that dangers abound and it is impossible totally to guarantee one's safety, but that you can reduce the chance of many traumatic experiences by taking appropriate precautions.

Use the *benefits calculation* (p. 65) to examine the wisdom of holding a safe-world belief. You could also use the *double standard technique* (p. 69) and ask yourself: 'Would I encourage a loved one to hold such a belief?'

Vulnerability

Following victimisation, people often jump from the illusion of personal invulnerability ('It won't happen to me') to the opposite extreme ('I have been singled out to suffer this'). The solution is to move towards the idea of universal vulnerability ('Everyone is equally vulnerable to negative experiences').

Self-blame and competence

Closely linked to the issues of vulnerability and self-blame is your perception of how competent or able you are to keep yourself safe in the future. After a traumatic experience, you may view yourself as weak, powerless, helpless, out of control, or even deviant because of what happened. This is the result of core beliefs like 'Bad things only happen to people who deserve them.'

Begin by clarifying what you are blaming. Is it your *behaviour* ('It happened because of what I did'), particular *character traits* ('It happened because I'm unassertive/thoughtless/etc.') or your *total self* ('It happened because I'm a bad person')?

If you blame your behaviour or character traits, check out the evidence. If it turns out that your behaviour was indeed wholly or partly the cause of what happened, there are three things to do. First, take responsibility for your actions. Second, *accept yourself* in spite of those actions (p. 79). Third, consider what you can do to reduce the likelihood of a repeat.

If you doubt your ability to keep yourself safe in the future, check out exactly what your deficiencies are and address them. To do this you may require additional education and training in particular skills.

Trust

If you have experienced trauma at the hands of another person or people whom you trusted, you may find yourself swinging from a pre-existing belief like 'People can be generally trusted' to an extreme opposite like 'No one can be trusted.' It is important to adopt a more realistic outlook, e.g. 'People can be trusted to varying degrees — some very little, others more, some a lot.'

Are you *too* trusting? Seek guidance on how to assess the degree to which it is wise to trust other people. A counsellor may be able to help with this, or you could talk to people you know who seem to have a sensible attitude to trust.

The search for meaning and demands for fairness and order

If you understand why the traumatic event happened you will probably be less distressed than if you can't make sense of it, so it may be helpful to clarify this — if it is possible to do so. But take care. Asking 'Why did this happen to me?' may keep you locked into your bad feelings, because the question is really a statement — 'This should not have happened to me' — so can never be answered. The underlying issues here are just-world and fairness demands. There are several things you can do to deal with these.

First, dispute them. One way to dispute the demand for fairness is to move from 'Why me?' to 'Why *not* me?'

Then work towards acceptance of reality. This involves two steps. First, acknowledge that the event has happened and that it could do so again, although you naturally hope it doesn't and will work hard to minimise that possibility. Second, change any demands that it 'shouldn't' have happened, or 'mustn't' happen in the future, to *preferences*. You may find it helpful to review the material on *acceptance of reality* (p. 82).

Anger

Are you having difficulty with anger? You may be angry with yourself for not avoiding the traumatic event, for your behaviour during it, or for the way you have 'coped' since. You may also be angry with yourself for surviving when others died (so-called survival guilt). On the other hand, you may be angry with others for failing to be understanding or supportive, or with those you perceive as the perpetrators of the event, or with God or 'the world'.

Anger is not always a problematical emotion — it can be an appropriate response, commensurate with the situation. However, if you are sitting on excessive anger that is not leading to constructive action, this may result in distressful symptoms and prevent you resolving the trauma.

Check: is your anger helpful for you, or is it destructive? Use the *benefits calculation* (p. 65) to work this out. Dispute any underlying demands that are fuelling your anger. Remember that 'shoulds' and 'musts' do little more than create internal upset — they rarely change anything for the better.

Most importantly, move towards acceptance — of yourself and your own behaviour, of other people and their behaviour, and of the world and what happens in it. This doesn't mean viewing what happened as acceptable, or that you give up trying to change the consequences. Rather, it involves putting a stop to an emotion that is eating you up from the inside.

Low tolerance for anxiety symptoms
As we have seen, post-trauma anxiety is usually perpetuated by overreaction to its symptoms. If you fear your intrusive thoughts or bad dreams, this focuses your attention on them and so gives them life. The solution is to decatastrophise flashbacks, nightmares or other unpleasant manifestations. Techniques to use include the catastrophe scale (p. 70), reframing (p. 71) and rational-emotive imagery (p. 73).

Ensure you tackle any tendency to catastrophise about your *current symptoms*, not about the event itself. View your symptoms as 'unpleasant' rather than 'terrifying', as 'uncomfortable' rather than 'unbearable'.

Intimacy
Following some traumatic events, especially those involving sexual assault, intimate behaviour may trigger anxiety. Plan exposure assignments in which you gradually increase the level of intimacy you share with your partner while using rethinking and other coping skills.

From trauma to accommodation

Here are some common beliefs that block the integration of traumatic experiences, with rational alternatives:

Trauma beliefs	*Accommodation beliefs*
The world should be a just and fair place.	I want the world to be just and fair, but it isn't now and never has been; so demanding this will only make me feel alienated and disillusioned.
The world should be a safe place.	I want the world to be a safe place, but it will be much safer for me to accept the world as it really is than demand how it 'should' be.
People get what they deserve and deserve what they get.	People get what they get, and what they get has little to do with what they do or don't 'deserve'.
Bad things do not happen to good people.	Bad things happen to everyone. The universe does not differentiate between 'good' and 'bad' people.
The reminders/flashbacks/bad dreams are terrible and I can't bear them.	These symptoms are unpleasant, not terrifying. I can — and do — stand them, albeit uncomfortably. And I will tolerate them better if I avoid catastrophising about them.
I must not experience significant emotional pain.	I prefer to avoid emotional pain, but some pain is inevitable for human beings, so better I stop making it worse by demanding it not happen to me.
Given what I have been through, other people should be fully supportive towards me.	Where is it written that anybody 'should' support me at all? And, anyway, demanding they do so is more likely to make people back away from me.
I should be able to keep myself safe and avoid significant danger at all times.	Keeping myself safe is wise, not a moral imperative. Demanding safety will only make me unnecessarily distressed when things go wrong, as they inevitably will on occasion.

Trauma beliefs	*Accommodation beliefs*
Because I failed to keep myself safe, I'm a weak/bad/immoral/ etc. person.	I'm not a weak/bad/immoral/etc. person, just a person who sometimes fails to keep him/herself safe (but who is going to learn how to do this better in future).
Not being able to control my feelings shows I'm a weak, stupid, pathetic person.	Having difficulty controlling my feelings shows I'm a person with a problem — nothing more.

The end of therapy

Your therapy will be at an end when you have achieved three things. First, you are able to experience reminders of the traumatic event with manageable levels of anxiety. Second, you can enter all of the situations you were previously avoiding. Third, any other problems associated with your anxiety, such as depression, substance abuse or relationship difficulties, have been resolved.

As with all types of problem anxiety, be ready to dust off your coping skills as and when symptoms recur, so you can deal with them quickly and with minimal disruption to your life and happiness.

Finally, make sure you prevent new post-trauma anxiety from taking hold. If you have the misfortune to undergo further traumatic experiences, take action as soon as possible afterwards. Don't delay. Make use of your existing support systems — family, friends, etc. Obtain professional assistance if necessary, or use the self-help procedures you have learned.

How did Martin get on? It took him a while to seek help, but once he did, he made rapid progress. Within a matter of weeks he was starting to manage his feelings when reminded of the assault. As he learned to handle his symptoms, fewer and fewer things triggered unpleasant memories. Occasionally the fear comes back, but he is able to manage it with one or other of his coping skills. He resumed walking to the post office, perhaps a little more warily than before but acknowledging that there would always be risks in life that were worth taking.

There are no guarantees that extremely unpleasant things will never happen in the future to Martin, you or me — but we do have the power to control how we react when they do. We can't always control the world; but — and this is the most reassuring thing of all — we can control ourselves.

24 Health anxiety

To be concerned about your health is a good thing. It motivates you to take care with your diet, to exercise regularly and to visit a doctor if you suspect you have a health problem.

Unfortunately, concern for one's health can escalate and become counterproductive. A person may notice some symptoms and conclude they have a serious illness. They then begin searching for a medical explanation of the symptoms. A growing conviction that they are ill persists in the face of reassuring medical findings or other evidence to the contrary. They start to notice normal bodily functions and characteristics and to misinterpret them as signs of illness. Catastrophic evaluations follow. The end result is anxiety, avoidance behaviour and compulsive reassurance-seeking and body-checking.

Checking and the search for reassurance usually involve numerous doctors, specialists and other health professionals, as well as family and friends. Unfortunately, because anxiety has taken over, the person disbelieves any reassurance they receive. Their anxiety steadily grows and they feel increasingly desperate, whereupon they seek even more reassurance — and so it goes on. There is a Latin proverb that sums up the outcome: 'He who lives medically lives miserably.'[1]

Avoidance behaviour may entail staying away from sick friends or shunning exercise that might trigger 'symptoms'. The anxiety is not about these *external* factors; they simply act as potential reminders of the real fear, which is that something *inside* is wrong.

Stephen, whom we met in chapter 1, suffered from health anxiety. A divorced, middle-aged man with two grown-up children, he was perfectionistic, hard-working, careful to avoid risks — and prone to worry. He had been anxious about his health for some years, but his anxiety became apparent to others only when he began repeatedly to visit his doctor (and, before long, other health practitioners) with concerns about a discoloured patch of skin on his left arm. He believed the patch was slowly spreading, and feared it signalled cancer. His children, irritated by his constant health-talk, came to dread his phone calls and reduced their visits. Fortunately, their response helped Stephen realise his anxiety was excessive and that he needed to do something about it.

What causes health anxiety?

Like other forms of problem anxiety, health anxiety is the product of a vicious circle. You misinterpret innocuous physical signs and symptoms as indications of a serious illness. You catastrophise about these, which creates anxiety. The symptoms of anxiety fuel your fears, and you obsessively check your body for more symptoms. This increases your anxiety, which leads you to misinterpret normal bodily functions and characteristics. And so the circular process is perpetuated. See the diagram below:

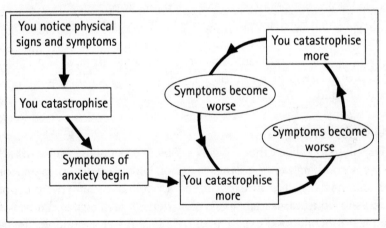

Stephen interpreted his skin discoloration as evidence of cancer. Reassurance from various sources, including his family doctor, a skin specialist and a cancer specialist, sustained him for only a few days, then his fears returned.

Behaviours driven by health anxiety can reinforce the belief in a serious illness. Checking may actually create symptoms. Stephen was forever fingering and prodding the patch on his arm, which made it red and sore — a sure sign, as far as he was concerned, that it was a cancer.

The behaviour of health practitioners can have a similar effect. If your doctor, to try and reassure you, carries out tests, you may take this as evidence that he or she thinks something could be wrong. And any reassurance that you do accept, far from putting a stop to your obsessive thinking, will provide only temporary relief — which encourages you to seek further reassurance.

Inappropriate diagnoses and treatment reinforce the belief in a serious illness. Sufferers of health anxiety frequently approach alternative health practitioners, who may diagnose problems such as 'toxicity' or 'imbalance', which are vague and lack supporting evidence. Also, it is not unknown for a doctor to tell a patient there is nothing wrong with them but still to prescribe some benign medication 'just in case' — which the patient interprets as proof that the doctor really does think something is the matter.

Avoidance behaviour perpetuates itself. If you have come to associate anxiety with illness situations, such as doctors' surgeries, hospitals, sick people or medical information, you may shun these. The relief this provides will then reinforce your belief that such situations are best avoided.

Where does it begin?

Health anxiety, like other types of problem anxiety, probably results from a combination of biological factors and early-learning experiences. As we have already seen, it appears some people are predisposed towards high levels of anxiety. If such a person also has unpleasant childhood experiences of ill health — for example, a parent dying of cancer — or is fussed over as a child when only mildly ill or hurt, they may form distorted beliefs about illness or health.

Such beliefs can involve both discomfort and self-image issues. Here are some common discomfort-based beliefs:

- To be in good health I must be symptom-free.
- I must always be able to know what my symptoms mean.

- If you worry about things, you can stop them happening.
- If you don't worry about things, they will creep up on you.
- Physical symptoms always mean there is something seriously wrong.
- I must get help immediately, otherwise the worst could happen.

Here are some common self-image beliefs:

- Perfect health is possible, and I should be able to attain it.
- I couldn't bear to develop a major health problem, especially through carelessness on my part.
- To develop a major health problem would show I was a weak, incompetent person.

What sets it off?

An episode of health anxiety may be triggered by a health-related experience. A friend may die of cancer, an unexplained symptom may occur, such as tenderness in some part of the body, or two such events may take place close together in time.

Stephen, who was probably predisposed to anxiety (as evidenced by his tendency to worry), had lost his mother to cancer when he was in his early teens. The skin discoloration on his arm, diagnosed as a harmless by-product of the ageing process, had almost certainly been present for a long time, but it happened to come to his notice after his unexpected and rather sudden separation from his wife — a time of great stress for him.

The separation and his noticing the patch triggered several of Stephen's core beliefs, including 'I must never allow any unexpected event to catch me unawares' and 'I should maintain perfect health; if I don't, it will show I'm a failure.' These led to thoughts of a catastrophising nature, e.g. 'I might have cancer', 'That would be terrible' and 'I must get reassurance that I don't have cancer.' These in turn prompted changes in physical functioning and emotional arousal, resulting in reassurance-seeking and obsessive thinking. The process Stephen went through is typical of those with health anxiety.

An introduction to self-treatment

In the past, health anxiety has been considered difficult to treat. However, there is increasing evidence that CBT offers an effective approach,[2] so if health anxiety is a problem for you, have hope.

An important first step is to understand what the problem really is. It isn't that you may have a medical condition — rather, it is your *anxiety* about the possibility of having one. It is this that leads you to seek unnecessary reassurance, to undergo expensive and perhaps even dangerous medical procedures and to engage in avoidance behaviour — and to experience the unpleasant symptoms of anxiety itself.

Reduce your anxiety and you will gain, whether you have a medical condition or not. If you do have one, you will at least avoid exacerbating any symptoms. If you don't, you will save yourself unnecessary distress.

There are three main cognitive-behavioural approaches to treating health anxiety:

- You could work on your *inferences*, correcting misinterpretations of your symptoms as evidence of a medical condition.
- You could work on your *evaluations*, addressing what it means to you to have a medical condition should you indeed have one.
- You could develop your ability to *cope with your symptoms*, whatever their cause, and with the *anxiety* they trigger.

You can choose either one of these, although probably the most effective approach is to selectively use all three. Whatever your choice, keep the following in mind:

- It is normal for humans to become anxious when they perceive the possibility of danger, whether social, economic or physical.
- Such anxiety becomes dysfunctional if you believe you can't cope with the perceived danger and then *evaluate* your inability in a highly negative way.[3] A vicious circle is set up: anxiety itself becomes the problem. You become worried and tense about being worried and tense.

- A key aim of self-therapy is to break this cycle by learning skills to manage anxiety. This will give you a sense of being in control.

Do you believe you can't cope? Focus some of your self-help work on the fear of failure. Developing the coping skills outlined in this chapter will increase your confidence that you will in fact be able to overcome your problem.

The main steps of self-treatment are as follows:

1. *Assess* the problem.
2. *Educate* yourself about health anxiety.
3. Set your self-therapy *goals*.
4. Develop appropriate *coping skills*.
5. Undertake *exposure with response-prevention*.
6. Address your *core beliefs*.

1. Assess the problem

Consider the history of your anxiety
How was illness dealt with in your family when you were growing up? What factors may have precipitated your current concern?

Clarify your current problem

- What physical symptoms are you experiencing?
- What kinds of behaviour — checking your body, seeking reassurance, etc. —keep you focused on your symptoms? Describe them, and how frequently you engage in them.
- Identify any avoidance behaviour in which you engage. What things do you not do because of your anxiety? What do you do instead?
- Do you have any other condition that may need attention? In particular, do you suffer from *depression* (p. 45), have a tendency to *worry excessively* (p. 138) or have any other kind of problem anxiety?
- What is it you fear about your physical symptoms? What thoughts

263

do you have when you are aware of the symptoms?
- Are any aspects of your life under significant stress, e.g. family, finances, work?

Keep an *ABC diary* (p. 57) of your symptoms, thoughts, emotions and behaviours for two to four weeks. Note that analysing your problem in depth using a diary may form part of your treatment (see step 4).

2. Educate yourself about health anxiety

Reading the first part of this chapter will help you understand the ways in which health anxiety can show itself and how it is caused and maintained. In particular, note the varieties of avoidance behaviour — use the examples given to identify your own. Also note how repeated body checking and reassurance-seeking can reinforce the problem.

3. Set your self–therapy goals

The main focus of a self-therapy programme for health anxiety is to develop skills to cope with the physical symptoms, whatever their cause. To do this you will find it helpful to set specific subgoals, like the following:

- To check the lump on my leg no more than once a week.
- Whenever I worry about my health, to do a self-analysis instead of making a doctor's appointment.
- To resume visiting my aunt in the rest home once a week.
- To keep my anxiety below 3/10 when I notice my symptoms.
- To reduce my day-to-day muscular tension.

4. Develop appropriate coping skills

The most important coping skill is rethinking.

Tackle your anxiety thinking
After you have kept your ABC diary for a few weeks, select some of the entries for *rational self-analysis* (p. 52). Gradually build up your

understanding of the connection between your thoughts and how you feel and behave. Note especially the vicious circle of catastrophising ⇒ worsening symptoms ⇒ avoidance behaviour ⇒ worsening symptoms ⇒ catastrophising.

Correct mistaken inferences
Check out your belief that your symptoms indicate a serious illness:

- *Look at the evidence* for and against your beliefs about your symptoms. Stephen measured the discoloured patch of skin on his arm every day and after a month was able to conclude that it wasn't, as he had feared, getting any larger.
- *Develop alternative explanations* for your symptoms. For example, tenderness may be the result of constant prodding or fingering, or a headache may be caused by stress.

Correct faulty evaluations
Use *inference chaining* (p. 59) to dig beneath the surface and find out what you *really* fear. Then identify how you evaluate your fears by, for example, awfulising or demanding. *Dispute* any dysfunctional evaluations (p. 63).

Stephen did this and discovered his real fear was that if he developed a fatal illness, it would prove he had failed *at life* (especially so soon after his marriage had come to an end). Beneath this was the fundamental belief that it would prove he was a failure *as a person*. After disputing these beliefs, Stephen opted for the more rational belief that to fail is *a part* of one's life and doesn't make the *total person* a failure.

Develop additional coping skills
In addition to the strategies outlined above, you will probably benefit from some kind of training in directly managing your anxiety symptoms and intrusive thoughts. For example:

- *Progressive relaxation training* (p. 114).
- *Breathing control* (p. 126).
- *Distraction* and *thought-stopping* (p. 108).

5. Carry out exposure with response-prevention

As we have seen, excessive body checking, reassurance-seeking and passive avoidance of feared situations perpetuate health-related fears, and checking may actually *create* symptoms. The way to break this cycle is to stop the behaviour. This will increase your anxiety temporarily but decrease it in the long term. The best way to change unhelpful behaviour is to use *exposure with response-prevention* (p. 99). Here are the steps:

1. List the ways in which you *check* your body (e.g. examining your skin for spots, scrutinising your gums and teeth in the mirror, flexing your joints to test for pain), *seek reassurance* (e.g. visiting your GP or other health professionals, reading medical textbooks, searching for medical information on the internet) and *avoid anxiety-provoking situations* (e.g. certain body positions, particular types of food, physical exercise, reading or listening to media items about diseases, conversations about medical matters or contact with ill or hospitalised people).

2. Grade the items on the list according to the degree of anxiety each arouses.

3. Plan an exposure hierarchy (p. 96). This may involve activities such as repetitive physical exercise, reading an article or having a discussion about a particular medical matter, eating foods you normally avoid or visiting an ill person. If you are especially anxious about any particular task, prepare a separate hierarchy for it.

4. Carry out the exposure while using response-prevention, i.e. refrain from checking your body or seeking reassurance.

Here is the hierarchy Stephen developed to deal with his constant checking of the patch on his arm. His goal was 'To completely stop touching the patch except when washing my arm; and to wash no more than once daily.' As he carried out each step on the hierarchy, he was to refrain from touching the patch and instead use coping skills such as relaxation, eating something he enjoyed, rational cards, distraction or thought-stopping. He was to practise each step five times a day, except for steps 8 and 9, which he was to carry out once a day, and step 10, which he was to carry out once a week.

Step	Item	Anxiety level
1.	Think about (visualise) the patch for one second.	3
2.	Think about (visualise) the patch for five seconds.	3.5
3.	Think about (visualise) the patch for 30 seconds.	4
4.	Look directly at the patch for one second.	5
5.	Look directly at the patch for five seconds.	6
6.	Look directly at the patch for 30 seconds.	7
7.	Look directly at the patch for one minute.	8
8.	Think about having skin cancer for two minutes.	9
9.	Read article on types of skin cancer.	9.5
10.	Visit Bruce* and stay for half an hour.	10

*An old friend of Stephen's who had been successfully treated for cancer but whose face had been disfigured by surgery.

6. Address your core beliefs

As you begin to gain control over your anxiety, start working on the core beliefs that underlie your health fears. *Rational self-analysis* (p. 52) is a useful way to go about this. See the examples of rational beliefs below.

From health anxiety to realistic concern

Here are some common beliefs that underlie health anxiety, with rational alternatives:

Health anxiety beliefs	Health concern beliefs
I must always be able to know what my symptoms mean.	It is preferable to know what symptoms mean, but not always possible. Demanding to know can be expensive, time-consuming and potentially injurious to my health.

Health anxiety beliefs	Health concern beliefs
Bad health doesn't happen to good people.	Bad health can happen to anyone. Health conditions don't differentiate between 'good' and 'bad' people.
If you worry about things, you can stop them happening.	It is wise to be *concerned*, but worrying doesn't prevent bad health; if anything, it makes you sick.
Physical symptoms always mean there is something seriously wrong.	Physical symptoms can have many possible meanings, not all of them serious. Overreacting to symptoms, though, can be serious.
Perfect health is possible and I should be able to attain it.	There's no such thing as *perfect* health. I would be wiser to avoid disillusionment and aim for *good* health.
I couldn't bear to develop a major health problem, especially through carelessness on my part.	I don't want to develop a major health problem, but if one occurred I could adapt to it (and will do so better if I get rid of my can't-stand-it-itis).
I should be able to keep myself safe and avoid significant danger at all times.	Keeping myself safe is wise, but it's not a moral imperative. Making it a demand will only make me anxious now and screw me up whenever things do go wrong for me.
If I fail to keep myself healthy, it will show I'm a weak, careless person.	If I become ill, it will show I'm a person who isn't always healthy.
Being anxious about my health shows I'm a weak, stupid, pathetic person.	Being anxious about my health shows I'm a person with a problem — nothing more.

Overcome the blocks to successful treatment

There are several things that might block you from overcoming your health anxiety. Fortunately, both have solutions.

First, you may think the suggestion that you work on your anxiety rather than the health condition about which you are anxious implies your problem is 'all in the mind'. You might find this demeaning and so resist dealing with it. The solution is to remember that whether or not a genuine medical condition underlies your symptoms, reducing your anxiety will be worth the effort.

Second, you may fear that learning to manage your anxiety will mean any medical condition you have will go untreated, with catastrophic results. This can make it especially hard for you to deal with your anxiety. The solution is to identify how you would evaluate the consequences should they occur. In particular, watch for any catastrophising about these outcomes and demands that they not happen. Then rigorously dispute these beliefs, using the rethinking tools you have learned about in this book.

Last but not least, consider some lifestyle changes. Begin to develop interests and activities that do not involve illness.

The end of therapy

Your self-therapy will be at an end when you have achieved the goals you set at the beginning, when you are able to notice physical changes in your body with only moderate anxiety, and when you are confronting all of the situations you previously avoided.

How did Stephen get on? Through a combination of rethinking and exposure with response-prevention, he was able to overcome his fear of cancer — not by telling himself that it would never happen, rather by accepting that perfect safety could never be guaranteed, and that even if he did develop cancer, that would say nothing about the kind of person he was.

As with all other types of problem anxiety, it is important to keep in mind that you are not 'cured' when your anxiety abates. It is likely to return from time to time, especially during particularly stressful periods in your life. But if you expect this to happen, and are ready to dust off your coping skills and put them to use once more, you need never live medically and miserably again.

Part IV
Extra self-help resources

25 How to sleep well[1]

Anxiety can make getting to sleep and staying asleep problematical. There can be a variety of causal factors, so the first step is to identify which ones may be involved for you. The questionnaire below will help you with this. The section that follows explains how to analyse your answers.

The sleep questionnaire

Tick any boxes that apply to you.

1. Sleep environment

Noise ☐	Too cool ☐	Other . . . . . . ☐
Shift-work ☐	Too warm ☐	. . . . ☐
Time-zone changes ☐	Bed partner restless	. . . . ☐
Uncomfortable bed ☐	or noisy ☐	. . . . ☐

2. Sleep routine

Irregular bed- and getting-up-times ☐	Work in bed or in your bedroom ☐	Tense while lying in bed ☐
Heavy meal close to bedtime ☐	Read or watch television in bed ☐	Tell yourself after not sleeping well it will be hard to cope with the day ☐
Little exercise during the day ☐	Hard to switch off your mind when you go to bed ☐	Other . . . . . . ☐
Exercise close to bedtime ☐	Uncomfortable bed ☐	. . . . ☐

3. Substance use

Prescribed sleeping pills ☐	Slimming pills/ diet suppressants ☐	Thyroid supplements ☐
Over-the-counter sleep aids ☐	Oral contraceptives ☐	Cold remedies ☐
Tranquillisers ☐	Diuretic or water- reducing medication ☐	Bronchodilators ☐
		Beta-blockers ☐
		Stimulants ☐

☐ Caffeine: _____ cups of tea, coffee or other caffeinated drinks per day,
   last cup at _____ p.m.

☐ Other fluids: _____ cups/glasses in evening, last at _____ p.m.

☐ Chocolate: _____ during the day, last used at _____ p.m.

☐ Alcohol: _____ standard drinks per day, last drink at _____ p.m.
   (standard drink = 200 ml beer, small glass wine, one measure spirits)

☐ Nicotine: _____cigarettes/cigars/pipes per day.

☐ Drugs such as heroin, cocaine, cannabis, amphetamines, LSD or other
   hallucinogens.

4. Emotions

Anxiety/worrying	☐	Stress ☐	Other ☐	
Panic attacks	☐	Anger ☐	☐	
Depression	☐	Guilt ☐	☐	

5. Physical health

Pain ☐	Cough ☐	Starvation (including	
Heart problems ☐	Stomach and	anorexia) ☐	
Breathing problems ☐	digestive disorders ☐	Significantly over-	
Emphysema ☐	High blood pressure ☐	or underweight ☐	
Asthma ☐	Arthritis ☐	Toothache ☐	
Hiatus hernia ☐	Cancer ☐	Other ☐	
Enlarged prostate ☐	Kidney failure ☐	☐	
Food allergies ☐	Parkinson's disease ☐	☐	

6. Miscellaneous symptoms

☐ You wake in the early-morning hours and cannot get back to sleep, no
   matter what you do.

☐ You fall asleep uncontrollably at odd times during the day, either for a few
   seconds or for longer periods.

☐ After you have experienced a strong emotion (such as hilarity, anger or
   surprise) your muscles feel weak.

☐ Just before going to sleep and just after you wake up you are unable to
   move or speak.

☐ At the moment when you are falling asleep or waking up (including during
   the day) you experience vivid, dreamlike images.

☐ You have a restless, uncomfortable feeling in your legs that you can relieve
   only by moving or stimulating them, e.g. by walking around.

While asleep, you experience:

☐ Frequent leg or arm jerks, or general thrashing around.
☐ Snoring.
☐ Irregular breathing or gasping for breath.
☐ Intense anxiety (not associated with any dream) that leads you to cry out (as an adult).
☐ Sleepwalking (as an adult).

7. Beliefs about sleep

Indicate to what extent you agree or disagree with each of the following statements, using this scale:

Strongly disagree	Disagree	Unsure	Agree	Strongly agree
1	2	3	4	5

☐ Going for one or two nights without sleep can lead to a nervous breakdown.
☐ Chronic insomnia will inevitably have serious consequences for a person's physical health.
☐ By spending more time in bed, it is possible to get more sleep and feel better the next day.
☐ When it's hard to get to sleep, the best thing is to stay in bed and keep trying.
☐ If I have a poor night's sleep, I'll feel lousy and won't be able to function the next day.
☐ It's better to take a sleeping pill than have a poor night's sleep.
☐ There's nothing wrong with using sleeping pills on a permanent basis.
☐ Everyone needs eight hours of sleep to feel refreshed and function well during the day.
☐ Insomnia is a result of ageing and there isn't much that can be done about it.
☐ Feeling bad or not functioning well during the day is mostly caused by not sleeping well the night before.
☐ Insomnia is mainly caused by biochemical factors in the body.
☐ I must be able to feel and function at my best every day, and to do this I need a good night's sleep.
☐ Alcohol before bedtime is a good way to get a night's sleep.

☐ There's little I can do to handle the tiredness, stress and poor functioning that result from poor sleep.

☐ It's awful to have a sleepless night and I can't stand the way I feel the next day.

☐ I absolutely must get a good sleep every night.

☐ I should be able to sleep well every night, no matter where I am or what's happening in my life.

☐ Having a sleep problem makes me an insomniac.

☐ Insomnia is ruining my ability to enjoy life and stopping me from achieving my goals.

Analysing your answers

- *Substances*. If you ticked any of the medications, see your doctor and explain that you are having trouble sleeping. It may be possible to change your medication or its dosage. If you ticked any other items in this section, you need either to modify your intake or to give them up entirely. Be wary of any consumption of caffeine within six hours of bedtime, or more than one standard drink of alcohol after your evening meal. Any use of nicotine at all can make sleep difficult, as can any of the other drugs mentioned.

- *Emotions*. Deal with any you have ticked using the strategies you have learned in earlier chapters.[2]

- *Physical health*. Seek appropriate medical advice for any problems in this section. Even if a condition cannot be fully cured, it doesn't mean you have to be sleepless forever. What it does mean is that dealing with other contributing factors and using the strategies outlined later in the following pages will be even more important.

- *Miscellaneous*. The items listed all warrant seeking medical advice.

- *Beliefs*. Look at any items in this section for which you gave yourself a score of 4 or 5. All the statements listed are either myths or irrational beliefs about sleeping. We shall examine the myths shortly. For now, let's look at the beliefs characterised by awfulising, can't-stand-it-itis, demanding and self-rating.

* You may have noticed that worrying about sleeplessness causes it! A vicious circle is set up: you dread having a bad night, so you have a bad night, which makes you worry more, so your sleep gets worse — and so it goes on.

* Demanding that you sleep will keep you awake. Getting to sleep involves 'letting go', so trying too hard to sleep makes it less likely you will drop off.

* Exaggerating and awfulising about the consequences of not getting a 'good night's sleep' can create self-fulfilling prophecies. If you tell yourself you are going to have a bad day, you are likely to make yourself have one.

* Do you believe that you 'need' a certain number of hours' sleep? Many people can make do with less as they get older, but may worry about not sleeping as long as they used to. This gets the vicious circle going: 'I *need* eight hours sleep' leads to anxiety, anxiety leads to sleeplessness, and so it goes round.

* Many people make the assumption that disturbed sleep is inevitable with increasing age. This is not true. Researchers, using principles like those outlined in this chapter, have demonstrated that appropriate treatment can help older people sleep well.[3]

Some facts about sleep

Most people seem to benefit from between six and 10 hours' sleep a night, with the average being about seven-and-half. As you get older, your sleep requirements may reduce. What matters is not how many hours you spend in bed but how you feel in the morning.

Occasionally, people go without sleep for several nights in a row, perhaps following some kind of shock or trauma, but the need for sleep eventually takes over. It is possible to catch up on lost sleep. If you miss a night or even two, one good night's sleep will usually be enough to make up the deficit.

There are a number of stages to sleep. Each is important, and probably serves a specific function in restoring the body and mind.

For example, the stage known as rapid eye movement (REM) sleep (so-called because during it the eyes move rapidly under their lids) is associated with dreaming and an accelerated flow of blood through the brain. One theory has it that this process restores the brain. The other main stage of sleep — non-REM, or quiet, sleep — may serve to restore the body.

The basics of sleeping well

Whatever the original trigger, most sleep problems can be solved by modifying certain sleep habits. This involves paying attention to such matters as diet, how you handle stress, what time you go to bed and get up, and what you do just prior to bedtime and after you have gone to bed. No matter what type of sleep problem you have, the following recommendations are basic to getting a good night's sleep.

Analyse your daytime activities
What you do during the day affects how you sleep at night:

- *Keep daytime stress under control.* Problem-solve the things you worry about; accept things you cannot change; manage your time effectively; take regular exercise; be able to relax and shed physical tension; have at least one noncompetitive, creative hobby; deal with any dysfunctional emotions, especially anger and anxiety.
- *Practise good eating habits.* Eat foods high in L-tryptophan, a sleep-enhancing amino acid, e.g. milk, eggs, meat, nuts, fish, cheese and soybeans; have at least one hot meal each day; eat meals in a relaxed manner, sitting down, at regular times; avoid heavy meals too close to bedtime.
- *Exercise regularly during the day*, even if you are tired from insomnia. But see the comments below on exercise in the evening.
- *Is it wise to nap during the day?* For some people, daytime napping makes it hard to sleep at night; for others, it helps

them sleep better. You need to experiment. If you find that napping disrupts your sleep at night, avoid it no matter how tempting it is. Most people find that short rest periods during the day when they do not completely fall asleep refresh them without affecting their night-time sleep. Try the *breathing-focus* relaxation technique (p. 126). Because this reduces daytime drowsiness, it will, if anything, make you more ready for sleep at bedtime.

Ensure your environment is conducive to sleep

Is your bed comfortable? Keep your bedroom at a moderate temperature — not too warm, not too cool. Make your bedroom reasonably dark, but with provision for light to get in when morning comes. Dark and light are perceived by the brain as cues for the body system to put itself to sleep and wake up.

Have regular sleeping hours

- *You will sleep better if your system is used to a regular routine.* Retire and get up at the same time each night and morning. Set your alarm for the same time each morning no matter how much sleep you had the night before or whether it is the weekend or you are on holiday. Sleeping in is not a good idea. Maintain your routine to within an hour every day.
- *Get up early.* The longer you are awake during the day, the quicker you will get to sleep at night.
- *Limit the time you spend in bed to the time you are asleep.* Resist the temptation to stay in bed when you are not fully asleep. Dozing in the morning, for instance, will only give you a light, fragmented sleep at best, and make it harder to get a deep sleep the following night.

Develop a good pre-bedtime routine

- *Close to bedtime* avoid vigorous exercise (this will stimulate you when you need to be winding down) and, at the other extreme, falling asleep in front of the television.

- *Watch your caffeine usage.* Ideally, have none within six hours of bedtime as (a) its stimulating effect can linger that long, and (b) withdrawal during the night may wake you up. But experiment, as not everyone is affected the same way.

- *Avoid alcohol or smoking within two hours of bedtime.* Alcohol can suppress REM sleep and speed up the shifts between sleep stages. Nicotine is an even stronger stimulant than caffeine, meaning withdrawal during the night is likely to be more severe. Again, though, experiment. Some people can take a small amount of alcohol in the evening without their sleep being affected.

- *Chocolate and some cheeses* contain substances that can keep you awake. If you suspect a particular food item is affecting your sleep, try going without it.

- *Prepare yourself physically.* Try to be more physically than mentally tired at bedtime. Take a light walk, then a warm (not hot) bath. To get some sleep-inducing L-tryptophan into your system, eat some cereal with milk or some bread and honey and/or have a warm milk drink.

- *Prepare yourself mentally.* Avoid dwelling on stressful matters that cannot be resolved before bedtime: arguments, unhappy thoughts, anger, unsolved problems. To shed any excitement, engage in winding-down activities for about an hour before going to bed.

- *Have a bedtime ritual.* This will help cue your mind to begin thinking 'sleep'. For example: lock up, have a warm bath, get some supper, brush your teeth, change into your nightclothes, set your timer or alarm clock, turn off the lights.

When you are in bed

- *Use your bed only for sex and sleep.* Avoid reading, watching television or working in bed. Such activities will weaken the connection your mind makes between being in bed and being asleep. (Some people, though, seem to benefit from reading in bed — you may need to experiment.)

- *Relax your body and mind.* The *breathing-focus* technique (p. 26) is a good way to relax both. Choose to postpone problems; if you worry you might forget them, write them down.
- *If you wake during the night,* give yourself 15 minutes to fall asleep again. If you are still awake after this time, get up. (See page 281 for suggestions on what to do next.)

When you get up in the morning

What you tell yourself immediately on rising can have a significant impact on how you feel during the day. Suppose you tell yourself: 'Oh no! I hardly slept a wink last night so I'm going to feel lousy all day and I won't be able to cope', you are likely to create a self-fulfilling prophecy.

On the other hand, suppose you think: 'Well, I haven't slept as well as I would have liked, but I have had some rest. If I give myself a push and get moving now, I'll soon perk up and be able to cope with the day', you are much more likely to manage the morning and afternoon and to end up in the evening feeling OK about the day and thus more ready for sleep.

Dealing with particular sleep problems

Most sleep problems come right when sleep habits are improved. If yours doesn't, check the following difficulties and the recommendations for each one.

Trouble falling asleep

- During the day, don't nap (unless experimentation tells you otherwise) or take any stimulants.
- Three to four hours before going to bed, have a meal high in carbohydrates — cakes, sweets, sugar, honey, jam, ice cream, fruit pie, dates, figs, breakfast cereal, bread, milk, chocolate, potatoes, spaghetti, etc.
- Don't go to bed until you are ready for sleep — tired, relaxed and calm.

- If you feel tense in bed, use a relaxation strategy. The *breathing-focus* technique (p. 126) can be particularly effective.
- When in bed, say to yourself: 'I'll fall asleep quickly tonight.'
- When you experience disconnected thoughts or muscle twitching, think: 'I'm falling asleep.'
- If you are still awake after about 15 minutes, get up and follow the suggestions below (*Lying awake in bed*).
- Finally, don't sleep late in the morning, including at weekends.

Lying awake in bed

If you have had trouble sleeping for some time, your mind will have come to associate being in bed with being awake. You need to break this unhelpful association.

- *Only go to bed when you are sleepy and unstressed.* Lie down only when you are ready for sleep. Don't have arguments in the bedroom. Use your bed for sex and sleep only — no reading, television, eating or weighty discussions with your partner.
- *If you do not fall asleep within 15 minutes, or if you find yourself awake at any time of the night for more than 15 minutes,* don't lie in bed any longer. *Get up.* Go into another room. Stay up until you feel tired, probably for 20–30 minutes. When you are ready, go back to bed. Here are some things you can do while you are up:
  * Read something boring. Stop at the end of each page and try to remember what it was about.
  * Have some herb tea, a milky drink, a bread and honey sandwich, some milk and cereal, or other food or drink containing L-tryptophan.
  * Do something physically tiring: ironing, exercises, cleaning, sorting out, reading while standing up.
  * Do crossword puzzles, logic exercises, anything that requires the brain to work in short, sharp bursts. (But don't read an exciting book that will leave you wondering what happens next.)
- *Repeat this process* as often as you need to during the night,

and for as many nights as it takes to break the wakefulness habit.

Remember that the aim of this procedure is to train your mind to associate getting into bed with falling asleep quickly. Adhering to it may well test your discomfort-tolerance: most people tend to stay in bed in the hope that they will eventually drop off, believing that if they get up they definitely won't. You may well be reluctant to get up, especially if you have to do so frequently. If so, remind yourself why it is important.

Restless sleep

- Experiment with avoiding sleep during the day.
- Exercise vigorously (but not too late in the evening).
- Identify and deal with any underlying anger.
- Establish a good *pre-bedtime routine* (p. 278).
- Immediately before going to bed eat a high-carbohydrate snack.
- Get up one hour earlier than usual.

You wake early in the morning and cannot get back to sleep

- Cut out any daytime or early-evening sleeping.
- Don't go to bed until you are absolutely ready for sleep. Make yourself stay awake until then (though not with stimulants such as caffeine or nicotine).
- Abstain from alcohol during the evening — withdrawal may be waking you.
- If you have been taking sleeping tablets for more than a few weeks, ask your doctor for advice.
- Check out the possibility of *depression* (p. 45). If you think you are depressed, see your doctor or other health professional without delay.
- Establish a good *pre-bedtime routine* (p. 278).

Worrying

If you find yourself worrying about something while you are in bed, turn on the light and write it down. Firmly remind yourself that the middle of the night, when you are not fully awake, is the wrong time to try to solve problems. Commit yourself to dealing with it the next day. For further details, see pages 152–155.

Use of sleeping pills

The use of sleeping pills is a controversial subject. On one side of the debate are those who believe that pills are essential to their survival, or can be used indefinitely without harm. On the other are those who believe that medication for sleeping is always bad and should be avoided at all costs.

As might be expected, the truth lies in the middle. Sleep medication is helpful for some people under some circumstances, but the consensus at present is that it is usually appropriate for short-term use only. 'Short-term' varies from as little as three days to as much as four weeks, depending on which authority you consult.

The main problem with sleep medication is that it suppresses the essential REM sleep, and if this goes on for long, general wellbeing suffers. There is also the danger of addiction, and the consequent difficulties of withdrawal. Moreover, some sleep problems can actually be made worse by sleep medication.

If you are regularly using sleep medication, discuss this with your doctor. If necessary, ask to be referred to an appropriate specialist.

Attitudes to sleep by

Self-defeating beliefs	*Rational alternatives*
I must be able to feel and function at my best every day, so I need a good night's sleep.	I certainly want to be at my best every day, but demanding this will only make me uptight and thus more likely to perform at less than my best.
There's little I can do to handle the tiredness, irritability and poor functioning that result from poor sleep.	There's a lot I can do to deal with the consequences of not sleeping well, providing I take responsibility for finding and implementing solutions to the problem.

Self-defeating beliefs	Rational alternatives
It's awful to have a sleepless night, and I can't stand the way I feel the next day.	It's uncomfortable to have a sleepless night, but hardly horrific. I dislike the way I feel next day, but I can — and do — stand it, and will do so even better if I stop catastrophising about it.
I absolutely must get a good sleep every night.	I'd prefer to get a good sleep every night, but I'm not going to die if I don't. Also, I'm more likely to get to sleep if I stop demanding I do.
I should be able to sleep well every night, no matter where I am or what is happening in my life.	It would be great to sleep well every night no matter what, but I'm a human being, not a robot that can be switched on and off.
Insomnia is ruining my ability to enjoy life and stopping me from achieving my goals.	Insomnia detracts from my feeling of wellbeing, but it will only ruin my life and stop me achieving my goals if I let it.

26 Dealing with difficulties

By now, hopefully, you will know that it is possible to overcome your problem anxiety. Experience, though, may have shown you that it won't necessarily be easy. We have already dealt with many of the difficulties you may encounter, in the chapters on particular kinds of anxiety, but it may help to summarise some of the more common ones and what you can do to overcome them.

Blocks to using coping strategies

Have you found that you read about coping techniques but don't actually use them, or give up after a short time? Start by checking out why.

Are you trying to protect yourself? Dealing with anxiety involves acknowledging things that may threaten your self-image. You may, for example, realise that your avoidance behaviour is more extensive than you had thought, or that some of your thinking is self-defeating. You may consciously or subconsciously resist practising self-help because you believe that to practise it would mean admitting there was something wrong with you as a person.

You might see it as 'artificial' to *make* yourself act in new ways, believing that people 'should only do what they feel like doing'. Consequently, you wait for the 'right' feeling to come — which it never does.

Low discomfort-tolerance — believing that you can't stand the discomfort involved in temporary increases in anxiety — will discourage you from carrying out behavioural assignments, which are essential.

You may also have trouble seeing how behavioural work is relevant to getting better. If you don't see the point, you are unlikely to try.

Strategies to overcome the blocks

Understand the importance of action

Here are some key points to bear in mind when you hang back from carrying out behavioural assignments:

- The only way to check out how well founded your fears are is to face them and see what really happens.
- To feel in control of yourself, you need to get your thoughts, emotions and behaviours working together. Specifically, to consolidate new thoughts, you need to act on them.
- Anxiety is paradoxical — the more you try to avoid something you see as fearful, the more fearful it will become to you. Avoidance behaviour puts out the message 'The fact that I'm avoiding it means it must be dangerous.' This is *behavioural reasoning* — thinking that because you feel anxious, there is something to be anxious about.
- Change in one area will lead to change in others. A key principle of CBT is that modifying one component — thoughts, emotions or behaviours — facilitates modification of the others. Consequently, working on all three areas is the most likely road to success.

Develop a new view of behavioural work

See exposure work as experimental. One aim is to *test hypotheses*; for example, to check out whether certain things do in fact occur in a particular situation, or to establish whether something really is 'unbearable'. Another is to collect data; for instance, to record your thoughts and feelings while you are in an anxiety-provoking situation, or soon afterwards.

What if your fears *do* in fact come to pass? The experiment will still have been successful, because you will have increased your knowledge and understanding of your problem and thus will be better equipped to deal with it. Experiments are 'no-lose' situations in which you almost always gain — by checking the validity of your thoughts, acquiring new knowledge, getting used to taking risks, practising self-help techniques, and so on.

Uncover and dispute demotivating beliefs

As you become aware of beliefs that create blocks to action, deal with them as you would any self-defeating belief, using *rational self-analysis* (p. 52) as well as the tools on pages 65–67.

Use aids to facilitate learning

- *Develop recall aids.* You may find it hard to recall key learning when you are in situations that trigger your anxiety. One of the simplest and most useful aids here is the *rational card* (p. 87). Use it repetitively — eight to 10 times daily for about three weeks — and have it handy immediately before you enter an anxiety-triggering situation, while you are in it, and after you come out. Repetition is important if you are to recall a rational thought when it is needed.

- *Read widely, and wisely, about your problem.* Reading material on anxiety generally and your type of problem anxiety in particular can be obtained from a variety of sources, including the internet (though beware of poor quality and misleading material, which is especially rife in cyberspace). If you can afford it, purchase books you see as useful and keep them to hand as you pursue your self-therapy programme.

Ensure your self-therapy plan is appropriate

Make sure that the strategies and techniques you select are appropriate to your needs and relevant to the self-help work you currently have in progress:

- *Tailor assignments according to your needs.* Different assignments will suit different people in different circumstances. Ensure those you plan are appropriate to your personality, life situation and current therapeutic requirements.

- *Plan activities you are able to carry out.* Are you clear about what you are going to do? Is it within your capabilities? Will you have the time, opportunity and financial resources to carry it out? Don't set unrealistic goals or assignments — you will end up disappointed, disillusioned and in a mood to give up.

- *Check out possible blocks to completion.* Before you commit yourself to any course of action, anticipate what blocks there might be to carrying it out and problem-solve them.

If you slip up

If you fail to start an assignment, or don't manage to complete it, don't moralise or put yourself down. Instead, treat it as a therapy issue. Carefully analyse what the blocks were, then do some therapeutic work on them.

Overcome the fear of change

You are unlikely consciously to resist getting better, but there may be some advantage to staying as you are. If you have been avoiding certain situations for many years, such as crowded public places or travelling in a car, you may have adapted to a certain 'comfort zone' and justify staying there — to yourself as well as others — on the grounds that you have an anxiety condition. To get better would entail giving up that justification. Consider the relative merits of tolerating a short-term increase in discomfort and putting up with the permanent discomfort of staying as you are. Accept discomfort as a normal part of life. Remind yourself that facing it is in your interests. Then you will feel less afraid of beginning the process of personal change. You may find it helpful to refresh your understanding of *emotional and behavioural responsibility.*

Be realistic about change

Beware of demanding that you be able to change anything and everything you dislike. This will lead to disillusionment. Adopting the principle of *acceptance* (p. 82) will help you avoid this danger while still working hard at change. Begin your self-help programme with optimism and a determination to achieve the change you want — but keep in mind that you can't change everything. How do you do both? Desire change, but think of your desire as a *preference*, not a *demand*.

27 Outside help

You can go a long way with self-help — but there are limits. Sometimes a problem is too ingrained or complex to work out on your own. Recognise when it is time to seek help. Some suggestions follow.[1]

Where to get help

There are three main sources of external help for people with problem anxiety: self-help support groups, skills trainers and professional therapists.

Support groups
Sometimes it can be helpful to get together with others who have problems similar to your own. Check out any potential support group before committing yourself. Some tend to focus on complaining about problems rather than learning how to deal with them, so ensure you choose one that is intent on developing solutions. Talk to others who have been involved with it, or attend a trial session.

Skills training
Skills training can help you develop ability in areas such as assertiveness and communication. Some counsellors train one on one, although it is more usual to work in small groups. Group training is often available through polytechnics, adult education classes or social service organisations.

Professional therapists
Sometimes, because of the difficulty or complexity of a problem, professional help is required. Professional therapy may be available from a psychiatrist, psychologist, social worker, mental health nurse,

counsellor/psychotherapist or member of some other professional group. The label a professional therapist works under doesn't guarantee a good therapy experience, so don't attach too much importance to what someone calls themself. Instead, go on the recommendations of a trusted adviser or someone who has actually consulted the therapist you are considering. It is also important to ascertain that the therapist uses methods that are appropriate for treating problem anxiety — more on this below.

Where to get advice on sources of help
If you are unsure where to go for help, consult your family doctor, pastor or local Citizens Advice Bureau, or any other reputable service advertised in your phone book.

Before committing to a counsellor

You will increase the chance that counselling or psychotherapy will be a safe and helpful experience if you do some advance checking and monitor your ongoing contact with the counsellor or psychotherapist. The following suggestions are drawn from a checklist developed by Stephen Palmer and Kasia Szymanska,[2] as well as from my own experience.

- Does the counsellor have relevant qualifications and experience?
- Does the counsellor have training in Cognitive-Behaviour Therapy (CBT — the method on which this book is based) and are they predominantly using this approach? CBT has a number of variations: the best known are Rational-Emotive-Behaviour Therapy (REBT) and Cognitive Therapy (CT).
- Does the counsellor receive supervision from another professional counsellor or supervision group? Most professional bodies consider supervision to be mandatory.
- Is the counsellor a member of a professional body with a clear code of ethics? Obtain a copy of the code if possible.
- Discuss with the counsellor your goals and what you expect to get from counselling.

- Ask about fees, if any, and discuss the frequency and estimated duration of your counselling.
- Finally, do not enter into a long-term counselling contract unless you are satisfied this is *necessary* and will be *beneficial* to you. If in doubt, get a second opinion.

Once you are seeing a counsellor

- *Regular reviews.* Ask for periodic evaluations of your progress towards your specified goals.
- *Keep the focus on your problems.* Self-disclosure by a counsellor can sometimes be therapeutically useful, but speak up if sessions are dominated by the counsellor discussing his or her own problems.
- *Maintain appropriate boundaries between yourself and your counsellor.* Do not accept significant gifts (apart from relevant therapeutic material, such as reading) or social invitations (unless they are part of the therapeutic work itself — for instance, facing social anxiety by going with your counsellor to a busy cafe). If your counsellor proposes a change in venue for your sessions — for example, from a centre to his or her own home — without good reason, do not agree. Finally, it is not beneficial — in fact, it is almost always damaging — for clients to have sexual contact with their counsellor; and it is unethical for counsellors or therapists to engage in any such contact with their clients.
- *Express any concerns.* If at any time you feel discounted, undermined or manipulated, or have any doubts about the counselling you are receiving, discuss this with your counsellor. Try to resolve issues as they arise rather than sit on them. If you are still uncertain, seek advice. Talk to a friend, your doctor, your local Citizens Advice Bureau, the professional body to which your counsellor belongs, or the agency, if any, that employs him or her.

Overcoming the blocks to asking for help

Know that change is possible

If you don't see much chance of anything changing, you will let things drift. Challenge the idea that it is pointless to accept help. How do you know that change is impossible until you have given it a try? And dispute any 'magical' thinking that your emotions are controlled, or your life mapped out, by external forces.

Accepting help does not mean dependence

Do you believe that people shouldn't need help with personal problems and should be able to 'stand on their own feet'; or that to accept help is somehow proof of 'weakness'? Do you worry that if you seek help from other people you will become dependent on them?

Know what your limits are. Know how far you can go with helping yourself, and when it is time to turn to other people for support and guidance. Accepting help does not prove you are a 'weak person'; all it proves is that you are a person who sometimes requires assistance.

Trust your own judgements about the advice you get; decide which parts are right for you, and leave the rest. Remember that you create your own emotions and behaviours, and only you can change them. Other people can show you what to do, but only you can do it. If you keep this in mind, you are unlikely to lose your independence.

You can stay in control

Do you worry that you will be made to do things against your will, such as taking medication, entering a psychiatric facility or adopting beliefs that are contrary to your values? You need take from others only what will work for you — you can leave the rest. If you sense a helper is trying to force something on you, discuss it with them. If they don't listen, exercise your choice to go elsewhere.

Confront fears about revealing yourself to others

Do you fear that a counsellor will regard you as insane, or that you will end up with a formal psychiatric diagnosis? Do you think that if you expose your thoughts and feelings to another person they will use what they learn to harm you or get power over you, or at the very least will look down on you?

There are risks in accepting help. Sometimes people do make inappropriate use of what they learn; sometimes they do look down on others. The risk, though, will be minimal, especially if you adopt the suggestions made earlier and check out a therapist in advance. And keep in mind three questions. Just how damaging would these things be if they did happen? How likely are they to happen? And is the risk worth it, bearing in mind the potential gain (or the certainty of staying where you are if you do nothing)?

As you move from self-rating to *self-acceptance* (p. 79), you will become less concerned about what others may think when you reveal your thoughts and feelings to them.

28 Putting it all together

Problem anxiety may be the scourge of modern industrialised societies, but the key message of this book is that you can do something about yours.

Understanding is the first step: knowing that anxiety is not all bad, that it is part of being human and alive, and that it is problematical only when the alarm becomes worse than the fire. This will help you get anxiety into perspective and avoid overreacting to your own feelings. Understanding also involves learning about the *types of thinking* that contribute to problem anxiety, so you know how to recognise them in yourself.

The second step is to carefully *assess* your anxiety, set some self-therapy *goals* and draw up a *plan of action*. Then you will be clear about where you are heading and how to get there. You may be tempted to pass over this step and get on with trying out some self-help techniques; but time spent planning will save time later. You will be directing your efforts where they will deliver the best results.

Learning some *initial coping skills* comes next, as you will almost certainly want to obtain some immediate relief from your unpleasant symptoms. These skills will also be useful later. Basic rethinking techniques, such as *rational self-analysis* and *rational cards*, are essential. Many people will also find symptom-relieving techniques helpful, such as *relaxation training* and *breathing control*. Choose techniques that are appropriate to your situation.

Once you are using your new coping skills effectively, it is time for the next step: 'walking the talk', or *behavioural* work. The main behavioural strategy is *exposure*. Using *imagery exposure* can be a helpful first step for dealing with many situations; ultimately, though, most problem anxiety has to be tackled with *real-life exposure*, which entails facing the situations you fear in a graduated, step-by-step fashion, using your coping skills to manage your anxiety. This is another step you may be tempted to put off, but it is essential for dealing fully with your fears. It isn't as frightening as it perhaps sounds; remember, you enter the situations you fear only after you have learned to cope with them.

As you begin to get on top of your problem anxiety, you can start dealing with what underlies it: *self-defeating core beliefs*. Work on those demands for security and avoidance of discomfort, the belief that your difficulties make you a lesser person, and the fear of what others may think. This will not only help alleviate your anxiety, but will also lay the groundwork for a happier life in all respects.

Is this process a tall order? When you see the whole thing presented like this, it may seem so. But there is a trick to getting through it: take one step at a time, and get used to each step before taking the next. Also, keep clear in your mind why you are making such an effort. Your self-help therapy has nothing to do with 'becoming a better person'. You are not doing all this work because you 'should'. Nor are you doing it for your loved ones, even though they will almost certainly benefit as you get better.

What is your real motivation? You are doing the hard work of self-therapy because you want to be happier. You need no other incentive. Keep that before you throughout your therapeutic journey and you will arrive at your destination.

Notes

Chapter 3

1. Cloninger, C.R., Svrakic, & Przybek, T.R. (1993). A psychobiological model of temperament and character. *Archives of General Psychiatry*, 50, 975–90; and Gregson, O., & Looker, T. (1994). The biological basis of stress management. *British Journal of Guidance and Counselling*, 22:1, 13–26.

2. Warren, R., & Zgourides, G. (1991). *Anxiety Disorders: A rational-emotive approach*. New York, N.Y.: Pergamon Press.

3. I adapted this from the phrase 'The alarm is worse than the fire', a chapter heading in Beck, A. (1988). *Cognitive Therapy and the Emotional Disorders*. New York, N.Y.: Meridian.

Chapter 5

1. If you are interested in learning more about the possibilities and limitations of self-improvement, you can read about both in Seligman, M.E.P. (1994). *What You Can Change and What You Can't: The complete guide to successful self-improvement*. Sydney: Random House.

2. Bushnell, J., et al. (1998). *Guidelines for Assessing and Treating Anxiety Disorders*. Wellington: National Health Committee.

Chapter 6

1. Pokorny, A.D., & Lomax, J.W. (1988). Suicide and anxiety. In Last, C.G., & Hersen, M., (eds.). *Handbook of Anxiety Disorders*. New York, N.Y.: Pergamon Press.

Chapter 7

1. For a more detailed description of rational self-analysis, as well as some practice exercises, see Froggatt, W.

(1993). *Choose to Be Happy: Your step-by-step guide*. Auckland: HarperCollins.

Chapter 9

1. DiGuiseppe, R., (1991). Comprehensive cognitive disputing in RET. In Bernard, M. (ed.). *Using Rational-Emotive Therapy Effectively: A practitioner's guide*. New York, N.Y.: Plenum.

2. Palmer, S., & Neenan, M. (1998). Double imagery procedure. *The Rational Emotive Behaviour Therapist*, 6:2, 89–92.

3. Lazarus, A.A. (1968). Learning theory and the treatment of depression. *Behaviour Research & Therapy*, 6, 83–9.

Chapter 10

1. These values are elaborated on in Froggatt, W. (1997). *GoodStress: The life that can be yours*. Auckland: HarperCollins.

2. This subject is dealt with more extensively in Froggatt, W. (1993). *Choose to Be Happy: Your step-by-step guide*. Auckland: HarperCollins.

3. This list borrows from Beck, A.T., Emery, G., & Greenberg, R.L. (1985). *Anxiety Disorders and Phobias*. New York, N.Y.: Basic Books. pp.256–7.

Chapter 11

1. A good selection of tapes is obtainable from the Albert Ellis Institute, 45 East 65th Street, New York 10021-6593, USA. Phone 001-212-535-0822, fax 001-212-249-3582, internet http://www.rebt.org/

Chapter 12

1. Adapted from various sources, especially Bourne, E.J. (1995). *The Anxiety & Phobia Workbook*, 2nd edn. Oakland, Cal.: New Harbinger; and

Warren, R., & Zgourides, G. (1991). *Anxiety Disorders: A rational-emotive approach*. New York, N.Y.: Pergamon Press.
2. For a useful list of hierarchies relevant to a range of anxiety problems see also Bourne (1995).

Chapter 13
1. Adapted from Beck, A.T., Emery, G., & Greenberg, R.L. (1985). *Anxiety Disorders and Phobias*. New York, N.Y.: Basic Books.
2. Adapted from Bourne, E.J. (1995). *The Anxiety & Phobia Workbook*, 2nd edn. Oakland, Cal.: New Harbinger.

Chapter 14
1. Beck, A.T., Emery, G., & Greenberg, R.L. (1985). *Anxiety Disorders and Phobias*. New York, N.Y.: Basic Books.

Chapter 17
1. Froggatt, W. (1997). *GoodStress: The life that can be yours*. Auckland: HarperCollins.

Chapter 18
1. For a more detailed discussion of perfectionism and how to deal with it, see Froggatt, W. (1993). *Choose to Be Happy: Your step-by-step guide*. Auckland: HarperCollins. pp.163–72.

Chapter 19
1. Adapted from Beck, A.T., Emery, G., & Greenberg, R.L. (1985). *Anxiety Disorders and Phobias*. New York, N.Y.: Basic Books. p.110.
2. Adapted from Weekes, C. (1997). *Complete Self-Help for Your Nerves*. Sydney: HarperCollins.
3. Adapted from Bourne, E.J. (1995). *The Anxiety & Phobia Workbook*, 2nd edn. Oakland, Cal.: New Harbinger.

Chapter 20
1. Harvard Mental Health Letter, October 1994. Retrieved 27 November 1998 from http://www.mentalhealth.com/mag/1p5h-soc1.html.
2. Carduccci, B., & Zimbardo, P.G. (1995).

Are you shy? *Psychology Today*, 28:6 (Nov.–Dec.), 34–82.
3. Carduccci & Zimbardo (1995).
4. For further information on disapproval and how to deal with it, see Froggatt, W. (1993). *Choose to Be Happy: Your step-by-step guide*. Auckland: HarperCollins. pp.139–49.

Chapter 21
1. See Warren, R., & Zgourides, G. (1991). *Anxiety Disorders: A rational-emotive approach*. New York, N.Y.: Pergamon Press. The authors point out that the primary focus of both panic disorder and specific phobia is the harmfulness of one's own anxiety and bodily sensations, but that the harmfulness of the stimuli looms larger for phobic people (e.g. heights, spiders, flying) than for people with panic disorder.
2. For further examples covering, among other phobias, driving, being a passenger, giving presentations, shopping, entering elevators, crossing bridges, using public transport, flying, and visiting dentists and doctors, see Bourne, E.J. (1995). *The Anxiety & Phobia Workbook*, 2nd edn. Oakland, Cal.: New Harbinger.
3. Walen, S. (1982). Phrenophobia. *Cognitive Therapy & Research*, 6, 399–408.
4. A resource that may help is Ellis, A. (1972). *How to Master Your Fear of Flying*. New York: Institute for Rational Living.
5. One of the best resources for understanding and dealing with the fear of dying is Ellis (1972). See also Ellis, A. & Abrams, M. (1994). *How to Cope with a Fatal Illness: The rational management of death and dying*. New York, N.Y.: Barricade.

Chapter 22
1. It has been suggested that, with suitable training, some people can learn to use thought-stopping on the obsessive thought but that it is difficult to do so. Help from a therapist may be required. See Salkovski, P., & Kirk, J.

(1989). Obsessional disorders. In Hawton, K., et al. (1989). *Cognitive Behaviour Therapy for Psychiatric Problems: A practical guide*. Oxford: Oxford University Press.
2. Salkovskis & Kirk (1989).

Chapter 23

1. If symptoms have been present for less than a month, the condition is known as acute traumatic stress disorder (ATSD). ATSD and PTSD are not the same as stress. Every human being experiences a degree of stress. For the most part this is beneficial, in that it motivates action and enhances performance. It can become excessive and dysfunctional, but even then it does not constitute a psychiatric condition comparable with ATSD or PTSD. There is also a condition known as adjustment disorder, sufferers of which react to an identifiable stressor with symptoms that seem excessive for the degree of stress imposed. (How to define 'excessive' is, of course, a matter of debate; but, unlike with PTSD, the stressor is not considered life-threatening.) The symptoms last less than 12 months following easement of the stressor or its consequences.
2. Yehuda, R. (1997). Reported in *Psychology Today*, 30:6 (Nov.–Dec.), 9.
3. Victims often find themselves the focus of disapproval when they are victimised. People may blame victims to maintain their own just-world beliefs.
4. Adapted from Warren, R., & Zgourides, G. (1991). *Anxiety Disorders: A rational-emotive approach*. New York, N.Y.: Pergamon Press.
5. Adapted from Beck, A.T., Emery, G., & Greenberg, R.L. (1985). *Anxiety Disorders and Phobias*. New York, N.Y.: Basic Books.
6. It has been stated that for fear to be reduced, (1) the fear memory must be activated, while (2) new information is provided that is incompatible with the current fear structure. Only in this way can a new memory be formed. See

Resick, P.A., & Schnicke, M.K. (1992). Cognitive processing therapy for sexual assault victims. *Journal of Consulting & Clinical Psychology*, 60:5, 748–56.

Chapter 24

1. Barksy, A.J. (1988). *Worried Sick: Our troubled quest for wellness*. Boston, Mass.: Little, Brown.
2. Bouman, T.K., & Visser, S. (1998). Cognitive and behavioural treatment of hypochondriasis. *Psychotherapy & Psychosomatics*, 67, 214–221.
3. A belief that one lacks ability to cope is considerably more anxiety-provoking when followed by an irrational evaluation, e.g. that one should be able to cope, that it is awful or unbearable that one cannot cope, and/or that being unable to cope proves something negative about one's self. See Froggatt, W. (1997). *GoodStress: The life that can be yours*. Auckland: HarperCollins. pp. 17–18).

Chapter 25

1. This is a summary of chapter 12 in Froggatt, W. (1997). *GoodStress: The life that can be yours*. Auckland: HarperCollins. If your sleep problem is not covered adequately here, consult the original for further information.
2. Depression, anger and guilt are covered extensively in Froggatt, W. (1993). *Choose to Be Happy: Your step-by-step guide*. Auckland: HarperCollins.
3. Morin, C.M., et al. (1993). Cognitive-behavior therapy for late-life insomnia. *Journal of Consulting & Clinical Psychology*, 61:1, 137–46.

Chapter 27

1. Adapted from Froggatt, W. (1997). *GoodStress: The life that can be yours*. Auckland: HarperCollins.
2. Palmer, S., & Szymanska, K. (1994). A checklist for clients interested in receiving counselling, psychotherapy or hypnosis. *The Rational Emotive Behaviour Therapist*, 2:1, 28–31.

Bibliography

Literature on Cognitive-Behaviour Therapy

There is a huge literature supporting the effectiveness of Cognitive-Behaviour Therapy (CBT). Here is a tiny selection, including items that relate specifically to the CBT treatment of anxiety:

Abrams, M., & Abrams, L. (1997). The paradox of psychodynamic and cognitive-behavioural psychotherapy. *Journal of Rational-Emotive & Cognitive-Behaviour Therapy*, 15:2, 133–56.

Becker, I.M., & Rosenfield, J.G. (1976). Rational Emotive Therapy: A study of initial therapy sessions of Albert Ellis. *Journal of Clinical Psychology*, 32, 872–6.

Bernard, M.E. (1995). It's prime time for Rational-Emotive-Behaviour Therapy. *Journal of Rational-Emotive & Cognitive-Behavior Therapy*, 13:1, 9–27.

Bushnell, J. et al. (1998). *Guidelines for Assessing and Treating Anxiety Disorders*. Wellington: National Health Committee.

DiGiuseppe, R., Leaf, R., & Linscott, J. (1993). The therapeutic relationship in Rational-Emotive Therapy: Some preliminary data. *Journal of Rational-Emotive & Cognitive-Behavior Therapy*, 11:4, 223–33.

Flett et al. (1991). Dimensions of perfectionism and irrational thinking. *Journal of Rational-Emotive & Cognitive-Behavior Therapy*, 9:3, 185–201.

Nathan, P., & Gorman, J. (1998). *A Guide to Treatments that Work*. New York, N.Y.: Oxford University Press.

Nottingham et al. (1992). Evaluation of a comprehensive inpatient Rational-Emotive Therapy Program: Some preliminary data. *Journal of Rational-Emotive & Cognitive-Behavior Therapy*, 10:2, 57–81.

O'Donohue, W., & Szymanski, J. (1993). Change mechanisms in Cognitive Therapy of a simple phobia: Logical analysis and empirical hypothesis testing. *Journal of Rational-Emotive & Cognitive-Behavior Therapy*, 11:4, 207–22.

Seligman, M.E.P. (1994). *What You Can Change and What You Can't: The complete guide to successful self-improvement.* Sydney: Random House.

Silverman, McCarthy & McGovern (1992). A review of outcome studies of Rational-Emotive Therapy 1982–1989. *Journal of Rational-Emotive & Cognitive-Behavior Therapy*, 10:3, 111–86.

Simpson, H.B., Gorfinkle, K.S., & Liebowitz, M.R. (1999). Cognitive-behavioral therapy as an adjunct to serotonin reuptake inhibitors in obsessive-compulsive disorder: An open trial. *Journal of Clinical Psychiatry*, 60:9, 584–90.

Solomon, A., & Haaga, D.A.F. (1995). Rational-Emotive-Behaviour Therapy research: What we know and what we need to know. *Journal of Rational-Emotive & Cognitive-Behavior Therapy*, 13:3, 179–91.

Resources on the internet

The following is a list of resources relating to anxiety management and associated topics that were available on the internet at the time this book was written. If you cannot connect to a particular site, the server may be down or overloaded, so try again later. If you still have trouble, try using an internet search engine. Should you still have no luck, it may be that the address has changed or no longer exists. You can also use a search engine to locate resources not listed here.

If you do not have a computer with an internet connection, your local library will probably be connected and have terminals for public use for a small hourly fee. Print the information you want and take it away with you.

Anxiety management
Anxiety Disorders Association of America —
http://www.adaa.org/

Effective speaking —
            http://www.effectivespeaking.co.nz/
Generalized anxiety home page —
            http://www.anxietynetwork.com/gahome.html
National Centre for Post-Traumatic Stress Disorder —
            http://www.ncptsd.org/
National Institute of Mental Health —
            http://www.nimh.nih.gov/anxiety/anxietymenu.cfm
Panic disorder home page —
            http://www.anxietynetwork.com/pdhome.html
Panic/anxiety disorders (miningco) —
            http://panicdisorder.miningco.com/
Social anxiety home page —
            http://www.anxietynetwork.com/sphome.html
Social phobia/Social Anxiety Association —
            http://www.socialphobia.org/

Healthy living

Healthy.Net — *Nutrition Information Center* —
            http://www.healthy.net/nutrit/
Keeping healthy — *Exercise information sheet* —
            http://www.mcchiro.com/keeping.htm
Mind tools on nutrition and exercise —
            http://www.mindtools.com/smhealth.html
Virtual Nutrition Centre —
            http://www-sci.lib.uci.edu/HSG/Nutrition.html

Relaxation

Obtaining a three-stage relaxation tape & manual —
            http://www.rational.org.nz/public/relaxtape.htm
Relaxation, imagery, breathing control —
            http://www.mindtools.com/smpmr.html

Sleep problems

The sleep medicine home page —
            http://www.cloud9.net/~thorpy/

301

Sleepnet list of resources —
> http://www.sleepnet.com/

Problem-solving
Brainstorming —
> http://www.mindtools.com/brainstm.html
Decision trees —
> http://www.mindtools.com/dectree.html

Seeking help
Online support groups —
> http://www.supportpath.com/
Psychologist's code of conduct —
> http://www.apa.org/ethics/code.html
Questions about counsellors and psychotherapists —
> http://www.counselorlink.com/
Rate your psychotherapist —
> http://www.cybercouch.com/library/rati.tag.html
Types of therapists —
> http://members.aol.com/therapy678/freud/choice.htm

Self-help tools
Internet mental health —
> http://www.mentalhealth.com/p.html
Mind tools —
> http://www.mindtools.com/

Cognitive-Behaviour Therapy
Albert Ellis Institute (New York) —
> http://www.rebt.org/
Beck Institute for Cognitive Therapy and Research —
> http://www.beckinstitute.org/
Centre for Rational-Emotive Behaviour Therapy, London —
> http://www.rebt.org.uk/
New Zealand Centre for Rational Emotive Behaviour Therapy —
> http://www.rational.org.nz

The Australian Institute for Rational Emotive Therapy —
    http://www.go.to/airet

Further reading

Anxiety in general
General
Bourne, E.J. (1995). *The Anxiety & Phobia Workbook*, 2nd edn. Oakland,
    Cal.: New Harbinger.
Hauck, P. (1974). *Calm Down*. London: Sheldon Press.
Hauck, P. (1975). *Overcoming Worry and Fear*. Philadelphia, Pa.: The
    Westminster Press.
Hauck, P. (1975). *Why Be Afraid?* London: Sheldon Press.
Weekes, C. (1997). *Complete Self-Help for Your Nerves*. Sydney:
    HarperCollins.

Professional
Barksy, A.J. (1988). *Worried Sick: Our troubled quest for wellness*. Boston, Mass.: Little, Brown.
Beck, A.T. Emery, G., & Greenberg, R.L. (1985). *Anxiety Disorders
    and Phobias*. New York, N.Y.: Basic Books.
Bushnell, J., et al. (1998). *Guidelines for Assessing and Treating Anxiety Disorders*. Wellington: National Health Committee.
Michelson, L., & Ascher, L.M. (eds.), (1987). *Anxiety and Stress Disorders: Cognitive-behavioral assessment and treatment*. New York,
    N.Y.: Guilford.
Treatment Protocol Project (1997). *Management of Mental Disorders*,
    2nd edn. Sydney: World Health Organisation.
Warren, R., & Zgourides, G. (1991). *Anxiety Disorders: A rational-emotive approach*. New York, N.Y.: Pergamon Press.

The causes of anxiety
General
Gribbin, J., & Gribben, M. (1993). *Being Human: Putting people in an
    evolutionary perspective*. London: Dent.

Professional

DiGiuseppe, R. (1996). The nature of irrational and rational beliefs: Progress in Rational-Emotive-Behaviour Therapy. *Journal of Rational-Emotive and Cognitive-Behaviour Therapy*, 14:1, 5–28.

Ellis, A. (1986). Discomfort anxiety: A new cognitive behavioral construct. In Ellis, A., & Greiger, R., (eds.). *Handbook of Rational-Emotive Therapy*, vol. 2. New York, N.Y.: Springer.

Ellis, A. (1987). A sadly neglected cognitive element in depression. *Cognitive Therapy and Research*, 11, 121–46.

Ruth, W.J. (1992). Irrational thinking in humans: An evolutionary proposal for Ellis' genetic postulate. *Journal of Rational-Emotive & Cognitive-Behaviour Therapy*, 10:1, 3–20.

Toates, F. (1988). *Biological foundations of behaviour*. Milton Keynes: Open University.

Relaxation training
Professional

Goldfried, M.R., & Davison, G.C. (1976). *Clinical Behaviour Therapy*. New York, N.Y.: Holt, Rinehart & Winston.

Palmer, S. (1992). *Stress Management: A course reader*. London: Centre for Stress Management.

Assertiveness
General

Ellis, A., & Lange, A. (1994). *How to Keep People from Pushing Your Buttons*. New York, N.Y.: Citadel Press.

Hauck, P. (1976). *How to Do What You Want to Do*. London: Sheldon Press.

Hauck, P. (1981). *How to Stand Up for Yourself*. London: Sheldon Press.

Hauck, P. (1988). *How to Be Your Own Best Friend*. London: Sheldon Press.

Jakubowski, P., & Lange, A.J. (1978). *The Assertive Option: Your rights and responsibilities*. Champaign, Ill.: Research Press.

Professional

Carmody, T.P. (1978). Rational-emotive, self-instructional and behavioral assertion training: Facilitation maintenance. *Cognitive Therapy & Research*, 2, 241–53.

Lange, A., & Jakubowski, P. (1976). *Responsible Assertive Behaviour: Cognitive-behavioural procedures for trainers*. Champaign, Ill.: Research Press.

Robb, H.B. III. (1992). Why you don't have a 'perfect right' to anything. *Journal of Rational-Emotive & Cognitive-Behavior Therapy*, 10:4, 259–69.

Wolfe, J.L., & Fodor, I.G. (1975). A cognitive-behavioral approach to modifying assertive behavior in women. *Counselling Psychologist*, 5:4, 45–52.

Perfectionism
General

Burns, D. (1980). The perfectionist's script for self-defeat. *Psychology Today* (Nov.), 34–52.

Froggatt, W. (1993). *Choose to Be Happy: Your step-by-step guide*. Auckland: HarperCollins.

Professional

Flett et al. (1991). Dimensions of perfectionism and irrational thinking. *Journal of Rational-Emotive & Cognitive-Behavior Therapy*, 9:3, 185–201.

Worrying
General

Copeland, M.E. (1998). *The Worry Control Workbook*. Oakland, Cal.: New Harbinger.

Professional

Borkovec, T.D. (1985). What's the use of worrying? *Psychology Today* (Dec.), 59–64.

Borkovec, T.D. & Inz, J. (1990). The nature of worry in generalized anxiety disorder: A predominance of thought activity. *Behavior*

Research & Therapy, 28, 153–8.

Warren, R., & Zgourides, G. (1991). *Anxiety Disorders: A rational-emotive approach*. New York, N.Y.: Pergamon Press.

Panic and avoidance
General

Bourne, E.J. (1995). *The Anxiety & Phobia Workbook*, 2nd edn. Oakland, Cal.: New Harbinger.

Weekes, C. (1997). *Complete Self-Help for Your Nerves*. Sydney: HarperCollins.

Professional

Beck, A.T., Emery, G., & Greenberg, R.L. (1985). *Anxiety Disorders and Phobias*. New York, N.Y.: Basic Books.

Ellis, A. (1979). A note on the treatment of agoraphobics. *Behaviour Research & Therapy*, 17, 162–4.

Ruddell, P. (1993). Panic disorder. *The Rational-Emotive Therapist*, 1:2, 68–71.

Treatment Protocol Project (1997). *Management of Mental Disorders*, 2nd edn. Sydney: World Health Organisation.

Warren, R., & Zgourides, G. (1991). *Anxiety Disorders: A rational-emotive approach*. New York, N.Y.: Pergamon Press.

Social anxiety
General

Dryden, W. (1997). *Overcoming Shame*. London: Sheldon Press.

Robin, M.W., & Balter, R. (1995). *Performance Anxiety*. Holbrook, Mass.: Adams Publishing.

Professional

Heimberg, R.G., & Juster, H.R. (1994). Treatment of social phobia in cognitive-behavioral groups [review]. *Journal of Clinical Psychiatry*, 55 (supp.), 38–46.

Hudson, J.L., & Rapee, R.M. (2000). The origins of social phobia. *Behavioral Modification*, 24:1, 102–29.

Juster, H.R., & Heimberg, R.G. (1995). Social phobia: Longitudinal course and long-term outcome of cognitive-behavioral treatment. *Psychiatric Clinic of North America*, 18:4, 821–42.

Mersch, P.P., et al. (1992). Somatic symptoms in social phobia: A treatment method based on Rational-Emotive Therapy and paradoxical interventions. *Journal of Behavioral Therapy & Experimental Psychiatry*, 23:3, 199–211.

Taylor, S. (1996). Meta-analysis of cognitive-behavioral treatments for social phobia. *Journal of Behavioral Therapy & Experimental Psychiatry*, 27:1, 1–9.

Warren, R., & Zgourides, G. (1991). *Anxiety Disorders: A rational-emotive approach*. New York, N.Y.: Pergamon Press.

Specific fears
General

Bourne, E.J. (1995). *The Anxiety & Phobia Workbook*, 2nd edn. Oakland, Cal.: New Harbinger.

Ellis, A. (1972). *How to Master Your Fear of Flying*. New York, N.Y.: Institute for Rational Living.

Raeann, D. (1997). *The Sky Is Falling: Understanding and coping with phobias, panic, and obsessive-compulsive disorders*. New York, N.Y.: Norton.

Seligman, M.E.P. (1994). *What You Can Change and What You Can't: The complete guide to successful self-improvement*. Sydney: Random House.

Professional

Beck, A.T., & Emery, G. (1985). *Anxiety Disorders*. New York, N.Y.: Basic Books.

Ellis, A. (1991). Rational-emotive treatment of simple phobias. *Psychotherapy*, 28, 452–6.

Walen, S. (1982). Phrenophobia. *Cognitive Therapy & Research*, 6, 399–408.

Warren, R., & Zgourides, G. (1991). *Anxiety Disorders: A rational-emotive approach*. New York, N.Y.: Pergamon Press.

Obsessions and compulsions
General

Raeann, D. (1997). *The Sky Is Falling: Understanding and coping with phobias, panic, and obsessive-compulsive disorders.* New York, N.Y.: Norton.

Steketee, G., & White, K. (1990). *When Once Is Not Enough.* Oakland, Cal.: New Harbinger.

Professional

Ellis, A. (1994). Rational-Emotive-Behavior Therapy approaches to obsessive-compulsive disorder. *Journal of Rational-Emotive & Cognitive-Behavior Therapy,* 12:2, 121–41.

Enright, S.J. (1991). Group treatment for obsessive-compulsive disorder. *Behavioral Psychotherapy,* 19, 189–92.

Hawton, K., et al. (1998). *Cognitive-Behaviour Therapy for Psychiatric Problems.* Oxford: Oxford University Press.

Warren, R., & Zgourides, G. (1991). *Anxiety Disorders: A rational-emotive approach.* New York, N.Y.: Pergamon Press.

Post-trauma anxiety
General

Seligman, M.E.P. (1994). *What You Can Change and What You Can't: The complete guide to successful self-improvement.* Sydney: Random House. Chapter 10.

Professional

American Academy of Child and Adolescent Psychiatry. (1998). Practice parameters for the assessment and treatment of children and adolescents with posttraumatic stress disorder. *Journal of the American Academy of Child and Adolescent Psychiatry,* 37:10, 4S–26S.

Ellis, A. (1994). Post-Traumatic Stress Disorder (PTSD): A rational-emotive-behavioral theory. *Journal of Rational-Emotive & Cognitive-Behavior Therapy,* 12:1, 3–25.

Meichenbaum, D. (1997). *Treating post-traumatic stress disorder: A handbook and practice manual for therapy.* Brisbane: John Wiley.

Muran, E.M., & DiGiuseppe, R. (1994). Rape. In Dattilio, F.M., & Freeman, A., (eds.). *Cognitive-Behavioural Strategies in Crisis Intervention*. New York, N.Y.: Guilford.

Resick, P.A., & Schnicke, M.K. (1992). Cognitive processing therapy for sexual assault victims. *Journal of Consulting & Clinical Psychology*, 60:5, 748–56.

Warren, R., & Zgourides, G. (1991). *Anxiety Disorders: A rational-emotive approach*. New York, N.Y.: Pergamon Press.

Health anxiety
General
Barsky, A.J. (1988). *Worried Sick: Our troubled quest for wellness*. Boston, Mass.: Little, Brown.

Professional
Fishman, B. (1992). Therapy for an anxious patient who believes his symptoms are caused by a medical problem. *Hospital and Community Psychiatry*, 43:6 (June), 583–5.

Salkovskis, P. (1989). Somatic problems. In Hawton, K., et al. (1989). *Cognitive-Behaviour Therapy for Psychiatric Problems*. Oxford: Oxford University Press.

Sleep problems
Professional
Morin, C.M., et al. (1993). Cognitive-Behavior Therapy for late-life insomnia. *Journal of Consulting & Clinical Psychology*, 61:1, 137–46.

Sloan, E.P., et al. (1993). The nuts and bolts of behavioral therapy for insomnia. *Journal of Psychosomatic Research*, 37 (supp. 1), 19–37.

Dealing with difficulties
General
Dryden, W., & Gordon, J. (1993). *Beating the Comfort Trap*. London: Sheldon Press.

Professional
Ellis, A. (1985). *Overcoming Resistance: Rational-Emotive Therapy with difficult clients*. New York, N.Y.: Springer.

Ellis, A. (1995). Rational-Emotive Therapy approaches to overcoming resistance. In Dryden, W., (ed.). *Rational Emotive Behaviour Therapy: A reader*. London: Sage Publications.

Meichenbaum, D., & Turk, D.C. (1987). *Facilitating Treatment Adherence: A practitioner's guidebook*. New York, N.Y.: Plenum.

Outside help
General

Palmer, S., & Szymanska, K. (1994). A checklist for clients interested in receiving counselling, psychotherapy or hypnosis. *The Rational Emotive Behaviour Therapist*, 2:1, 25–2.

Seligman, M.E.P. (1994). *What You Can Change and What You Can't: The complete guide to successful self-improvement*. Sydney: Random House.

Index

Choose to be Happy

Do you want to choose how you feel?

Do you want to be your own therapist?

You can learn to help yourself — with a proven method of psychotherapy that emphasises the use of your own reasoning powers to achieve personal control and growth. This book introduces the method step by step, allowing you to understand and change the way you react to events in a rational and realistic manner.

Choose to be Happy offers more than inspiration and 'positive thinking'. It holds out the prospect of permanent change.

HarperCollins*Publishers*

Speak Easy

In her many years as a communications consultant, media trainer and performer, Maggie Eyre has developed a thorough understanding of what is involved in public speaking. Whether you are facing a business presentation or an after-dinner speech, Maggie can guide you from initial concept to final delivery. Included in *Speak Easy* are chapters on body language, voice, health, warming up, managing your audience, fear, media skills, grooming and learning your lines. Along the way Maggie recounts many anecdotes and case studies based on her own work and experience, with useful tips and summaries. This practical and authoritative handbook is destined to become the manual of choice for anyone looking to improve their public speaking and presentation skills.

HarperCollins*Publishers*